Craig Kielburger | Marc Kielburger | Shelley Page

THE WORLD NEEDS YOUR KID

Raising Children Who Care and Contribute

Updated and Revised

me to we BOOKS

GREYSTONE BOOKS
D&M PUBLISHERS INC.
Vancouver/Toronto/Berkeley

12 13 14 5 4 3 2

Greystone Books
An imprint of D&M Publishers Inc.
2323 Quebec Street, Suite 201
Vancouver BC Canada V5T 4S7
www.greystonebooks.com

Me to We Books
225 Carlton Street
Toronto ON Canada M5A 2L2
www.metowe.com/books

Cataloguing in Publication data available from Library and Archives Canada
ISBN: 978-1-55365-586-2

Cover design by Barb Williams (www.barbwilliamsdesign.com)
Cover photograph by Getty Images and iStockphoto
Interior layout & design by TurnStyle Imaging Inc. (www.turnstyleimaging.com)
Interior photos by Free The Children, iStockphoto, Corbis and Getty Images or as otherwise noted
Printed and bound in Canada by Friesens
Text printed on acid-free, FSC-certified paper
Distributed in the U.S. by Publishers Group West

We gratefully acknowledge the financial support of the Canada Council for the Arts, the British Columbia Arts Council, the Province of British Columbia through the Book Publishing Tax Credit and the Government of Canada through the Canada Book Fund for our publishing activities.

FSC
www.fsc.org

MIX
Paper from
responsible sources
FSC® C016245

To our parents, who will always be our greatest teachers

Contents

07 THE FIRST C: COMPASSION

P. 125
Elie Wiesel speaking
at We Day 2009

P. 207
Jason Mraz

FOREWORD

His Holiness
the Dalai Lama

October 17, 2009

WE ARE NOW AT THE beginning of the 21st century and when we look back on the 20th century we can clearly see that while there were important human inventions, particularly in the fields of science and technology, it was also a century of bloodshed. Some say that more than two hundred million people were killed as a result of war during the last century. This painful experience came about because many people assumed that they could solve problems through recourse to violence. Learning from their mistakes, I believe we should all try instead to make this 21st century a century of peace.

Peace does not mean that all our problems will disappear. As long as human beings exist, there will always be some differences among us. Peace means restraining from violence and using our common sense when there is a possibility of conflict. Genuine peace can be engendered through understanding that all human beings are like us in wanting happiness and not wanting fear and stress. The idea of distinction between "us" and "them" is now outdated because in today's reality everything is interdependent. Therefore, we should embrace the idea that the entire six billion human beings are part of "us."

The children of today belong to the 21st century and can give a new shape to a new

era. All of us should aim to make this a century of peace and compassion. How can we go about this? Believe that in order to have the confidence to trust, understand and respect others, some kind of inner disarmament is necessary. To begin with, we need to embark on the difficult task of developing love and compassion within ourselves. Only in this way can we address the underlying causes that disturb us and prevent our finding peace and happiness. Machines cannot generate the inner peace we require, nor can peace be bought in a shop. Peace is something that has to come from inside, through transforming our hearts and minds.

Everyone has the potential to be more compassionate and loving, since we have all received a genuine seed of compassion from our mother. But these seeds need to be nurtured through education. Children require an all-round education that not only exercises their intelligence, but also teaches the value of being warmhearted. I am therefore pleased to see that this book highlights the importance of training in compassion and other inner strengths in the upbringing of children. I hope that parents and teachers will take the time to read it and come to appreciate the positive qualities they can encourage in their children and students.

His Holiness the 14th Dalai Lama

Everyone has the potential to be more compassionate and loving..."

Me to We and the Three Cs

THE WORLD NEEDS YOUR KID. Seriously, the world needs *your* kid.

You probably don't need us to tell you that your child is extraordinary, but you should know that he — or she — can make the world a better place.

Through our work with Free The Children, the world's largest organization of children helping children through education, we have met tens of thousands of kids who want to make a difference. Many are looking for a place to begin — and that's where you come in.

There is no greater privilege and no more important responsibility in life than to raise the next generation. If children are the future, it's the job of parents, grandparents, mentors and teachers to shine the light and guide the way. (No pressure!)

You're in an extraordinarily influential position. The work you do now can guide the decisions your children make throughout their lives. It's our hope that this book will help you to nurture global citizens — kids who care and contribute. Raising your child to be compassionate is not just good for the world — it's good for your child. We'll show you how small actions can make a big difference when it comes to friendships, grades and self-esteem. Studies show that caring kids are healthier and less likely to

Raising your child to be compassionate is not just good for the world — it's good for your child."

use or abuse drugs and alcohol.

One of the greatest gifts you can give a child is the opportunity to help someone else. Our work has convinced us that every child has a gift to share. Maybe it's a love of music or art or research. Perhaps it's the ability to make people laugh. We've also learned that kids have the capacity to care deeply about matters large and small, near and far — the stray cat in your yard, the frogs in the pond down the street, girls in Afghanistan who are not allowed to go to school. When children combine their gifts with their passions, they become unstoppable forces of goodness. And that's why the world needs your kid!

It's a point that was driven home to us when we received an unexpected invitation from the world's most famous monk. When His Holiness the Dalai Lama calls, you answer. Or, to be more precise, you do after his people dial your people (a.k.a. Mom). Odds are we were outside playing soccer when Mom took the message from Stockholm where the Dalai Lama was gathering philosophers, historians, teachers and religious leaders to contemplate the greatest challenges of our times. We were humbled, honored and hugely surprised to be recruited. We'd only recently founded Free The Children. At the time, it was still a novelty for kids to campaign for children's rights.

The Dalai Lama invited his gathered guests to consider a single but profound question: "What is the greatest challenge facing our time?" We had a week to come up with an answer. Some suggested nuclear annihilation posed the greatest threat. "It's poverty," others argued. One expert spoke passionately about the tragic disparity between the rich and poor. Another worried about peace in the Middle East. There was a long discussion about genocide. We suggested it might have something to do with the education of children.

The Dalai Lama was also deep in thought. After contemplating all that had been said, he spoke. To this day we remember his words: "The greatest challenge facing our time is not weapons of mass destruction or terrorism or ethnic cleansing," he said. "It is that we are raising a generation of passive bystanders."

The Dalai Lama argued that children today are afraid to stand up, stand out or be counted. He blamed parents, grandparents, teachers and mentors for shielding the world from this generation on the sidelines.

The warning inspired us to consider how we could all do better. The Dalai Lama inspired us, as he might inspire you, to want more for our children and their future. His words became our call to action. This book is the result.

Our travels have convinced us that the world needs more active and compassionate global citizens. We know from our work that young people crave responsibility. Once they discover they can make a difference, they thrive on doing so. Each day presents itself with opportunities to nurture compassion. Not sure where to begin? Start by opening the morning paper. Archbishop Desmond Tutu once told us he considers the newspaper God's to-do list. "It's delivered right to my door every day," he explained. "In this way, I know the issues on which to act."

People often ask us if we were raised to be "activists." In fact, the word rarely came up. However, we were raised to be active citizens ready to engage at home, in school or out in the community. Our parents have been our greatest teachers. They were educators by profession, in fact, but fully aware that life's greatest lessons take place outside the classroom.

Witness a scene from our childhood: One December day, just before Christmas, Mom was heading downtown to do some last-minute shopping. She invited us to tag along. We kids from the suburbs were blown away by the traffic, caught up in the chaos and mesmerized by department store windows decorated with holiday scenes. Dashing along busy sidewalks slick with ice and snow, we stumbled on the outstretched feet of a homeless man. His pants were torn and a tattered scarf flapped around his neck like a piece of frayed rope. He was trying to keep warm in the bitter cold. We didn't think to stop, but Mom did. She took us by the hand and approached the man with a smile.

"Hello, how are you?" she said.

She asked his name and inquired if he'd been able to find shelter the previous night. The man seemed shocked that anyone — especially someone with children — would stop to "see" him as a person. Mom opened her purse, fumbled for her wallet and slipped a few dollars into his gloveless hands. As she did so, she gathered us closer and into their conversation. It was a bit unnerving. It would not be the last time Mom drew us into such an exchange. She never lectured us — then or ever — about helping the needy, but she always took time to explain why someone might not have a family or a home or a job or presents under the tree. She always invited us to consider how we might help. In refusing to turn away — or to let us walk by — Mom taught us that every person is unique and worthy of acknowledgement. She showed us that we should help; not out of guilt but because we have so much to give. Years later, we thanked Mom — something kids don't do nearly enough — for opening our eyes. She taught us a lesson that we now teach.

Mom could never have anticipated the Dalai Lama's urgent appeal, yet she and Dad seemed to know instinctively that children want and need to contribute. With that in mind, they guided us on a path that led us to create Free The Children. Along the way, they recruited the wisdom of our grandparents, teachers, friends, coaches and mentors — all of whom taught us so much.

Thanks to Free The Children, we've had the privilege to work with more than one million school kids across North America as they've rallied to the challenge and helped us build more than five hundred schools in the developing world. We've encountered hidden heroes, subversive world-changers and unrepentant extroverts who can't help but get everyone involved. We know how much each and every child has to offer the world.

We hope you'll consider this book a roadmap to the future. Our landmarks along the way will be what we have come to call the Three Cs — compassion, courage and community. We've divided the book into three sections to explore each "C" in detail. Between each chapter, you will find stories from remarkable individuals who were inspired by a parent, a teacher or perhaps a mentor to live compassionately and courageously: Jane Goodall, Jason Mraz, Archbishop Desmond Tutu, Betty Williams, Steve Nash, Jane Fonda and many others.

Our conversation with the Dalai Lama moved us to talk to hundreds of experts — developmental psychologists, teachers, coaches, volunteers, parents and, of course, kids. We also sat down with our parents and grandparents and aunts and uncles to hear stories of our childhoods and of theirs. We enlisted the interviewing and writing help of journalist and mother, Shelley Page. We needed someone to ask questions that can only come from a parent who has stayed up all night with a cranky baby, soothed temper tantrums, quieted bullies and made tough choices — all while trying to raise kids who contribute.

This is also an intensely personal book. It reflects stories from our lives that have profoundly influenced who we are. We share them humbly, if only because they are the ones we know best.

If the Dalai Lama is right — the greatest challenge facing our time is that we are raising a generation of passive bystanders — it follows that the most important work at this moment belongs to parents.

The world needs your kid!

Craig Kielburger

Marc Kielburger

THE FIRST C
Compassio

In the first section of this book, we will show you how the smallest of gestures — caring for a toy, a plant, a sibling, a friend — yield the greatest lessons in caring.

Our work with children has taken us from the richest nations to the poorest countries on this planet. We have come to know, and be inspired by, some of the greatest spiritual, political and social luminaries of this time. In the same way, we have been moved by youngsters in the streets of Salvador, on the grasslands of the Maasai Mara, and in the bustling offices of Free The Children in downtown Toronto.

Amidst the worst that life has to offer, we have seen the best that humans can give. In the slums of Calcutta, we've been greeted with simple meals of rice and *roti*. In the war-torn villages of Sierra Leone, we've been welcomed by children whose limbs were amputated by savage militias. We've spent time in battle zones where terror reigns and also in refugee camps where hope is found again. In the face of the inconceivable, we have witnessed breathtaking acts of compassion.

Across languages and cultures, almost without exception, we have found that compassion begets compassion. We are all connected. When we are able to see ourselves in others, we begin to move with a felt sense that our actions influence everyone around us.

Imagine waking each morning knowing that your actions could inspire change in

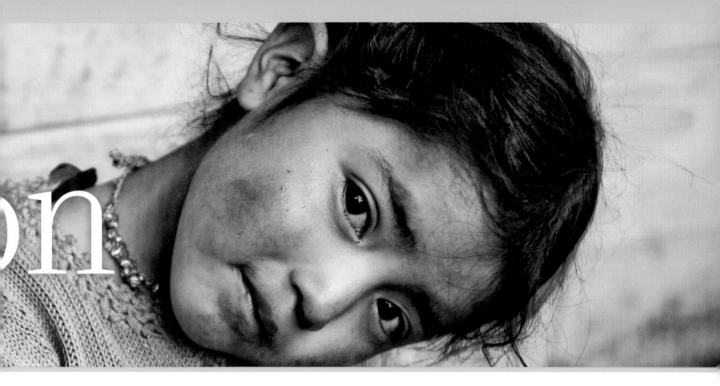

on

your family, your community, your world. We call this living *me* to *we*.

If we hope to nurture compassion in our children, we must help them discover the connections from one to another to another. Just as reading is a fundamental — one of the Three Rs — compassion is paramount, the first of our Three Cs.

In the first section of this book, we will show you how the smallest of gestures — caring for a toy, a plant, a sibling, a friend — yield the greatest lessons in caring. We will also consider how to nurture empathy in your child. You will learn the importance of teaching your son or daughter to be responsible in the home — a necessary step if they are ever to take ownership for the problems in their community. You will learn how to develop your child's unique gifts and awaken their passion for a cause. When a child combines a gift with a passion, the world is a better place.

Where to start? The Dalai Lama says he tries to treat anyone he meets as an old friend. "This gives me a genuine feeling of happiness," he explains. "It is the practice of compassion."

And so, as if old friends, let us begin.

Inside Our House

Welcome inside our upbringing. It has been a long journey for us not only with Free The Children, but as brothers. A strong, insightful adventure nonetheless. Join us as we explore how we got to where we are today. Heads up: Our parents had a lot to do with it.

MANY PEOPLE ASSUME THAT as brothers we are interchangeable. It's understandable. Through our work at Free The Children, we are dedicated to making the world a more just and compassionate place. At an early age, we each decided we would not wait to step up or speak out. Now we spend our days telling people about *me* to *we*, a way of being that is dedicated to feeding the positive into the world — one small act at a time. On all this we agree, but we are not one and the same.

Marc is older — wiser, too, he insists. He'll tell anyone who'll listen that he got the looks in the family. He'll tell them even if they're not listening, truth be told. In the same way, Craig insists he's the one in the family who ended up with the sense of humor. While Craig is bookish, Marc is a natural athlete. He claims to have learned about empathy during his rugby days, a sport that's been compared to a bar fight with finesse. There was no compassion during the rucks and mauls, of course, but in between matches, Marc rallied his team to go an extra mile for charity.

Marc is analytical and leads with his head. Craig is passionate and follows his heart. Still, we end up in the same place, convinced that by embracing *me* to *we*, we truly can be the change we want to see in the world. Our hope is that children — yours and, one day, ours — can stop dreaming about a better world and begin to live in one.

Now you're probably assuming our parents raised us to be do-gooders — that instead of chauffeuring us from soccer practices to piano lessons they hustled us from penny drives to bake sales. Not entirely so. When we were asked as young children what we wanted to be,

"activist" never came up. Mom and Dad dropped hints and hopes: "How about a doctor?" "Why not a lawyer?" It only makes sense they had high hopes for us. We found our calling in Free The Children, an international charity for kids.

Mom and Dad were determined to give us what they never had. There was actually a time when Mom's family was homeless. And Dad, when he was not at school, spent his childhood working at his family's corner store. For this reason, they dreamed we'd go to good schools and on to great careers. In fact, Marc did grow up to become a lawyer, though he has never practiced. Craig, meanwhile, spends much of his life in hotel rooms in city after city, never tiring of speaking to young people and their parents about social engagement. To be sure, we embrace as many invitations as we can to share the *me* to *we* philosophy.

During the summers, Craig makes pit stops in Kenya where he helps Free The Children volunteers build schools for African kids. And although he is not the doctor that Mom and Dad thought he'd grow up to be, Craig has dedicated his life to helping people all the same. Like many physicians, he works long hours and often grabs sleep in short intervals on the fly. Thankfully, he can sleep anywhere and never, ever drools. (So far as he knows.) Many people wonder how we ended up becoming activists when our parents dreamed our futures would be in law and medicine. Where did we go astray? Truth be told, we were following Mom and Dad's lead all along.

Mom thinks it's crucial that parents help their children look critically at what they see. It's far too easy to turn away. "If we want to raise children to be caring citizens, we must teach them from an early age to open their eyes to their world," she reminded us recently. "Kids need to seek information and answers to help them understand, to look at all sides of an issue, to put themselves into a situation mentally and see how they would feel. In their own small way, they must take action so they do not feel powerless."

Dad helped open the eyes of Craig, er, Marc... "whichever one you are." To this day, he mixes us up. Disconcerting, yes. Worse when you realize he has perfect recall when it comes to Coco and Muffin — our dogs! Every morning when we were kids, Dad would spread the newspaper on the table in our sunny, plant-filled kitchen and point out world happenings and local injustices. War in Bosnia. Drought in Ethiopia. Cat stuck in tree in local neighborhood. We'd talk about the issues at the heart of each story. Sometimes — but not always — we'd muse about how we might get involved or learn more. Research Bosnia, raise money, get a ladder. Even if he mixed us up from time to time, Dad always listened to our ideas. Each and every day, we drank up lessons in kindness.

Nature + Nurture = Future

Forgive us if we go on about Mom and Dad. It's just that they've given us so much to go on about. We've always relied on them for guidance and inspiration and encouragement, in the same way the young people in your life are counting on you. Our friend, Reverend John Niles, says parents have a sacred responsibility to their children and to the world. "When a parent truly grasps this, they come to understand they have been given an opportunity to change the world."[1] Think about it. Had it not been for their parents, Nelson Mandela, Mother Teresa and Martin Luther King, Jr. might never have achieved what they did. We share these childhood stories in part to show you that we were ordinary in every way. Our last name is not Buffett or Gates. We are not born of wealth, though our parents always sought out the best for us — material goods, sure, but also a solid foundation from which to move through the world with compassion. Thanks to them, we began to discover the richness and complexities of life.

At United Nations conferences, we've sat on panels with heads of state and royalty. Yet we've learned just as much talking with street children from Brazil to Thailand. We've met with tens of thousands of students, parents and educators in schools around the world. And we've acquired important lessons from everyone — human rights workers in war zones, moms and dads in suburbia, executives in corner offices and people without any place to call home. We believe passionately that parents, teachers, coaches and role models can nurture compassion and altruistic behavior

FREE THE CHILDREN
children helping children through education

me to we

FREE THE CHILDREN is the world's largest network of children helping children through education. More than one million youth are involved in our innovative education and development programs in forty-five countries.

Founded in 1995 by international child rights activist Craig Kielburger, Free The Children has a proven track record of success. The organization has received the World's Children's Prize for the Rights of the Child (also known as the Children's Nobel Prize) and the Human Rights Award from the World Association of Non-Governmental Organizations. It has formed successful partnerships with leading school boards and Oprah's Angel Network.

The primary goals of the organization are to free children from poverty and exploitation and free young people from the notion that they are powerless to affect positive change in the world. Through domestic empowerment programs and leadership training, Free The Children inspires young people to develop as socially conscious global citizens and become agents of change for their peers around the world.

www.freethechildren.com

ME TO WE is a new kind of social enterprise for people who want to help change the world with their daily choices. Through our media, socially responsible choices and leadership experiences, we support Free The Children's work with youth creating global change. Every trip, organic T-shirt, song, book, speech, thought and choice adds up to a fun, dynamic lifestyle that's part of the worldwide movement of *we*.

Through donations and in-kind contributions, Me to We is designed to help bring Free The Children's already low administrative costs to zero while, at the same time, encouraging people to change the world with their daily choices. Me to We is not only a way of life but also a social enterprise designed to help support the work of Free The Children. Half of its annual profits are given to Free The Children with the other half reinvested to sustain the growth of the enterprise.

Each enterprise – Me to We Trips, Speakers, Style, Leadership, Music and Books – represents something Craig and Marc Kielburger wished they had as kids. These are the opportunities, experiences and products that help improve the world and fit within a young person's daily life. Think *we*.

www.metowe.com

in young people. The research is on our side. Some scientists believe we inherit the desire to help. In fact, genes were found recently that apparently account for about 50 percent of our altruism and generosity. Upbringing and environment likely influence the rest. One way or the other — and probably a bit of both — parents are the key to nurturing compassion in the next generation.

A recent survey of one thousand young Americans, aged fifteen to twenty-five, revealed that by donating their own time and resources to the community, parents nurture the importance of service and inspire their children to volunteer throughout their lives.[2] Another study in Holland found that children are most likely to volunteer if their parents give time to the community.[3] In other words, the volunteer work you do today will inspire the volunteers of tomorrow.

Parents don't always appreciate that they set a powerful example. Many of the thousands of young people we work with tell us they took cues from their parents — not from their words, but from their actions. Moms and dads are bombarded with warnings: Bad parenting produces delinquents or depressed kids. Workaholics raise apathetic and disengaged children. Abusive parents bequeath their behavior to the next generation. What often gets overlooked are the positive ways parents can influence their children's actions and beliefs. There is solid evidence that when parents — as well as teachers and mentors — display helping behavior, children stand a good chance of internalizing and adopting this worldview.

In laboratory settings, children mimic the selfish or giving behavior of adult role models.

In studies in which kids play "donating" games, they model what the adult does. In a study of civil rights workers, most said their parents demonstrated altruistic behavior and reported warm, cordial and respectful relationships with one or both parents. And so it goes, from benevolent adult to impressionable kid, one generation to the next. In other research, volunteers who finished a six-month work commitment tended to report good relationships with altruistic parents. In contrast, those with relatively poor relationships with parents who were not considered altruistic completed volunteer commitments primarily if they trained with a cohesive group. Those who did not like their training group tended not to finish. Individuals with poor relationships with their parents tended to complete volunteer commitments primarily for social rather than altruistic or moral reasons.[4]

Planting the Seeds

We know first hand what experts have shown many times over: The ability to care for others does not spring spontaneously from the hearts of children. It can, however, be coaxed out in simple ways. Love a child and they learn to love. Care for a child and they learn to care. When life begins in the womb, a child is a circle of one, writes Dr. Charles A. Smith of the School of Family Studies and Human Services at Kansas State University. "Greeted by at least one other loving person, their circle expands to two. The circle widens as other caring family members are added. Even though 'I' remains important, a 'we' emerges that also has to be nurtured and protected."[5] In this way, a child

FACTORING THE FATHER FIGURE

A shout out to dads, before we move on. Fathers play a crucial role in the success of their children. Here's a fascinating study that underlines the point:

For more than two decades, Greg Duncan and his colleagues at Northwestern University studied children born to some one thousand families between 1956 and 1962. They examined factors thought to influence the future of these children. A mother's schooling was found to benefit the outcome of her daughters, for example. Researchers also looked at a father's wages and the time he devoted to housework.[8] In *Raising Cain: Protecting the Emotional Life of Boys*, authors Dan Kindlon and Michael Thompson highlight one of the study's most important findings: "Of the dozens of factors they considered, father attendance at PTA meetings was the most influential in terms of the child's income at age twenty-seven."[9]

"It doesn't mean the mother is not important," Kindlon told us. (It's rare for a mother to be uninvolved with her kid.) "The statistic indicates that when a father is involved, there's a huge advantage for the child."

Our family fishing excursion

David Suzuki's daughter, Severn

WE ARE ALL IN THIS TOGETHER

Severn Suzuki was just twelve when she stood to address politicians and dignitaries at the 1992 Earth Summit in Rio de Janeiro, Brazil. These days in Canada the word "environmentalist" is synonymous with "Suzuki" — thanks to Severn, yes, and to her father, David, both of whom have inspired millions to consider how individual choices influence us all. "I am here to speak for all generations to come," the young activist told the audience that day.

Here is just some of what she went on to say:

"In my life, I have dreamt of seeing the great herds of wild animals, jungles and rainforests full of birds and butterflies, but now I wonder if they will even exist for my children to see.

Did you have to worry about these little things when you were my age?

All this is happening before our eyes and yet we act as if we have all the time we want and all the solutions. I'm only a child and I don't have all the solutions, but I want you to realize, neither do you!

You don't know how to fix the holes in our ozone layer.

You don't know how to bring salmon back up a dead stream.

You don't know how to bring back an animal now extinct.

And you can't bring back forests that once grew where there is now desert.

If you don't know how to fix it, please stop breaking it!

Here, you may be delegates of your governments, business people, organizers, reporters or politicians — but really you are mothers and fathers, brothers and sisters, aunts and uncles — and all of you are somebody's child.

I'm only a child, yet I know we are all part of a family, five billion strong, in fact, thirty million species strong and we all share the same air, water and soil — borders and governments will never change that. I'm only a child, yet I know we are all in this together and should act as one single world toward one single goal."[10]

moves from *me* to *we*.

Children watch parents closely to learn how to respond to situations. By nine months, a baby's face will mirror the happiness and joy in her mother's expressions. By age

one, compassion is usually part of a child's repertoire. It's like two forks in tune, explains Dr. Smith: Strike one and the other vibrates. Researchers at the National Institute of Mental Health in the U.S. asked both strangers and family members of one-year-olds to simulate sadness by

Our grandfather, Peter

sobbing, pain by yelling "ouch" and distress by coughing or choking. The babies reacted to each outburst by patting and hugging the sufferer or by rubbing the "hurt" spot.[6] The babies appeared most concerned about their mothers but also extended compassion to strangers. At first a child is unable to tell the difference between his distress and that of another. For example, an eighteen-month old responds to his mother's tears with tears of his own. If he tries to comfort his mother, it's only to ease his own distress. True compassion comes a little later. By the time he's ready for Grade 1, he will be able to appreciate his mother's separate perspective and her sadness or pain.

Our earliest memories are something like a highlight reel of faded home movies that features us splashing in a pool, playing cards or curling up in a lap for a story. We can't recall every detail, but we remember the deep sense of love we experienced. Like many kids today, we were enrolled in a crowded schedule of extracurricular activities that included piano,

soccer, tennis and swimming. In addition, Mom and Dad took Craig to speech therapy each week, determined to help him overcome a severe impediment caused by chronic ear infections. In between, they helped out with homework. In return, we were expected to pitch in around the home.

Under our roof, Mom and Dad cared for our grandfather, Peter. His spartan bedroom off the kitchen contained his collection of fedoras, a few canes and treasured photographs — one of his parents in Romania, another of him as a young man in a band. (He could play half a dozen instruments.) Wherever he went, he chewed an unlit cigar. Although we bellyached at the time, we realize now that we were extremely lucky when our grandfather enlisted our assistance with chores. In the autumn, we helped him rake leaves. When he wasn't chatting with the neighbors, he'd entertain us with stories. We never tired of his tales — especially the one about his first attempt to leave Germany for North America. (To make a long story — and journey — short, the boat sank!) He was nineteen when he finally arrived in Toronto during the Great Depression. He had little money and less English. He earned "suicide pay" fighting champion boxers. Every punch, bruised rib and black eye brought him closer to his not-so-humble dream. Once he'd saved enough, he opened a small grocery store where he and our grandmother worked day and night, three hundred and sixty-five days a year for more than twenty years.

Our parents also care for Mom's mom, Mimi, who is now well into her nineties. Mom, the second youngest of four, was born in Windsor, Ontario, across the border from

Children are both our near and distant future. It is by them and through them that we feel linked to the immortality of the human race."

Elie Wiesel
Auschwitz survivor and winner of the Nobel Peace Prize

Detroit. She was nine when her father passed away. In his absence, life was a struggle. Mom and one of her sisters found work at a local store where they sorted pop bottles and tended to customers. One summer, finances were so dire that the family was forced to sleep in a tent. Another year, they ate bologna sandwiches for Christmas dinner. (It's pretty easy to see why Mom cares so much for those who have so little.) Mimi, with a Grade 8 education, taught herself to type and then worked her way up from housekeeping to an office job at Chrysler Corp. Eventually, she headed her department. She sent everyone of her children to university. Mom, determined to help others, studied to be a teacher.

Until we started this book, we had no idea that Mom had worked with the homeless (we've seen photos in which she looks very much like a hippie!) or that Dad once spent a summer volunteering in a community for the mentally disabled. Although they'd never shared specifics, it was clear they'd always been motivated by an inexhaustible concern for others — starting with those at home. When we were kids, we didn't talk about changing the world, but we often discussed how we could make it better for the people in our lives. When we were planning a birthday party, for example, Mom would encourage us to include kids who were often excluded. She asked us to reflect on how we'd feel in their place. Inevitably, we'd end up inviting the entire class! If we burst in the door buzzing about a playground dust-up, Mom and Dad would ask who did the bullying and to whom. Just as important, they'd want to know what we did or didn't do about it.

People assume we woke up overnight determined to help child laborers, save the environment and care for street people with AIDS. In truth, our early steps were tentative. When we were kids, for example, we discovered that a housing development was going to replace the pond where we skated in winter and chased tadpoles in the summer. We didn't chain ourselves to a tree or lie down in front of a bulldozer. Instead, Marc jotted a few sentences on a piece of paper, then took it to our neighbors and asked them to sign. It was his first petition. Inspired by his brother, Craig spoke up a few years later when he learned that a local library was slated to close. (Even then, Craig was a nerd.)

We could never have anticipated that any of this would lead to a lifelong commitment to others. Mom and Dad laid the groundwork by ensuring we contributed to the family, the neighborhood and our school. Yet, as you will see, our accomplishments come from the ordinary, day-to-day, best wishes of parents who wanted the world for us. You picked up this book, so presumably you are equally committed to nurturing compassion, courage and community. Perhaps you've been living *me* to *we* and are trying to figure out how it applies to new additions in your household. You are not alone.

Well-meaning parents often approach us for advice. Many want their kids to kick-start a revolution, some for less than altruistic reasons. On one occasion, Craig was buttonholed by a mother whose fourteen-year-old son was closing in on his Ph.D. His academic success was not enough — now she wanted him to "change the world." The teen stood quietly behind his mother. Craig asked if he had a passion for any specific issue. "I guess I want to help people," the boy mumbled. Craig started to explain how Scouting had changed his life. "He can't join Scouts!" she interjected. "It already exists!" Forget community building — it was pretty clear her only interest was in résumé padding.

We hope it goes without saying that you don't have to found an organization to make a contribution. We all have gifts and talents to share. Someone needs to make the cookies for the bake sale. Someone else needs to design the posters to get the word out. Others need to research the cause and follow through on the fundraising efforts. It doesn't just take a village to raise a child; it takes a village to raise awareness.

Your children are watching. If you are compassionate, so they will also try to be. If you counsel compassion but are not that way yourself, there is a good chance you'll end up raising a cynic. For better — and sometimes for worse — you are the guiding force. As you move through this book, you'll see that compassion is contagious. We'll show you how it can be passed from one generation to the next. As Kahlil Gibran wrote, "Your children are not your children ... You may house their bodies not their souls, for their souls dwell in the house of tomorrow."[7]

SMALL ACTIONS › EVERY DAY

1. EARLY TO RISE:
Set the alarm twenty minutes early to avoid the weekday morning rush. With luck, you'll spend less time hustling your kids out the door and more time checking in with them about the day ahead. Connecting leads to caring.

2. EVERY CONTRIBUTION COUNTS:
Enlist your children to aid with chores. Young kids especially love to "help." Let them know their efforts are important to the running of your household. Helpers around the home are helpers around the neighborhood.

3. DINNER TIME CONVERSATION:
Encourage kids to discuss highlights and low points in the day. Get them talking about outrages and injustices they've witnessed, then help them figure out how to react — and act.

4. DINNER AND A MOVIE:
Set aside a family night to play games or watch a movie or make a meal together. Go international! Cook a meal from a world away. Watch a movie about a different culture.

5. TURN COMMUTES INTO COMMUNICATION:
Make the backseat of the car a no iPod, gadget-free zone. Encourage your kids to talk. If they won't, take the lead and share stories from your day.

6. NOT-SO-RANDOM ACTS OF KINDNESS:
Show your kids the beginning steps of living *me* to *we*. Open a door for someone. Help someone out who is short changed. Buy lunch for a stranger. Clean up someone else's mess.

Damn the Consequences

*The two-time Academy Award-winning actor and political activist, **Jane Fonda**, spoke to us about how her father, actor Henry Fonda and the Vietnam War shaped her social conscience. When she visited Cairo as the UN Goodwill Ambassador, her experiences with young women forever changed her perspective on the world and how she sees others.*

MY FATHER DIDN'T TALK MUCH, but through the roles he chose to play he conveyed a social ethic of justice and equality that had a profound effect on me. In *The Grapes of Wrath*, he was a union organizer and in *The Wrong Man*, he played an innocent man charged with a crime he didn't commit. He was a cowboy in *The Ox-Bow Incident*, stopping a mob from lynching innocent men. In *Young Mr. Lincoln* he portrayed one of America's most revered presidents. The effect his example had on me has manifested itself in many ways throughout the course of my life, particularly during the Vietnam War and later, working to prevent teenage pregnancies in Georgia.

The Vietnam War had been going on for a number of years before I joined the anti-war movement. I have asked myself many times, "Why did I choose not to know for so long what was going on in Vietnam?" I think unconsciously I knew that if I allowed myself to know then I would not be able to turn away. And my life would not be the same anymore. What was my life? I had just turned thirty, had a new baby and was living a relatively superficial, relatively hedonistic life with blinders on. I could continue as I was, or I could throw myself into the fray. Because I am my father's daughter, I chose the latter. Damn the consequences.

As I spoke out against the war, I met people at rallies, vigils, fasts and GI coffee houses that were very different than people I had ever known before. These were college-educated people who could have done different things with their lives, but chose to use their lives in very generous and altruistic ways. These people had a profound effect on me. I am indebted, for example, to a woman named Terry Davis, who I met at a GI coffee house in Killeen, Texas, near Fort Hood. It was 1968 and my movie *Barbarella* had just opened and some people I had met in the movement were using my acclaim to gain attention for the cause. I didn't mind so much. But Terry treated me like a human being. She asked my opinions and made sure I was included in discussions. It was like getting into a warm bath. It made me understand the type of world we were fighting for, and it's also one of the things that allowed me to survive the controversy and attacks against me for my involvement in the anti-war movement.

For the rest of my life, whether it was the raising of children or grandchildren, or making movies or writing books, I wanted to feel that I was moving in the direction of humanity and love. I have tried to do what Terry did for me. I try to listen to others, be open to what they say and see them as human beings.

When you see others as human beings, you want to help them. That was the case after I attended the United Nations Conference on Population and Development in Cairo, Egypt, in 1994. At the time, I was the UN Goodwill Ambassador to the UN Population Fund. I was frankly surprised that the entire conference was organized under the aegis of gender. Until then, I hadn't fully understood that women in the developing world have no social or economic power. They also don't have the power

to negotiate with their husbands about the use of contraception. If they say, "I don't want more children. I'm going to use contraception," they will be beaten and perhaps killed. Their only status is very often having large families.

When I was in Cairo, I visited a community of garbage pickers. They dumped the trash they'd scavenged into their living rooms and their children, mostly girls, picked through it. A local social services organization had tried unsuccessfully to convince their parents to educate the girls. So instead they started a program where the girls were paid $17 a month to turn trash into recycled goods. As they sat in a circle, using scrap fabric to fashion quilts or used paper to make stationery, the girls were taught to read. They were also educated about family planning. It may seem paltry, but that $17 a month allowed the lives of these girls to be changed profoundly. Because they were wage earners, they suddenly had value to their family. And because they were learning to read, they could negotiate with doctors and take charge of health care. And because they understood family planning, they could say to their families, "I am not going to get married. I am going to wait and have a smaller family." Something as simple as $17 a month altered the balance of power within the family.

I took the lessons I learned in Cairo back home to Georgia, which had extreme pockets of poverty and the highest rate of adolescent pregnancy in the United States. I spent a year researching this crisis and trying to figure out how I could help. I remember meeting a fourteen-year-old African American girl who was in labor with her second child. She lived in a tarpaper shack with no indoor plumbing. She looked straight into my eyes and unblinkingly challenged me to judge her. I realized that unless I could change her life circumstances and create a future for her, I had no business talking to her about birth control.

If you want to reduce teen pregnancy, and all risky behavior, then you have to give hope. Hope is the best contraception. A year after going to Cairo, I founded the Georgia Campaign for Adolescent Pregnancy Prevention. We describe our work as "above the waist" because what goes on between the ears of young people is more important than what goes on between their legs in terms of determining their behaviors. This work is not just some charity work for me; it's part of my gut. Just like Terry Davis taught me, even though I'm white and privileged, I know that if you listen to people from your heart, it changes them. And it changes you.

Try to listen to others, be open to what they say and see them as human beings."

Jane Fonda

EMPATHY

To See Yourself in Someone Else's Sneakers

From the playground to the grocery store to the living room sofa, our day-to-days are filled with moments that can be considered from someone else's perspective. When we can imagine being another person, it becomes next to impossible not to want to help when they are suffering.

ONE ICY WINTER DAY, five-year-old Hannah Taylor was driving down a back lane with her mom, Colleen, when she noticed a shivering man eating out of a garbage can. "What is that man doing?" she screamed. Her mom struggled to explain in simple but honest language that some people are poor, hungry, down on their luck. "Until that moment, Hannah believed everyone had what she had," Colleen recalls. "A

home, a bed, love and care."

Hannah says she'll forever remember the sight of that homeless man. "I actually think I felt my heart crack," she says now. "I knew immediately that what I had seen was wrong." For more than a year, Hannah struggled with what she had witnessed. Colleen recalls her daughter's many questions:

"Where is that man?"

"What is he eating?"

"Where is he sleeping?"

"Who loves him?"

Hannah could imagine with every fiber of her tiny being what it might feel like to be in that hungry man's scuffed shoes. With the help of her parents, she learned as much as she could about the homeless. "Even though I was little, I knew I had to do something. I think caring is doing. You cannot ever say you care about someone or something and then do nothing to help." One night Colleen tried to reason with Hannah. "I said, 'Maybe if you do something to help the problem your heart won't be so sad.'" Two days later, Hannah decided to share what she had learned with her Grade 1 class. Many of her classmates were eager to help. Some asked why she liked "stinky, dirty people." The homeless are not bad people, she explained. "They are great people wrapped in old clothes with sad hearts."

Hannah could imagine walking in the shoes of the homeless. She was filled with empathy, which moved her to step up. She organized fundraisers in her school and later on in the community to collect donations for missions

Hannah Taylor is all smiles

> *Hannah has taught us as a family and as parents the importance of looking beyond our insular, safe world. The real reward in life is not what we get but rather what we give."*
>
> **Colleen Taylor**
> Hannah's mother, on the life lessons her own daughter taught her

and shelters. Using her talent for crafts, she transformed her sister's baby food jars into spray-painted "ladybugs," distributing them wherever she could collect change. She also formed strong friendships with street people.

These days, almost a teenager, Hannah runs the Ladybug Foundation, which in a short time has become an influential advocate for the homeless. She and her partners have raised more than one million dollars. She travels across North America urging school kids to give the homeless a chance.

Many people ask Colleen and her husband, Bruce, if they raised Hannah to be an activist. Just like our parents, they offer a resounding, "No." They did raise their children to be in touch with their own feelings and to consider the feelings of others. Little did they know Hannah would take their lessons to heart. At one point, when Colleen was having difficulty grasping the urgency of the cause, she spent a night on the streets with a heroin addict named Grace. Colleen, a marathon runner, had never been so tired. "Hannah has taught us as a family and as parents the importance of looking beyond our insular, safe world. The real reward in life is not what we get but rather what we give."

Do we really expect five-year-olds to campaign to eradicate homelessness? Hannah is an exception, of course, but her story reminds us that parents provide the building blocks when they help kids contemplate the plight of others. Moms and dads can't predict what or when their children will be drawn to an issue. They may find themselves, like Hannah, swept up in a large campaign that involves many. Or they may infuse their days with good deeds, large and small.

E is for Empathy

In 1967, four young Brits sang, "All You Need Is Love." While "All You Need Is Empathy" is not as catchy, it really does have more potential. In order to raise children to be participants — instead of bystanders — we must teach them how to adopt the perspective of someone else, even a stranger. Before children can think *we* instead of *me*, they must experience feelings for the *we*. Empathy is a prerequisite.

There are loads of good reasons to nurture empathy. For starters, emotionally literate children are more likely to get along with parents and siblings. (Come to think of it, maybe this is what motivated Mom and Dad!) Kids who lack empathy grow into hard-edged adults — a demographic in no danger of decline. Significantly, teaching kids to consider the feelings of others is an antidote to bullying, which remains a significant concern despite persuasive education campaigns. The National Institute of Child Health and Development found 29 percent of students — more than one in four — have been on the giving or receiving end of bullying.[1] Just as alarming, most kids who witness bullying fail to intervene.[2] In many cases, neither bullies nor bystanders can put themselves in the victim's position. However, kids who can empathize with others are less likely to bully and more likely to step to another's defense. On the flip side, children without this ability are more likely to grow into insensitive, apathetic adults. When you're looking out for number one, you're less likely to notice someone in need.

We don't mean to suggest that empathy can only be taught. Everyone is hardwired with the ability to feel for others. Scientists are only beginning to understand how the brain creates and responds to feelings of empathy and why its intensity varies from individual to individual.

From an early age, we teach children to identify and organize objects: A is for apple, B is for ball and so it goes. In the same way, we should help them to name and process feelings. It's as easy as talking about the weather. For example, "You must be happy the sun is shining, we can go to the playground." Or, conversely, "Perhaps you are disappointed it's raining and we can't visit the park." Boys and girls will only talk about their feelings if we give them the vocabulary, show them how and give them permission to express them. Start by sharing the highs and lows in your day. When you are facing a moral dilemma, talk about it with your kids. They don't need to know every detail to get the gist. When you make a mistake, apologize — not only is it the right thing to do, it shows kids how it's done.

From the playground to the grocery store to the living room sofa, our day-to-days are filled with moments that can be considered from someone else's perspective. A pint-sized power struggle at the playground swing-set could evolve into a lesson in sharing and perspective-taking: "How would you feel if you weren't allowed a turn?" At a restaurant, a brush with a curt waiter might serve up food for thought: "Why do you suppose he's so angry?" A bedtime story or children's movie that ends happily-ever-after might merit a follow-up: "What do you think you would have done in that situation?" When the younger daughter of our co-author, Shelley, feels sad because her big sister snagged

her bedraggled, formerly pink, stuffed poodle, Shelley helps her to process what she's feeling. As kids develop a repertoire of emotions, they are increasingly able to adopt the viewpoint of other groups, ethnicities and nationalities. The more we understand that "they" are just like "us," the less likely it is that we will tolerate their suffering.

Mom and Dad were teachers, so books filled our lives and home. One of our favorite places was the book-lined room where we stored our Hardy Boys books and Craig's treasured, leather-bound edition of *Tales of the Round Table*. In our younger years, Dad was especially fond of Dr. Seuss. (All together now: "One fish, two fish, red fish, blue fish.") Mom and Dad understood the potency of story to illustrate a lesson. We saw its transformative power in Mark Twain's *Adventures of Huckleberry Finn*, for example. Huck, a fourteen-year-old from the wrong side of the tracks, travels the Mississippi on a raft with his best friend, an escaped slave named Jim. Huck has a crisis of conscience when he is pressured to give up Jim's whereabouts. Forced to choose between salvation and damnation, he decides to give up his place in heaven. "All right then, I'll go to hell," he says, defiantly. When we can imagine being another person, it becomes next to impossible not to want to help when they are suffering.

The Care and Feeding of Others

Dan Kindlon, a renowned child psychologist, tells us the story of a mother and daughter who encounter a crying boy in the park. When the daughter asks why the boy is sad, the mom helps her speculate. "Maybe he's lost. Maybe

FOLLOW THE LEADER

For better or for worse, children mimic all they see. The good news is that this makes it easy to lead by example. Here are a few ways to get them off to an early start:

1. **Let children catch you in everyday acts of caring.** Take time to explain you are e-mailing an old pal or sending photographs to an elderly relative or running an errand for an over-scheduled friend.

2. **Make room to step back:** If you and your kids witness another child's tantrum, discuss what might have prompted the meltdown. "Do you think the little girl was hungry? Or tired? Do you remember how it felt when you asked to go to the playground and I said no?"

3. **Help kids imagine what it's like to be somebody else:** Ask your kids to consider what it might be like to be the teacher or a parent up against cranky kids at the end of the day. You will be nurturing empathy any time you can inspire your children to consider how someone else might feel.

4. **Make time to discuss the child's feelings:** Show them how.

**Trust walk at a
Take Action Academy**

he hurt himself." A mother with a son, however, is more likely to tell him not to dwell on the crying child. Kindlon says parents — and society — often protect boys from having to do the emotional work that helps them become whole people. The Harvard professor, who has spent much of his working life helping boys develop the skills to discuss their feelings, wrote *Raising Cain: Protecting the Emotional Life of Boys* with Michael Thompson.[3] The 1999 book remains a must-read title. Boys don't need special training, Kindlon assured us; they need opportunities to show off their natural capacity by caring for pets, siblings, grandparents, elderly neighbors or others in the neighborhood.

Studies show that parents emphasize achievement, competition, conformity and control of feelings with their sons, while they encourage their daughters to excel at interpersonal relationships. Parents express these expectations verbally and physically. Girls get more embraces and kisses, plus a lion's share of loving language.[4]

When we were little, we enjoyed an infinite supply of hugs. Now it's our default greeting. Free The Children is an organization where everyone embraces — even the guys. As kids, we watched our parents care for their ailing parents. Doing so taught us to help out. We also cared for fish, gerbils, hamsters, turtles, dogs and everything but cats. (Mom didn't like cats, much to Dad's chagrin.) We can now laugh about the time we all chased an A.W.O.L. gerbil from room to room. We had to suspend the search at dinner time when, as if on cue, it ran straight through the kitchen. Game on! Once it was back in its cage, Mom and Dad made us pledge to keep him there. We promised — until

the next time. Caring for animals teaches kids a lot about compassion. (It teaches parents just as much about patience.)

In our house, no matter what we were trying to express, Mom and Dad listened and supported us without judgment. Our parents did their best to expose our softer side. We were never told, "Boys don't cry" — and thank goodness for that. Dad never ordered us to "Suck it up!" if we took a hit on the playing field. Bad enough to be knocked senseless, worse to be rebuked for shedding a tear. Dad did not measure his worth in our pursuits, fortunately. Nor was he wedded to macho traditions. He did the laundry, cleaning and most of the cooking, er, thawing, plus he packed our lunches. (Processed cheese slices on white bread with margarine. Every day! Now and then, Mom would supply gourmet sandwiches and decadent desserts, if only to remind us who really possessed the culinary skills in our family.) Watching Dad, we learned to contribute. We were nourished in every way.

Mom and Dad were launch pads from which we took off on our own time — and we're not just saying that because they're reading this book. (Hi, Mom. Sorry about the gerbil.) We've always known their support was crucial. Recently, we discovered that our appreciation is backed by research. Mothers who are responsive, non-punitive and non-authoritarian with their preschoolers raise kids who are more empathetic and caring.[5] It only makes sense. Numerous studies have shown that you can't rear empathetic kids if you employ threats or physical punishment.[6] The same goes for rejecting a child or withdrawing your support if you don't like a certain behavior.[7]

> **"The Roots of Empathy classroom is creating citizens of the world."**
>
> **Mary Gordon**
> Roots of Empathy founder

Just giving children the tools and permission to discuss their feelings can be liberating. While this is true of elementary school children, it's especially true for teenagers. Every year we organize Me to We leadership academies in places like Toronto, Vancouver, San Francisco, Halifax, Patagonia and Beijing. Children between the ages of eight and twenty show up for a jam-packed week of workshops on social issues, fundraising and public speaking. Day 1, though, is devoted to building trust, creating safe spaces and establishing ground rules.

TEACHING EMPATHY

Raising young people to be empathetic and caring demands a careful balancing act between exposure and protection.

Kids, like adults, may experience empathetic distress if they see a person in trouble. When children take on real or imagined feelings of suffering they may tremble, sweat or cry. To escape such feelings, a child may turn away or else reach out to relieve the distress.

When we were first exposed to homelessness, Mom and Dad understood we would be distressed. They took time to discuss why someone might not have a home or a job or food. We considered what it might feel like to live on the streets. Labeling and discussing emotions is the first step to teaching empathy.

The next step is to help children find a way to help. On the issue of homelessness, just for example, here are a few actions a parent could take with a child:

- Offer a smile or a sandwich.
- Collect change in a jar to donate to a shelter.
- Gather sleeping bags, winter coats and blankets.
- Research and find out why poverty is prevalent in the city.
- Discuss findings.

It's important to talk about each action. Ask the child how it felt to act on his feelings. If helping made him feel good, make the link. If it made him afraid, explore the reasons why. Reinforce and congratulate empathetic behavior. In this way, it will become a part of who he is.

In the decade that we've run this program, we've noticed that girls are better than boys at expressing sentiments and negotiating the rules of communication. We've discovered that most students, even the older ones, have never been in a place where discussing emotions was on the agenda. Many confess they've never truly opened up to parents, pastors and priests or siblings. Kids realize early on that it's easier to say what they think parents want to hear — especially when parents don't take the time to delve deeper.

Parents do a great service any time they can be concrete about their own values. Kindlon advises using everyday situations to demonstrate empathy. "That's what kids watch most of all." We vividly remember Mom's displays of generosity. In stopping to help another, she taught us to think about others less fortunate. If we balked on our way to dropping coins into a homeless man's cup, she would shove us forward. Not only did she discuss our fear, sadness and confusion, she helped us put ourselves in their well-worn shoes. The coins always made it into the cup.

When we were exploring ways that parents can nurture empathy, we had to wonder what might happen to children who don't discover it in their homes. We ended up spending time in the classrooms of renowned educator Mary Gordon. She assured us it is an ongoing journey. Kids in her program learn empathy from a very wise teacher. And, no, she's not boasting of her own prowess! In fact, it was another girl named Hannah who showed us where to find the roots of empathy.

You've Come a Long Way, Baby!

"Hannah is coming!"

The tweens at Dunlop Public School were sugar-high restless, wriggling on the floor after lunch, jabbing each other, ignoring admonishments to be quiet and still. A diverse group that included immigrants from Somalia, Ethiopia and India, the Grade 4 students couldn't muffle their anticipation. "Hannah is coming!"

"She's here!" announced ten-year-old Janakan.

Hannah didn't strut into the classroom, nor did she walk. Rumors suggested that next time she might toddle. On the day of our visit, she arrived in her mother's arms.

Hannah was ten-months-old with two teeth, a dimpled smile and a pink bow in her hair. Her arrival signaled the start of Roots of Empathy, an innovative program taught in classrooms in Canada, the United States, New Zealand and Australia. How unusual? Well, for starters, Hannah is the teacher.

"Hello Baby Hannah!" the kids burst into song. "How are you today?" Hannah's mom told the class about her baby's first steps. The kids begged to see. Applause and marvel met Hannah's off-kilter steps. After all, when the students first met Hannah, she was not much more than a newborn. Laura Faller and her baby dropped into the school every three weeks. When the students were first introduced to three-month-old Hannah, they expected to see her crawl and to hear her talk. Now they know that first teeth, first smiles and first steps arrive in time, each a small miracle.

Speaking of extraordinary happenings,

HOW WOULD THAT MAKE YOU FEEL?

U.S. President Barack Obama has said the only time he ever saw his mother angry was when she witnessed someone being bullied or being treated differently because of who they were. "If she saw me doing that, she would be furious," he said in his video introduction at the Democratic Convention in August 2008. "She'd say to me, 'Imagine standing in that person's shoes. How would that make you feel?' That simple idea, I'm not sure I always understood it as a kid, but it stayed with me."

Later, traveling from town to town during his campaign for the White House, the candidate was reminded of his mother's words. "One person's struggle is all of our struggles," he said. "We recognize ourselves in each other."

"

We recognize ourselves in each other."

Barack Obama

Mary Gordon's program is a remarkable exercise in nurturing empathy. By watching the evolving relationship between a mother and her baby, children learn to see the world through the infant's eyes. A traincd instructor helps students label a baby's feelings. If, for example, a baby falls again and again while attempting to stand, the kids come to recognize that she might be frustrated. A young observer might then compare the baby's struggle to difficulties in her own life, analogies that are encouraged before and after each session.

On the day we visited, students were asked to consider how Hannah might feel to be the center of attention. Every hand went up. "I think she likes all the attention," said mop-topped Dillon. "It makes her happy."

"I think she's a bit scared," Hibbo added shyly, "but also she feels *un-lonely*. She is happy not to be alone."

An adult hand reached out to touch Hibbo's shoulder. It belonged to Mary Gordon, who also happened to be visiting. "I have learned a new word today," Gordon said. "Un-lonely. I like that word. It's what we all want to be. I learned something else recently. When you touch someone, the feeling of being touched causes new circuits in the brain to form, it grows larger. Being touched is good for your brain and your heart." Her words might have been over the children's heads, but the look on their faces suggested she'd spoken to their hearts.

We were drawn to the sublime world of Mary Gordon because she has demonstrated that schools have the power to teach children the Three Rs, the Three Cs — caring, compassion and community — and the Big E: Empathy.

Along the way, she's collected impressive evidence that supports her work. Independent studies have shown that program graduates are more socially sensitive and in touch with their emotions than other youngsters. These same kids have been found to be less aggressive and more likely to challenge nastiness and injustice. "The Roots of Empathy classroom is creating citizens of the world," says Gordon, who has earned the right to boast.

When she was a child, Mary Gordon was spoon-fed empathy. She was her father's shadow during his visits to the sick and dying in hospital. She also tagged along when her mother delivered clothing, food and coal to poorer families. Mary's mother always took time to share a cup of tea with the lady of the house. If Mary made a face at cracked cups or shoddy conditions, her mother would later put her in her place. "How dare you judge?" she'd demand.

Mary Gordon grew up to become an elementary school teacher, a promoter of literacy and an advocate on behalf of teenage mothers. As she contemplated the relationship between mother and child, she realized it had much to teach. She came to see that if children could put themselves in the shoes, er, booties, of a baby, they'd be able to put themselves in anyone's shoes.

She writes about nine-year-old Sylvie, for example. Several kids were laughing at the girl's shoes — cheap, tacky and done up with Velcro. Sylvie was crying on her way out to recess until her best friend convinced her to swap a shoe. In the schoolyard, the girls stood together in mismatched footwear. "This is my friend," their silent act told the tormentors. "Make fun of her and you make fun of me." This story, says Mary, shows how important it is to nurture empathy in the youngest of children.

We can't all enroll our children in a Roots of Empathy program, although Mary assures us she is working on world domination. The program is spreading throughout schools in Canada, the U.S. and other countries. But don't worry, she says: Attentive, loving and empathetic parents are the best role models for children. Empathetic children, she assures us, will become citizens of the world.

SMALL ACTIONS › EVERY DAY

1. IF THEY'RE HAPPY AND THEY KNOW IT:
Help children name and process what they are feeling. Once they can articulate their emotions, encourage them to think about the feelings of others.

2. HOW WOULD YOU FEEL IF...?
It's a question that's perfect for every occasion. Ask kids to put themselves in someone else's shoes — happy or sad.

3. CHAMPION A PET PROJECT:
Caring for an animal — large or small — is a natural way to nurture compassion in a child. When appropriate, older children can be asked to tend to younger siblings.

4. MAKE THANKS A HABIT:
Invite every person around the dinner table to express gratitude for something that happened during the day.

5. SHARE QUIET ACTS OF EMPATHY:
Morally courageous people don't often make front-page news, but don't let that stop you from highlighting acts and decisions that are worth celebrating.

My Great Hero in Life

*On August 10, 1976, **Betty Williams** was driving in Belfast when she turned a corner and saw a broken and mangled bike, a baby carriage and the bodies of Joanne, John and Andrew Maguire. A runaway car driven by an IRA member, Danny Lennon, crashed into the family. Lennon had been fatally shot while fleeing from British soldiers. All three children were killed. Their mother, Anne Maguire, was critically injured and later committed suicide. Williams' reaction to the deadly accident set in motion a series of profound events. Williams and Mairead Corrigan (Anne Maguire's sister) – co-founders of Peace People – were jointly awarded the Nobel Peace Prize in 1976 for their action to end the sectarian violence in Northern Ireland. We talked to Betty about why she rose up against the conflict in her community and how that led her to continue to work for peace.*

I WAS A PRETTY HARD CHILD. Very self-willed, especially if I thought I was right. My mother said trying to get me to change my mind was like trying to lift somebody out of a box of cement that had hardened. As stubborn as I was, my daddy, my great hero in life, saw beyond the tough shell to the softie inside.

I remember one day my mommy was having an awful time with me and she kept telling me, "Just wait 'til your father gets home." When I saw him walk up the path, I hid behind the coats in the hall. You could see my little spindly six-year-old legs sticking out. Daddy went to the sink and washed his hands while my mother recited an entire list of the naughty things I had done that day. I was shaking, anticipating his reaction. I

remember daddy turned to my mother and saying, "Well, what do you want to do Margaret?" She said, "Well should you smack her?" And he said, "Margaret, have I ever smacked you?" And she said, "Certainly not." "Well then I'm not going to smack someone smaller than you." Then he came out to the hall and lifted the coats so he could see my wee face, and he said, "Your mother says you and I need to talk. What would you like to talk about?"

It was an amazing moment. He removed all my fear I had inside of me and then we sat down and talked through the issues. He always told me there was nothing we couldn't accomplish if we just opened our minds and hearts to the matter. But the truth is, as I grew up, fear took away my courage.

Being a mother in Northern Ireland, I feared for my two kids all the time. I had seen terrible atrocities that I can't even talk about now because it hurts too badly. But I can tell you I had two cousins killed in the war. My cousin Danny, a pre-med student, was killed at the age of eighteen, when Protestant extremists shot him as he stood at the front door of his house. Another cousin, a postman, was killed when a booby-trapped car abandoned by members of the IRA exploded as he was driving past it. The Protestants killed one of my cousins, and the Catholics killed the other. My cousins, like me, were Catholic.

But the day the Maguire children were destroyed in one senseless act of violence — it was the straw that broke the camel's back. Those three hours following the accident will remain etched into my life as it would for any mother. I could never go back to being the person I once was. I was in shock. My next memory was standing in my garage screaming. And then just anger. *We can't go on like this*, I thought. *The next dead children could be my own.*

For years I had lived in fear of the violence and truthfully had done very little to change the situation. But that evening something snapped inside of me. Fear had crippled us. But no more.

I grabbed a writing pad, scrawled Peace Petition, and drove through Andersontown, through IRA territory, banging on doors. I thrust the paper at people who answered, urging them to sign my petition. It was to condemn the IRA's violence and demanding the IRA leave our neighborhoods. Within minutes I had hundreds of signatures. As I went door to door, women came out of their homes to help. They all knew about the death of the Maguire children. Everyone was devastated. We all thought, "No more." I was like the Pied Piper walking through the streets of Andersontown followed by a growing crowd of women. We collected and counted thousands of signatures that night.

There was no point in going to bed. I picked up the phone and called the local newspaper and told them of the petition. When the editor heard how many names had been collected, he said, "Hold the front page." The banner headline the next day shouted about my housewife's call for peace. We planned for a rally that Saturday afternoon on Finaghy Road where the Maguire children had been killed. I invited all women, Protestant and Catholic, to join this movement to protest all violence – legal or illegal. I gave out my phone number and my address. The police chief arrived at my house and told me I'd made myself a target. He said I would need security including police presence, barbed wire and cameras around the house. But I went on and told him that men with guns surrounding the house would only attract more guns. So I insisted on having no security. I didn't want to be afraid anymore.

A few days later almost 10,000 people — most of them women — descended on Finaghy Road North rally where the Maguires had been killed. Protestant mothers pushed through the neighborhood divide to join arms with Catholic mothers. We sang hymns and prayed. There was a moment of silence for the dead Maguire children.

Those events altered my life's path. They also reminded me of the early lessons my daddy taught me. If you sit back and accept life as it is then nothing is going to change. You are just going to be behind curtains or blinds or barbed wire forever. I had to make change, but I also knew it would come at a cost. When it was announced that we had received the Nobel Peace Prize I knew that this was both a gift and a curse. I was a mother myself and I had two young children. I knew that my whole life was going to be turned on its ear and so was theirs. My head was filled with so many "what ifs." But I accepted the Peace Prize as a gift and a tool that would allow me to move forward and help others.

If you sit back and accept life as it is then nothing is going to change. You are just going to be behind curtains or blinds or barbed wire forever. I had to make change."

Betty Williams

LESSON 3:
RESPONSIBILITY

The Case for "Home" Work

Start with small tasks — setting the table or emptying the dishwasher — so kids learn they have a role to play. Chores are not always a bad thing and sometimes they can be fun. And with chores comes responsibility — and maybe a future as a chef. It doesn't hurt that the whole household is coming together to lend a hand.

NAABALA IS A WARRIOR in the Maasai Mara of East Africa. As we walk the scrubby landscape, the twenty-one-year-old's necklaces jangle when he stoops to point out plants that save lives and others that kill. He wears a bright red *shukha* blanket over his shoulder with a baton-like weapon called a *conga* tucked into his belt. It's a scene out of pastoralist Africa — or at least it was until he stops to answer his cell phone. He speaks with another warrior who has called to discuss the chances that rain might bless this drought-stricken region.

When we first met Naabala, he was a scrawny, giggly boy at one of our schools. Today he is the future of his people. On a recent visit, the statuesque warrior and budding botanist talked to us about the evolving but critical roles he plays in his family. After walking awhile, we came to rest under a tree on the crest of a hill. Zebras grazed nearby. With no apparent dangers in sight — say, a hungry lion — the warrior put down his spear. Everything Naabala knows, he's learned from his father, also a Maasai warrior and the local plant expert. Naabala's father has seventeen children by several wives. Although he is busy, he is committed bring them home for dinner!

When we were very young, our parents did almost everything for us. They cooked and cleaned and chauffeured — important Three Cs, to be sure. Thankfully, for our sake, they realized we needed more. To help teach us responsibility, they decided to give us some, whether it was feeding the neighbor's cat (until it ran away) or helping around the house. In little ways, we took on bigger roles in our family and the community. In no time, these tentative steps became larger strides and bolder actions. You can't expect a young person to assist a stranger if they have not first experienced what it is like to help those they love. If a child is a bystander in her own household, she is almost certain to be one everywhere else. The channel-surfing tween who watches his mother whip up dinner, set the table and tidy up is not the most likely to become a teen who helps an elderly neighbor with groceries or volunteers time at a homeless shelter. Mom and Dad began by teaching us small gestures — holding open a door, for example, an antiquated courtesy that we insist on at Free The Children. In subtle ways, we were nudged to lend a hand. Asking kids to get up and chip in teaches them how it is done. Small acts in early days are almost certain to give way to later, greater acts. Take the 44th President of the United States as an example.

Get the Roller Rolling

On the day before his inauguration, President-Elect Barack Obama could have been sweet talking voters anywhere in the country, but chose to help paint the walls of an emergency shelter for homeless teens in Washington, D.C. He took off his jacket, rolled up his sleeves, dipped a roller in blue paint and showed the world how to give back — one roll at a time. He didn't make much of his painting technique. "Seriously, this isn't like rocket science," he joked with reporters and volunteers. "You take a pole and there's a roller at the end, and then you roll." But he made much of the power of his gesture. On that day, Martin Luther King Day, President-Elect Obama called on the entire nation to serve. It is every citizen's responsibility, he said. When people chip in for the common good, it makes a country great. "When all of our people are engaged and involved in making their community better, then we can accomplish anything," he said.

"Not simply as a call to sympathy or charity, but as something more demanding, a call to stand in somebody else's shoes and see through their eyes," he writes in *The Audacity of Hope*. His feeling of responsibility toward others came from his mother, Stanley Ann Dunham, who earned her doctorate at the University of Hawaii while helping craftsmen in Indonesia and Africa get small loans to improve their lives and their villages. She showed her son that it was possible to change the world by helping people help themselves. The President says his mother also disdained cruelty, thoughtlessness and any abuse of power, whether it was racial prejudice, bullying in the schoolyard or underpaying workers. Whenever she and her son witnessed "even a hint" of such behavior she'd ask him, "How do you think that would make you feel?" President Obama says he uses that simple question, "How do you think that would make you feel?" as a guidepost for the

**Maasai Mara
warrior Naabala**

to teaching his offspring to contribute to each other and eventually to the village, a collection of families that depend on one another for food and shelter. Naabala's mother teaches his sisters to cook, fetch water and tend children. Naabala, meanwhile, learns about the rugged landscape — which plants are toxic, which are healthful, which should be reserved for late-night parties. When he turned nine, he was given a spear and responsibility for a hundred cattle. Each night and every weekend, it was his job to count the cows returning from pasture.

From an early age, Naabala was expected to contribute to his family and to his village. We couldn't help but reflect on our own lives at age nine. Mom and Dad might have asked us to pitch in with a rake or a paintbrush or a dishtowel, but we were never in charge of the food supply — unless you count the times we were dispatched to the corner-store to buy milk. Imagine entrusting a kid in North America with the family's wealth? That's exactly what Naabala was protecting when he kept watch over the livestock. As he grew, so did his responsibilities. Now that he is a warrior, he is not just expected to ward off wild animals — he's supposed to way he tries to treat others.

The First Lady, Michelle Obama, was raised with an emphasis on education, achievement and service toward others. She grew up on Chicago's South Side in a one-bedroom apartment. Her father, the late Frasier Robinson, was a city pump operator and a Democratic precinct captain. Her mother, Marian, was a secretary who later stayed home to raise Michelle and her older brother, Craig. Brother and sister slept in the living room with a makeshift sheet dividing their room. Despite family hardship, Michelle was raised to help others first. It would shape her career. A professor who taught her at Harvard Law School recalls, "She made a commitment to her father, who did not go to college, that she would pursue her talents to help her community." And she did, working at the school's legal aid bureau, running a non-profit leadership training program for young people, and developing the University of Chicago's first community service program.

The First Family's passion for setting an example through service reminds us of how contagious the Three Cs—compassion, courage and commitment to community — are. Both the President and First Lady speak frequently about how this sense of responsibility to their community — both locally and globally — began at home, and can be passed from one generation to the next, like a favorite family recipe, or an organic carrot in the White House vegetable garden.

In our family, young Marc, maybe a bit like President Obama, enjoyed "helping" others with a paint brush.

It's Never Too Early to Start

Mom and Dad confessed recently that as much as they appreciated our "help" around the house — and, yes, they used the word in quotations — the goal was never to lighten their load. When Marc was four, for example, they recruited his assistance when they were redecorating a room. Taking time to train their young aide, they supplied him with wallpaper scraps and showed him how to glue it to the wall. Marc was assigned a small corner of the room where he spent the afternoon pasting strips. Though disappointed the ends did not line up, he went to bed happy. The next morning, he discovered every seam was perfect. He ran to tell everyone about the "wallpaper fairy." To this day, Marc remains almost comically naïve about who finished the job. (Maybe it was Barack Obama.) For the record, Mom and Dad did not usually redo our work — focusing on our efforts rather than the results. "Children have to feel they have a contribution to make, that their help is needed and welcomed," Mom says of such assignments. "They have to gain confidence and a sense of importance in taking those first steps to help and to share." By starting with small tasks — setting the table or emptying the dishwasher—kids learn they have a role to play. "They can help," Mom insists. "They can make people happy. They can improve a situation. They have talents they can share."

Here's the catch: Kids today have hockey practice and math tutoring and violin lessons — for some that's just on Tuesdays! There's little room in overcrowded schedules for grunt work. With so much on the go, parents are inclined to present children with fewer responsibilities rather than more. There was a time when kids could not escape their duties. Now, blessed with so much wealth, we give them all that is asked and demand little in return. Naabala reminds us that children in many cultures and countries still work crops, tend animals and care for siblings and grandparents. These, of course, are not make-work projects but tasks that are fundamental to a family's well-being. You can't send your city kid to tend the flocks, obviously, but there are equally important places within our communities that could use an extra hand. It's easy for kids today to be only and all about themselves. Yet if it's true that children learn what they live, we need to give some thought to what we are teaching them on the shuttle from studies to athletics to music classes.

At this point it would be easy to get defensive. After all, many parents work really hard to provide what they themselves never had — piano lessons, trendy clothes, winter getaways. Others with the best intentions want to delay the introduction of real-world responsibilities. Yet we know from our own lives and through our work that it's never too early to help a child develop social responsibility. Almost from the start, parents can encourage children to think about others. When they lend a hand, they'll discover what it feels like to be needed. Even the most straightforward of assignments will show them that they can make a difference.

Two Scoops and a Call to Order

Experts — Mom included — suggest the first opportunities for service begin in the home. The sooner, the better. The ranks of our volunteers at Free The Children are examples in action. One mom we know, Julie Weiss, moved all of the dishes to the bottom shelves in her kitchen so that her children

Marc happily helping out with the laundry

THE POWER OF "HOME" WORK

It's never too early to recruit your children to help around the house. Complete this worksheet to help figure out who should do what.

1. Write down the household chores that could be completed easily by the youngest in your household. We've started the list with a few examples:

   - Tidy toys.
   - Empty wastebaskets.
   - Put dirty clothes in the hamper.
   - Help to clear the table.

   _____

   _____

   _____

   _____

2. Now list jobs that a young child could take on with the help of an adult. We've jotted down a few ideas:

   - Rake leaves.
   - Sort the laundry.
   - Load the dishwasher.
   - Water houseplants.

   _____

   _____

   _____

   _____

3. List assignments an older child could do with the proper training. A few ideas to begin:

   - Walk the dog.
   - Wash the car.
   - Help make dinner.
   - Care for a younger sibling.

   _____

   _____

   _____

   _____

could set the table without help. The three kids took turns. No plates? No dinner. It's not exactly guarding the cattle, but you get the idea. Julie's kids were also expected to sort laundry and to load the dishwasher. The kids complied, not to earn an allowance but because it was their responsibility as contributing members of the family. They held Sunday meetings, usually over ice cream, at which they discussed plans for the week ahead and problems with the week gone by. "I wanted them to know they are part of something greater than themselves and their small actions can make a difference," Julie explains. "I also wanted them to know that their opinions and concerns matter." The children felt important because they had a say in planning and organizing family life. Julie tells us that she and her husband, Eric, wanted their children to feel connected. "I wanted the kids to feel it was important that they are in the family."

Julie's eldest, Jordana, now in university, attended one of our leadership camps when she was nine. She went on to become a motivational speaker, and has participated in many overseas volunteer trips. Jesse, now in high school, has also been an active volunteer. Julie remains very involved in FTC activities and is always available to support staff members. She is also on the board of One Child, an organization that combats the sexual exploitation of children. "Some kids don't like having their parents around," Jordana told us. "That's not true for me. The family meetings really made us feel like a team. We felt we were achieving something together."

As many parents well know, it's actually more work to enlist small hands in household chores. It helps to acknowledge that going in. It's a good idea to match the tasks at hand to the abilities of the children involved. Caring for the family dog is too much to expect of a seven-year-old boy, but he could be asked to ensure the animal always has fresh water. A ten-year-old wouldn't take on a solo shift at a soup kitchen. Yet it's an experience tackled easily if parents also commit to the outing. Even if the initial behavior is nothing more than a gesture, successive acts of a similar nature tend to grow in scale. Don't be afraid to ask too much of your child. Be afraid to ask too little.

Should kids get paid for chores? It's a question that has been debated almost as long as there have been teenagers. Like Julie Weiss, many parents believe every family member should contribute to the household — period. One expert suggests that if your kids want cash for shoveling the driveway, you should send them next door. Others say that earning an allowance teaches kids how to handle cash. At our friend Shelley's house, the girls receive an allowance independent of their chores. When the weekly handout takes place, the girls are reminded to save some and give some. The rest is theirs to spend. One Christmas, the girls pooled the money — $75 — with their friends James and Will Feschuk to buy a hamper of food for a family down on their luck. On another occasion, they made a $100 micro-credit loan to an entrepreneur in Uganda to buy used sports clothes to sell in a market. Next it was $22 to the Terry Fox Run. Ten dollars bought a mosquito net in Ethiopia.

No matter where you stand on allowance, we believe chores should be non-negotiable.

SEE SPOT TEACH. TEACH, SPOT, TEACH

Craig spending time with Muffin, Coco, Pepper and Chip

Kids have always enjoyed the companionship of pets. Studies show that children can learn important lessons from animals about empathy, responsibility and compassion.

Dr. Aubrey H. Fine at California State Polytechnic University-Pomona has been working with animals and humans for more than twenty-five years. "My interest in using animals originally was to figure out ways for the animals to act as a social catalyst to enhance rapport," he has said. "I've since learned to incorporate animals in a variety of other ways that take advantage of their gentleness, their sense of calmness and sometimes their silence in providing therapy."

Feeding a goldfish, walking a dog, grooming a horse — enjoying time with an animal companion fosters cognitive development and emotional maturity.

"Having an animal takes major responsibility," Dr. Fine says. "Kids become mentors to the animals, and they learn to be teachers, not only takers."

ADD IT UP!

- Families are so over-scheduled that in the past twenty years structured sports time has doubled, household conversations have become far less frequent and family dinners have declined 33 percent, according to over-scheduling expert Dr. Alvin Rosenfeld.

- Since the 1970s, children have lost twelve hours a week in free time; including a 25 percent drop in play overall, according to the University of Michigan's Survey Research Center.

- Students were found to be spending eight hours more each week in school than kids twenty years ago. During this period, homework time has nearly doubled, according to Michigan researchers.

- Although the National Sleep Foundation claims students need nine hours of sleep to be ready for school, most teens get between seven and seven-and-a-half hours of sleep each night.

- A 2004 study at the University of Minnesota found that teens who ate five or six meals a week with their families were seven to 24 percent less likely to smoke cigarettes or marijuana, drink alcohol, get lower grades or show signs of depression.

The Kielburger family on their European vacation

Helping at home — even on the most mundane of assignments — is a place to start. Underestimate your child's abilities, and they will never rise to the occasion. Watch your kid and look for emerging abilities or interests. If your son likes to help in the kitchen, encourage him to help plan a family meal once a week. If your daughter loves nature, put her in charge of watering the household plants. If your son is a budding interior designer, put him in charge of the wallpaper and painting.

Lost Arts and Life Lessons

Just as we learned from our parents, we also learned from our grandparents. Grandpa taught Craig to hold a rake, bag leaves and greet the neighbors. (Craig figured out on his own that before you bag leaves, you're supposed to jump in the pile!) Later, when our grandfather was ill, Mom and Dad showed us how to offer him care. There is so much wisdom to share among generations. Unfortunately, many of the avenues for this exchange no longer exist in North American households.

Shelley told us about a Saturday afternoon when her two children were visiting their grandparents. Shelley's ten-year-old, Cleo, noticed a couple of holes in her pants. It would have been easy for Shelley to patch the holes, easier still to drop them with a seamstress, or buy a new pair. Instead, Shelley's mom decided to teach Cleo the basics — just as she'd once taught Shelley. When the work was done, Cleo was proud and satisfied. The next morning, Cleo's younger sister, Scarlet, hopped on her grandma's lap with a torn shirt and the sewing kit.

When we were sixteen and ten, Mom and Dad took us to Europe. It was to be our dream vacation. We began with four weeks in Paris, the city Dad visited as a young man. We rented a small apartment in a historic part of the city. Just one problem: Marc had a new girlfriend and had made it no secret that he did not want to be with us. During the days, we hopped from museum to art gallery — the bottom of Marc's list of must-do activities. Aware of Marc's displeasure, Craig lobbied to fill the itinerary with more museums. He'd contemplate each masterpiece in every gallery, while Marc would give a glance before trudging out. In the evenings, he'd call his girlfriend and they'd scheme about how to get him home. Mom tried to convince him that it was his last chance to hang out with family before university. He didn't care.

Eventually Mom and Dad had to acknowledge that it was not "our" trip — it was "their" trip. They called a family meeting and invited us to take over the remaining four weeks of the summer getaway. They gave us a budget and urged us to get organized. We consulted travel guides and planned a family adventure by train through Italy, Switzerland, Germany and Greece. We planned sightseeing, found inexpensive places to stay and even took care of their luggage. Marc didn't forget his girlfriend entirely — he sent a postcard from every stop — but as chief organizer, he was immersed in every detail. Just a couple years later, we would travel on our own to Europe, Thailand, Kenya and South Asia. Mom and Dad are convinced we'd never have made those journeys had we not been empowered first at home and later on that vacation. Young people rise to a challenge. In our rush to do our best for our children, it's easy to assume tasks that they could take on. A job well done teaches kids a sense of accomplishment. Children deserve an opportunity to revel in newfound abilities and take on challenges in their school, community and, one day, the world.

SMALL ACTIONS › EVERY DAY

1. STEP BACK SO THAT A KID CAN STEP UP:
If you are forever tying his shoes, he might never try on his own. If you always intervene in playmate squabbles, she may never attempt to work things out on her own.

2. HAVE PATIENCE FOR TRIAL AND ERROR:
Spilt milk is truly no cause for tears, especially if it's the result of an ambitious preschooler learning to self-serve. Help your child deal with the consequences. "Here's a cloth to mop up..."

3. PRESENT OPTIONS:
Let your child choose — when safe and possible — and stand by his choices. Doing so demonstrates your faith in his abilities.

4. BOTTOM FEEDERS:
Move the plates to a low shelf so the kids can set the table. No matter what the task, enlisting kids teaches them responsibility and shows they are crucial to family functioning.

5. WILL WORK FOR COIN:
If you give your kids an allowance, encourage them to divide it into three: Save some, spend some and share some.

Helping Others Brings the Greatest Joy of All

*Acclaimed actor **Mia Farrow** is a Unicef Goodwill Ambassador who has traveled to such places as Angola, Chad, Central African Republic and Darfur to highlight the plight of women and children while urging the world to take more decisive action against poverty and injustice. She spoke to us about nurturing a social conscience.*

I'VE BEEN INCREDIBLY LUCKY. I started working as an actor when I was eighteen. There were plenty of actors who were better, more talented, more beautiful than I, but artistic success, fame and fortune came my way while I was still in my teens. There are people who spend much of their lives looking for these things. I was and I am profoundly grateful. And I am grateful too for the most useful piece of knowledge that came out of it all — the discovery that those things in themselves do not make you happy.

So I began the search for a life that would be meaningful to me and hopefully to others. This search took me along various paths. I needed to find a life that involved helping others but I didn't know how to go about it.

Eventually I became the mother of fourteen children. They came from many countries and with

many disabilities. They have been my teachers, my joy and more. I tell my children that we are part of a larger human family. When one of us is suffering then we all suffer. If we turn away from that suffering, then we are diminished in the most essential way.

We know that on this same Earth, as we go about our business, ten million children die from hunger every year. More than a billion children do not have safe drinking water. Countless children are caught in conflict — they are not safe.

People often ask me what is the most important thing I could teach my children. If I had to boil it down to one word, that word would be "responsibility." I hope they will have a true sense of responsibility to their family, their community, to the planet they have inherited, and to their brothers and sisters everywhere in the human family. We can all find ways to do our part to serve those in need.

In our family, well before learning the alphabet, my kids knew the Two Rs — responsibility and respect. If our actions and decisions are made with a sense of responsibility and with respect, I think we won't go too far off track.

I try to help them discover their own strengths

and gifts that they can share. An opportunity to do something for someone else is a gift. The most closely guarded secret is this: Helping others brings the greatest joy of all.

My son Ronan, for example, is a Unicef spokesman for youth. He has been to Darfur twice. He worked in the slums of Kibera in Kenya this summer. He speaks about what he has seen in Africa and writes opinion pieces. My daughter Malone and my daughter-in-law Gillian run my website. So many of my children are finding their own ways to help others.

"With knowledge comes responsibility," I tell my children.

That doesn't mean that my children don't want things. These are materialistic times. The culture is materialistic. But how do you make your children see that who they are is separate from what they have? I tell them that the only time you really own anything is in the moment that you give it away.

At times I have asked them, "If I gave you more things would you be better? If I gave you a bigger TV or three iPods would you be a better human being than you are now? How about if I gave you ten of them? Would you be better if I gave you thirty of them? And what if you had none of them? Would you be less of a person?"

I hope they see that it is by that which cannot be taken away that we can measure ourselves.

"An opportunity to do something for someone else is a gift. The most closely guarded secret is this: Helping others brings the greatest joy of all."
Mia Farrow

Every Child Has Something to Give

Just imagine how much better the world would be if we recognized that everyone has something unique to contribute. The gift is also beside the point. What is key is that kids are encouraged to share their talents.

WHEN WE WERE KIDS, there was no such thing as a day off school — at least not for Kielburgers. When schools in our board were closed, we'd have to tag along to Mom's in downtown Toronto. At the timeworn elementary school, we'd climb four floors to her classroom where there was no air conditioning in June and little heat in January. In winter, the students, many newly arrived from countries that do not know cold, kept their sweaters and coats on all day long. Come to think of it, so did we!

From our seats in the back corner, we watched Mom teach. In her class of special needs students, there were autistic children, slow learners and immigrants who had yet to master English. While others saw only their weaknesses, Mom worked hard to identify

"Be Kind whenever possible. It is always possible."

—The Dalai Lama

If you dare to dream of becoming an artist, you will dare to be different. This will take courage... to be an artist is to have the gift of seeing the world in a unique way; a gift you can share with the world for the rest of your life.”

Wendall Minor
Author and
illustrator

their strengths. In doing so, she taught us that all students are gifted no matter what they're up against. As she uncovered new abilities in her students, she taught us that each and every kid — not just those who score highest on intelligence tests — has a knack or unique skill to offer the world. Like pieces of a puzzle, these gifts and abilities come together to create the big picture. Alice Paul, author of the Equal Rights Amendment passed in 1923, once likened the women's movement to a great mosaic: "Each of us puts in one little stone." In the same way, all children must be encouraged to contribute so that the world can shine a little brighter.

We learned a lot in Mom's classroom. We followed a new immigrant as he learned to read and watched a girl with learning disabilities tackle rudimentary math. From our corner, Mom would recruit us to help. The experience was profound and empowering, especially for Craig. He'd struggled with a speech impediment and had trouble pronouncing many sounds, including 'Rs' — a concern when your first and last names contain three! He didn't enunciate and often spoke too quickly. He was teased mercilessly. Yet in this work with children who did not speak English as a first language, Craig was the expert. He borrowed from speech therapy, teaching them where to place their tongues to form words. Together they pondered the age-old question: "How much wood would a woodchuck chuck (if a woodchuck could chuck wood)?" In other moments, Marc was encouraged to sit with an outcast. Emulating Mom, he'd touch the child's shoulder in encouragement and look her in the eyes. It's hard to say who benefited more from

the exchange.

Mom has always had the ability to help the shy and self-conscious find their voice. Early in her career, she taught a class of ten, ranging in age from eight to thirteen, all of whom struggled with speech or language. At the start of the school year, the principal let Mom know her class would not be expected to take part in school assemblies. Mom turned the pass into a challenge. "I sensed these kids already felt isolated," she explained. "I thought we should at least try."

She gathered her students and started to rehearse for Christmas celebrations. First, she pulled together pictures and images of the holiday. Next she wrote each student's name on the blackboard. "Every time a child said something, I wrote the exact words, thought or idea under his or her name." She filled every inch of the board. "It was a huge jigsaw puzzle of words and ideas. All I had to do was put them together — carefully respecting what each child had said and making sure their own words would be their part in the play." On the day of the assembly, the classmates performed for their school. It was a giant first step. The best part, Mom says, was watching "sparkling little eyes come alive."

Despite the odds, Mom went on to prepare six of her students for a public speaking contest. They rehearsed in front of anyone who would listen. "I cannot tell you the shock that permeated the school." One of her students placed second, another captured third. Thanks to Mom, we learned to uncover hidden talents. We grew to understand that her gift was helping others to find their gifts.

What to Say About the Gift of Gab?

It's probably no coincidence we became public speakers, but it was never a given. Marc was a shy and self-conscious boy. The thought of speaking in public filled him with fear. But Mom helped him find his confidence for a Grade 3 speaking contest. She sat at home with him as he recited and memorized "Alligator Pie," a poem by the beloved Dennis Lee. She taught him that preparation and passion were crucial. On the day of the competition, Marc was shaking in his shoes, and his brown corduroys and orange sweater. (Can you tell Craig wrote that sentence?) To everyone's surprise, including Marc's, he picked up a three-inch trophy. Better than that, he'd received a tremendous boost. He was still shy but more willing to take risks. By the time he reached high school, Marc had won local, provincial and even international contests. Since those days, he's shared the stage with Bill Clinton, the Dalai Lama and other great orators, speaking to audiences as large as fifty thousand — all thanks to Mom and "Alligator Pie."

When Craig was much younger, he auditioned for the church choir. "You sing like an angel," he was told. "Just try to do it more softly." Apparently, it's easier to identify areas in which you are profoundly ungifted! Inspired by Marc, he decided to try public speaking. Mom was anxious to shelter Craig from teasing about his speech impediment, but she knew better than to underestimate anyone — especially her headstrong second born. He was eager to be like his big brother, of course, though he would never have admitted it to Marc. He was also determined to do what he'd been told he could not.

In Grade 6, he entered a school-wide speaking contest. On the night before the event, he barely slept. Mom tried to convince him to stay home because he had a bad cold. Not a chance. He showed up to discover that he was up against the provincial champ. The subject of the contest? "Being a winner." At that

MOTHER KNOWS BEST

What we learned from Mom about making a speech:

1. Find a topic or issue about which you are passionate. Know your audience. Believe in yourself and in your ability to make a difference.

2. Paint a picture in words. Help people understand your passion. Make it interesting and creative. Speak slowly, loudly and clearly. Deliver from the heart.

3. Share what you have learned. Express how you feel and why. Find real-world examples. Make eye contact; look at your audience and smile.

4. End your speech by summarizing your main points. Briefly explain how audience members can help.

moment, Craig couldn't have felt more like a loser. Nervously and without notes, he took the stage. "Real winners are those who try hard and don't necessarily win," he began. He found confidence as he described playing hockey and watching dads yell at their sons for losing a puck or missing the net — wondering out loud why it mattered so much. The speech wasn't perfect but it came from the heart. Like something out of a Hollywood movie, Craig won first prize! Since that sleepless night, he's given thousands of speeches to students, educators, lawyers, judges and business people around the world — kind of amazing when you consider how many people doubted his abilities. These days, in fact, everyone complains that he talks too much! (Can you tell Marc wrote that sentence?) It's not about prizes, of course. It's about finding and sharing your gift.

Although we believe every child has a gift, society's definition of "gifted" is limited almost exclusively to stand outs in academics or sports. Just imagine how much better the world would be if we recognized that everyone has something unique to share. Some people have a talent for teaching, others for inventing, others still are natural-born leaders or artists or problem-solvers. The gift is almost beside the point. What is key, we think, is that kids — and adults — are encouraged to share their talents. Kids who like to mess around in the kitchen, just for example, could be encouraged to organize a bake sale for charity. Bookworms who love nothing more than to get lost in a story could volunteer to tutor those just learning to read. Inspired artists might create greeting cards to sell for a good cause. Would-be American Idols or aspiring gymnasts could show off their talents at a local retirement home. Teens who like to talk on the phone — which is to say all teens — could be asked to organize a phone tree to spread news about a social justice issue or event. And, in the same spirit, budding athletes could be encouraged to organize an equipment drive or a sports tournament to raise funds for charity.

Schools teach kids reading, writing and arithmetic. At the end of the day, we shuttle them from one activity to the next. So far, so fine. But what's missing, we think, is an equal emphasis on teaching kids to be caring, compassionate and contributing individuals. We want them to recognize what is truly valuable — putting *we* before *me* — as they make decisions about the way they want to live. Young or old, we all have gifts to give.

It's Tiny Talent Time

It is tempting for parents to try to tease talents out of their offspring — especially if they run in the family. Two-year-olds get drilled with flashcards. Three-year-olds take violin while mom imagines future gigs with the New York Philharmonic. Four-year-olds run backyard drills as dad contemplates NFL prospects. It would be funny if it weren't true. So maybe it can't go without saying that it's never too early for parents to check their egos at the door. Few children become class valedictorian, fewer still a professional football player. But every kid has a special *something*. The best thing parents can do is to help their child to shine in their own way.

When Tom Carr was a kid in Syracuse, New York, he was a lacrosse star. He never figured ball-handling skills would prove handy for anything but scoring goals. Indeed, he went on to become a guidance counselor in North Carolina where few could tell a lacrosse stick from hockey lumber. And yet sports came into play when Carr was working with a scrawny ten-year-old named Jim. Although the shy boy wasn't a jock, he fixated on the old wooden stick in Carr's office. Inspired by Jim's interest, Tom ditched the talk therapy. Instead, every Tuesday, he met Jim in the schoolyard for lacrosse therapy. "He could throw it, cradle it, and do tricks behind his back." The lost boy began to blossom, develop self-esteem and form friendships. "He got so good, cocky even. I had to tone him down a bit." The fact that Jim went on to earn a lacrosse scholarship was pure serendipity.

Carr, who later wrote *Every Child Has A Gift*, told us that parents and educators must help children find their thing. "Take them out in a rowboat and get them rowing," he advised us. "Who knows what will happen?" Younger children think they're good at everything, while older kids think they are good at nothing. At his school, there are more than two dozen after-school clubs from chess to yoga to poetry to wrestling. "It's our job as adults to plant seeds." Some don't sprout, others blossom. Psychologist Mary Pipher has observed that talents can be both gifts and burdens. "The finest innate characteristics can be mismanaged," she cautions in a recently published memoir. "Athletes can become role models or arrogant bullies. Likable extroverts can become great leaders or convincing psychopaths. Good communicators can be skilled therapists or snake-oil salesmen." We are all given a blueprint, she says, but the blueprint is not the building. "A man can be born brilliant, but if he spends his life parked on a sofa watching reality TV, he is unlikely to flourish or contribute much to the common good. A child can be born a slave, yet with courage and wisdom, he can lead his people into freedom."[1]

Start by seeing children for who they really are. We were inspired by one teacher who found a way to identify an expertise in every child. Sally couldn't catch, but she was good at skipping. Walter was a lousy speller, but could add in his head. Classmates were encouraged to seek guidance from each other. By year's end, each child had an experience of accomplishment and a long list of talents to his or her name.

It was not until years after Free The Children was founded that Craig fully appreciated the meaning of giftedness. He'd been invited to participate in a national television program about accomplished youth. Joining him on the show was a nineteen-year-old pharmaceutical executive who had completed his master's degree and Ph.D. No, really, this is true. Throughout the interview, the fresh-faced scholar kept dropping the fact that he was "gifted." Apparently from the time he'd passed an I.Q. test in Grade 3, parents, teachers and the media had been telling the boy just that. The phenom dropped the six-letter word a half dozen times before the host turned to Craig with a question.

"Are you gifted?"

"Nope!" Craig said with a shake of his head.

He was still thinking about the interview when he returned to the Free The Children office. He passed by our Webmaster, a whiz at designing pages visited by millions around the world. He observed FTC's young writing team, who use language to inspire others. And he considered all our amazing adult volunteers and mentors, who give tirelessly of their time and expertise. Stopping to think, he realized he'd given the wrong answer. Just a glance around the office showed him that we all have gifts to give.

From First Steps to I.Q. Tests

In North America, four-year-olds who can read *Harry Potter* or stack blocks in the shape of the Eiffel Tower are hand-picked for I.Q. testing and, if they score above a certain percentile, are sent to a program for the gifted. In many jurisdictions, Grade 3 classes complete standardized tests in math logic and abstract reasoning. For example, a child may be asked, "Right is to left, as winter is to ---?" (Spoiler alert: Summer.) Based on tests, students are placed within the intellectual hierarchy: Gifted children at the top; advanced students next; then regular kids, trailed by slow learners and students with learning disabilities. The "gifted" may be segregated into classes with other such students where they are taught by the best teachers and prepared for a future of academic success.

It only makes sense that parents would want the best for their children. What doesn't make sense is how much anxiety such labeling creates. William Damon, a renowned child psychologist and educator, once noted that of all the calls he'd received in his role as director of a human development center, the "problem" he heard about most was what to do with a precocious child. "What can the parents do to nurture the child's special talent? What extra attention, stimulation, resources must the parent provide? What sacrifices are needed from the child's family if the child's

FIND YOUR GIFT

Everyone has something unique to contribute to the world, even though we don't all have the confidence to admit it. Help your child think about what they love to do. Whether it's sports, or art, or even hanging out with friends, what lights your child up is often where you'll find his gift. We are all gifted in some way, but not in every way — so we have to share our talents to help one another, to lift one another up. Here are just a few examples:

GIFT	SERVICE
Good listener	Join a peer-counseling group; be known among your friends as the one who is always there.
Physical strength	Shovel your elderly neighbor's driveway.
Language	Tutor other students in one of your languages. Help new immigrants to adjust and get settled.
Writing	Start a school newspaper devoted to social issues; draft letters to politicians for a social cause.
Speaking	Run for student council and create positive change; speak at your school or place of worship about an issue that concerns you.
Athletic ability	Organize a sports tournament to raise awareness and funds for a charity.
Musical talents	Set up a charity concert or open-mic night at school.
Artistic sensibility	Start a community mural project that invites participants to express their thoughts about an issue in a group painting. Design greeting cards to sell during the holidays as a fundraiser for charity.

extraordinary gift is not to slip away?" We imagine he took many by surprise when he responded that early precocity is not always an indicator of budding genius. "The development of talent is a story played out over many years of life." Of course your child is gifted, he tells the parents, "just as is practically every other child whom I have encountered. The challenge, and joy, of raising children lies in discovering and bringing out each child's amazing talents."[2]

Consider some of the geniuses who budded late: Thomas Edison was dyslexic and a mischief-maker. Teachers said he'd never make a scholar. And what about

Albert Einstein? When he was a teen, he was rejected by a prestigious academy in Zurich because he had failed non-science subjects. Leonardo da Vinci is thought to have suffered from dyslexia and attention deficit disorder. Imagine how they would have fared in today's schools.

We've questioned the streaming of "gifted" students and have been criticized by educators who defend its value. The system may work for plenty of kids, but we believe there are drawbacks. Labels affect children profoundly. Kids in special needs classes may be filled with a sense of hopelessness while "geniuses" can feel isolated in their rarified world. At the end of the school day, we think everyone loses. In a study published in 1998, researchers compared one thousand and twenty kids labeled as gifted in segregated classes versus gifted kids in non-segregated classes. The gifted kids in mainstream classrooms exhibited greater academic self-confidence, lower test anxiety and better grades. Within the gifted classes, there was more competition, a greater fear of failure, lower self-esteem, test anxiety and, ultimately, lower performances.[3] We think it's time to recognize that most gifts cannot be measured by I.Q. tests. For example, it takes an extraordinary individual to stand up to bullies or to challenge the status quo or even — perhaps, especially — to make people laugh.

Consider the oft-maligned class clown. In 1991, Tami L. Fern studied kids who had been identified by their teachers and peers as having an evolved sense of humor. From over one thousand nominees, experts interviewed those with the most votes, then selected the thirteen children considered funniest of all. The study found that funny kids are imaginative and gifted communicators. Not surprisingly, they have a way of easing anxiety and tension and are considered a joy to be around except perhaps in classrooms where they are often considered troublemakers. "People inclined toward music are given music lessons. Children with a talent for drawing are offered art lessons," Fern said. "No one helps funny kids perfect their humor. Quite often the reverse is true."[4] It's funny when you think about it — funny "peculiar," not funny "ha ha" — we'd all agree there's room for more laughter in the world, yet few of us would ever think to develop a child's sense of humor.

Wisdom, Wonder and Pure Genius

We think every child is gifted. Dr. Thomas Armstrong thinks every child is a genius. The psychologist and learning specialist is the author of some thirteen books, including *Awakening Your Child's Natural Genius* and *In Their Own Way: Discovering and Encouraging Your Child's Multiple Intelligences*. As he explained to us, not every child can "paint like Picasso, compose like Mozart or score 150 on an I.Q. test." But if you consider the original meaning of genius — "to give birth" and "to be zestful or joyous" — the word applies to every child. Put another way, he says, the real meaning of the word is to "give birth to the joy" within each child. "Each child comes into life with wonder, curiosity, awe, spontaneity, vitality, flexibility and many other characteristics of a joyous being," he writes. "An infant has twice as many brain connections as an adult. Young children have vivid imaginations, creative minds and sensitive personalities."

Asked to name gifts that adults often fail to acknowledge, he cites wisdom and wonder. "Young children have a spiritual wisdom that is not recognized by rational culture," he says. "Wonder is another gift. Young children have 'first-time' encounters with things that adults take for granted." Dr. Armstrong says it is crucial that we preserve the genius of childhood — wonder, wisdom, playfulness and flexibility — no easy task in a world moving at hyperspeed. In some households, potential is limited by poverty or depression, anxiety or addiction. In others, children are pushed ahead or pulled along to no end of activities. Schools, he says, dampen genius with testing and grading, tracking and labeling, talk and tedium. "Creativity can't thrive in an atmosphere of judgment." Nor can it easily survive in the age of YouTube when children are exposed to "mind-numbing violence, stereotypical images, mediocre content and repugnant role models."

Before adults help children develop their natural genius, Dr. Armstrong says parents must first awaken their own. "If they're not passionate about learning, how can they expect their kids to be?" He advises adults and children to start with nature hikes, museum visits and storytelling. Parents must realize that each child's genius is unique and cannot be quantified by I.Q. tests. Dr. Armstrong has written extensively about "multiple intelligences," a controversial theory developed in 1983 by Dr. Howard Gardner. The Harvard professor proposed eight categories of intelligence to reflect a broader range of human potential including "musical smarts," "people smarts" and "nature smarts."

SMALL ACTIONS › EVERY DAY

1. OF COURSE YOUR CHILD IS GIFTED:
Your challenge and joy is to help them discover their talents.

2. GIVE THE PRESENCE OF TIME:
Don't rush. Let your child discover their own abilities at their own speed.

3. MAKE ROOM TO EXPLORE:
Your talents are your talents. Give your kids the freedom to find their own way to shine.

4. TAKE AN INTEREST IN THEIR INTERESTS:
If your child is fascinated with dinosaurs, take them to the library or the natural history museum. No matter the flavor of the month, help them explore.

5. NO PAIN, NO PAIN:
Dragging a kid to practice only works for so long. Help them find their groove.

6. ENCOURAGE EFFORT, NOT RESULTS:
Marks and scores are important to a point. At the end of the day, the real goal is for the child to feel a sense of accomplishment.

7. MODEL OPTIMISM:
Tell your children you have faith in them and believe they can succeed.

8. SHOW AND SHARE:
Encourage kids to share their talents with friends, family and community.

Find Something That Makes Your Heart Break

After winning Survivor: Africa *in 2002,* **Ethan Zohn** *used his prize money to start Grassroot Soccer, a non-profit organization that trains Africa's professional soccer players to teach children about HIV/ AIDS prevention. He works for many other charities including America Scores, an organization that helps inner-city kids participate in educational programs. He talked to us about small actions, little things and making happiness.*

ON *SURVIVOR,* CONTESTANTS ARE allowed to bring one "luxury item" from home — something that represents your identity. Because soccer is so much a part of my life, I brought a hacky sack — a kind of mini soccer ball.

During the filming of *Survivor: Africa*, I visited a little village in the middle of Wamba, which is in Kenya. In the parking lot of the Wamba hospital, I played hacky sack with Kenyan children. Before leaving, I gave my hacky sack to one of the little kids. It's a little silly talking about it now, but in the context of the show, it was a tough decision. In that instant, I understood that it is much better to give than to receive. That real-life experience in the middle of a cut-throat reality TV game was a turning point in my life.

After thirty-nine days in Kenya, I went on to win the title of *Survivor*, a Chevy Avalanche, a million dollars and instant celebrity. I was totally not prepared for the spotlight. Celebrity is ridiculous. Fame is ridiculous. But, as Bono has said, it is currency.

I had just finished *Survivor* when I got together with Dr. Tommy Clark and Kirk Friedrich. We'd played soccer together. Tommy was finishing his residency and Kirk was unemployed. As we like to say: Tommy had the idea. I had the celebrity and the money. Kirk had the time. It was just us with a blank piece of paper saying, "What are we going to do now?"

I went on to use every media opportunity to talk about Grassroot Soccer and the tragedy of HIV.

When I talk to kids about what I learned on *Survivor*, I tell them they don't have to be Bill Gates or Donald Trump. People always think they have to make a giant dent in the world, but it's through the small actions that things get done. It could be as simple as dropping balloons at a hospital or reading to a senior citizen or organizing an equipment drive. You don't have to go out and change the world tomorrow, but you have to at least try. Find something that makes your heart break, then go and join an organization dedicated to that issue.

To be able to use my name and my fame to create change in the world — saving lives in Africa or changing the way people think about HIV/AIDS — is an honor and something that can never be taken away from me.

On *Survivor* I was stripped of everything I thought I was — a New Yorker, a soccer player, a biology major in college, a Jewish kid — everything I thought I was meant nothing. But the skills I had learned growing up from my parents and from my family were inside me, burned into my identity.

My father passed away from colon cancer when I was fourteen. In his dying words to me, he said: "To make happiness real for others is truly the greatest gift. It provides the foundation for the celebration of life." I live by those words and cherish his memory.

My family of five was really close. We sat down for dinner almost every single night. It was a time when we sat around and talked about what happened in our days. One hundred percent, every Friday night, no matter what, we had to be there for Shabbat. Every Friday night, I put a quarter into a jar that would later be given to charity. It was a little thing, but it made me realize there was something bigger than me going on.

Since we first came up with the idea for Grassroot Soccer, two hundred and fifty thousand African kids have graduated from the program. In America, we visit schools with the Kick Aids program that tells schools about the global AIDS pandemic. It's my life goal to raise awareness and to connect the youth in America with the youth in Africa in this common cause. I want to create mini-revolutions of consciousness that make as many people on the planet of all ages aware of the issues at stake.

In the years since my father died, I have learned much about life. I have learned to separate the important from the trivial. I have learned what to throw away and what to keep. I can appreciate the precious nature of time and the passion that any part of a minute can bring. As my father taught me, making happiness real for others is the greatest gift.

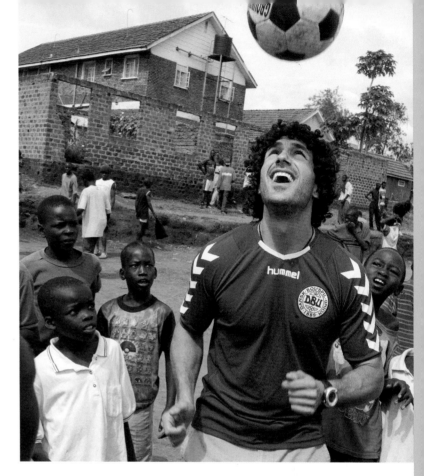

To make happiness real for others is truly the greatest gift. It provides the foundation for the celebration of life."

Ethan Zohn's father

Five Steps to Help Your Kid Step Up

Help your kids pay attention to what is going on in the world. Teachable moments that inspire passion are everywhere. Here are some practical steps to follow to help support your child and their endeavors, whatever they might be.

AT WHAT AGE DO YOU stop protecting kids from the sadness and tragedies of the world? When do you open the curtains and encourage children to peek out? Jamie Podmorow pondered such questions when she found herself with an extra ticket to a speech about the oppression of women in Afghanistan. She contemplated taking her fun-loving, soccer-playing, ten-year-old daughter, Alaina. It wasn't that Jamie sheltered her kids. Watching the TV news and debating the issues were routine in the Podmorow household. With minutes to spare, Jamie decided to invite Alaina. If the speech proved too much, they could always leave.

Sally Armstrong, Unicef's special representative to Afghanistan, spoke in searing detail about the dismal lives of Afghani women and girls, many of whom are kept out of classrooms, workplaces and public life. She painted a bleak picture of the limited freedoms of girls Alaina's age. "The worst thing you can do is nothing," the author and activist told the audience. Jamie tried to read her daughter's face. "I wondered if she was bored or maybe a bit lost." When Armstrong finished speaking,

Alaina's hand shot up. "I thought she might ask where the bathroom was," Jamie recalled in jest. Instead, her daughter had a question. "Has there ever been peace in Afghanistan?" Armstrong told the ten-year-old about life before the 1978 invasion by the Soviet Union. Later, after the speech, Armstrong told Alaina: "When I'm a grandmother in a rocking chair, you'll be doing big things."

On the way home, Jamie and Alaina talked about what it would be like to be without an education. Alaina couldn't imagine walking four hours in bare feet to find a classroom that would allow girls. Before falling asleep that night, she told her dad what she had learned. "I want to do something to help," she said. The next morning at breakfast, she announced her plan to raise $750 to hire someone to teach Afghani girls for a year. Alaina's parents were taken aback but offered unconditional support. Their newly-minted activist started to raise funds with donut sales and by collecting recycled bottles and cans. When that didn't bring in enough, she talked to her friends, who talked to their parents, who organized a silent auction and raised almost $2,000. After the local Rotary

Little Women for Little Women in Afghanistan, brainchild of Alaina Podmorow and her friends

Club matched the funds, they were able to pay for five teachers!

"The worst thing you can do is nothing." Alaina was haunted by Armstrong's words. During the speech, Alaina had learned about Canadian Women for Women in Afghanistan. Alaina wondered if she and her friends could create a similar chapter. Eighteen girls founded Little Women for Little Women in Afghanistan. Soon, Alaina was invited to speak across the country, which inspired new chapters to form. The government agreed to match the group's funds. So far they've hired five hundred teachers! We, too, were hugely impressed.

Since creating Free The Children, we have crossed paths with many budding activists and enthusiastic young people like Alaina, who discovered their passions in unique and unexpected ways. Some were guided gently. Others were moved to act when an issue in the community demanded action. Plenty more stepped up after tragedies such as 9/11 or Hurricane Katrina.

How to awaken a passion? We've broken it down into five easy steps. Step 1 is to help your kids pay attention to what is going on in the world. Teachable moments that inspire passion are everywhere. Let's look closer at each step.

Step 1: Stop, Look and Listen

In a world where life moves at breakneck speed, it's not always easy to stop to consider the big picture, let alone to talk about a small one. For this reason, it's crucial to do so. Speaking of teachable moments ... let's pause for a lesson on how to embrace one. Doing so is delicate work but it's not complicated. All you really need to do is help kids to stop and notice the bigger — or smaller — picture. Just as you might show a child the world in a grain of sand, so you can help them explore large-scale problems and overwhelming events. Whether you lead a child to think about something large or small, all that's required is your guiding presence. Truth be told, there's a bit of Zen in moments when you let go of everything that came before and all that will come next and simply stop to take something in, whether it is an injustice, a problem or unexpected beauty. All you have to say is, "Check that out," or "Look, did you notice this?"

As ethereal as we know it sounds, this is exactly how Mom and Dad awakened our passion for social justice. When Mom took us to her classroom or Dad pulled something out of the headlines, they'd make sure we noticed. They'd pause to put things in context. When appropriate, they'd ask us how we'd improve a situation. Each conversation reminded us that everyone is connected. Mom was teaching us, subconsciously she says, what she learned from her involvement with the Young Christian Workers: How to "Observe, Judge and Act." No pressure, by the way. Anyone who has tried knows you can't impose change and enlightenment any more than you can force a kid to eat lima beans, or, in Craig's case, watermelon. (He complains it's like crunchy water.) To be clear, we're not suggesting that you recruit your kids to your battles or causes. This is not about you — it's about them. The awakening is something like a dance in which you guide their tentative steps.

No matter where we were with Dad, he'd pull us in and show us something that we might not otherwise have noticed. When there was time, we'd discuss what was really going on in the world. He taught us so much, which is hardly surprising. He was a teacher's teacher — chatty and funny and inspired — the kind kids dream about having in a classroom. Teaching was his passion, whether in front of a blackboard, in the middle of nature or at the back of the line at the supermarket. We'd hide if he was approached by former students who wanted to prove they could still conjugate French verbs to the tune of *Farmer in the Dell* (a mnemonics ditty he liked to teach). Dad's view of the world was bigger than our neighborhood or city. He traveled the world and spent time volunteering in France (which seemed incredibly exotic to us). He wanted our world to be even bigger. It's up to parents and grandparents, teachers and mentors to look for teachable moments. Sometimes they are on the news, or sometimes they are at a talk at town hall. Often, they arrive in unexpected places and in unexpected ways.

Step 2: Find What You Love, Then Share

When Melody Dernocoeur turned six, her Auntie Barbie gave her a miniature horse. Not a plastic My Little Pony — a real, live horse. "I mean, honestly," says Melody's mom, Kate. "It seemed like a lawn ornament!" Although dumbfounded, Melody's parents decided it was no time to look a gift horse in the mouth. "It was whimsical, even magical." Kate, an active

WHAT LIFE'S *REALLY* ABOUT

Angelina Jolie's transition from actress to activist came about quickly after she starred as Lara Croft in *Tomb Raider*, a movie filmed in Cambodia. Jolie was so moved by the poverty in the developing nation that she adopted her first son from the country.

"Both my parents were very focused on charity," she has said of her upbringing. "I was raised by my mom to see the joy she had in doing things for others."

Jolie grew up in New York and L.A. She attended Beverly Hills High School. Though it may sound ideal, she's confessed to feeling lost during those years. "I think now that if somebody would have taken me at fourteen and dropped me in the middle of Asia or Africa, I'd have realized how self-centered I was," she once told an interviewer, "that there was real pain and real death to fight. I wouldn't have been fighting myself so much."

Now a mother of her own, Jolie spends part of each year visiting some of the world's most impoverished areas as Goodwill Ambassador for the United Nations High Commissioner for Refugees. On field missions to such places as Sudan, Pakistan and Cambodia, Jolie has met groups affected by war, poverty and natural disaster. "You go to these places and realize what life's really about and what people are really going through. These people are my heroes."

CHILDREN KNOW MORE THAN YOU THINK

How young is too young to expose children to social issues? Educators for Social Responsibility suggest parents acknowledge and discuss when a child has been exposed to disturbing current events. Let children lead with their questions. Make sure they are allowed to express their opinions, fears and ideas.

The Sesame Workshop, a non-profit organization that creates educational content for media, had two hundred and thirty-three children, aged six to eleven, in fifteen shopping malls across the United States answer questions, tell stories and draw pictures about the world. Guns, death and violence featured in almost two-thirds of the children's work. The younger children expressed fears of natural disasters or animals. More than two-thirds of the older children were worried about pollution and the environment; 65 percent were concerned their outdoor space would disappear because of development or neglect.

"Middle childhood is an age of enlightenment," Robin F. Goodman, a professor at the New York University School of Medicine, has said of the results. "Cognitively, children this age are more capable of understanding the complex adult world, no longer able to retreat with blinders to an age of innocence." Confronted with adult concerns but without effective coping tools, these enlightened children may be overwhelmed and in need of comfort and guidance to work through their fears, Goodman says. If you can help children to see they have a role to play, they may not feel so helpless.

volunteer in her rural Michigan community, imagined the joy this unconventional pet might inspire. So she sat down her young daughter to discuss the care and sharing of Rainbow. Melody still remembers the conversation in which her mom said she could keep the horse if she agreed to share it with others. "Rainbow was to become my equine ambassador."

On her first show and tell, Melody took Rainbow to visit some senior citizens. "Mom said, 'When I need to be put in a nursing home, someone better bring me a horse.'" Both mother and daughter still get emotional when they describe that day. "Residents buried their noses in her neck," Kate recalls. "Mom made me see that the people in these homes are human. A lot of times, people don't take the time to really see them and talk or listen." On that very first visit, Melody discovered that she loved to make people smile. "Just thinking about it makes me want to cry."

Next on the tour, Melody introduced Rainbow to her Grade 1 class. The visit would become an annual ritual until she graduated from high school. Thanks to such visits, Melody discovered it was her passion to bring happiness into the lives of others. She was a "people person," to be sure, most delighted when she was able to make those around her beam from ear to ear. She later took Rainbow to visit inner-city kids and disabled students, most of whom had never touched a horse. "My mom taught me it was important to share the gifts we receive." In reaching out, Melody was touched deeply, too.

Melody Dernocoeur's parents were always on the lookout for such moments. Not so long ago, Melody's mom uncovered a timeworn letter from a nature center thanking Melody for her

$8.53 donation. "The sky was always the limit and we'd tell her to reach for the stars," Kate says.

Those early encounters stoked Melody's passion for sharing a smile, especially with those who are marginalized or disadvantaged. Hokey but true. After high school and before university, she worked in a Bangkok orphanage. She recalls one special little girl named Fon. "In my valiant attempt to change the world, I gave her one month's worth of hugs, smiles, laughter, tears and love. It was only one month. She was only one child. I reveled in the instant gratification of a shared smile — our own moment of joy without words — but struggled to believe my actions had real impact."

Step 3: Get to Know the People You're Helping

Once your kids get started, you may sense they'd like to go deeper. Picking up garbage at the park is a noble undertaking in and of itself, but it may in turn inspire a child to offer to help an elderly neighbor with yard work. You can start small. Our friends James and Will Feschuk began by standing outside a supermarket handing shoppers paper bags to fill for a local food drive. James, ten, and Will, eight, also helped collect groceries during a citywide drive at Christmas. After the holiday rush, they recruited a group of young friends — no one was older than ten — to sort donations at the food bank. The small group sorted two tons of food — "as big as two elephants," they were told. The next year, James and Will pitched in at Operation Big Turkey, serving Christmas dinners to the hungry. Their next step could be to volunteer as a family once a week at a soup kitchen in order to meet the individuals who use it. By getting involved in this way, kids experience directly what it's like to make a difference in someone's life. Shelley's family routinely invites new immigrant friends, usually from China, to dinner to discover North American customs. The girls, who were adopted from China, learn about a less privileged immigrant experience than their own. They also enjoy having role models who can share stories of the country where they were born. In every teachable moment a spark flies.

Step 4: Be Ready With a Boost When Kids Step Up

We can't really tell this next story without a brief preface. Craig "was" a bit of a nerd growing up. Other kids hung out at the mall or the arcade or the skate park. Craig spent his time at the Gallanough Public Library. When he and his friends tired of soccer, they'd stop by to stock up on reading material. Craig would fill his backpack with novels, which he'd devour late into the night. When he was eleven, he arrived home one day with news that the library was going to be closed. He was shaken. Hell hath no fury like a nerd denied free reading material. Rather than downplaying his concerns, Mom and Dad asked pointed queries that ultimately led Craig to ask himself, "What am I going to do?"

He and his buddies arrived on a battalion of bikes at a public meeting where the closure was to be discussed. The friends pushed Craig forward. "Hi, my name is Craig," he began. "And I am a really angry bookworm." (Or something

ALL THESE THINGS ARE POSSIBLE

Leonardo DiCaprio may seem an unlikely environmental activist. With countless millions at his disposal, the megawatt star could live a secluded life of consumption and luxury. Instead, he drives an energy-efficient Prius and devotes much of his time to promoting environmental sustainability.

DiCaprio was raised in Los Angeles, one of the most polluted cities on Earth, but also a stronghold of the green movement. His hippie parents inspired the young actor to find his purpose, though he didn't seize on environmentalism until 1999 after filming a movie called *The Beach* in Thailand. Production of the film caused environmental damage to Phi Phi Le Island, which outraged Thai officials. When DiCaprio returned home, he started to speak out about global warming and species protection.

"I know there's this idea people have that I'm this spoiled, cocky punk of an actor," DiCaprio told the *London Sunday Times*. "Honestly, that's not who I am. I really care that so many species have been wiped out. I decided I want to be an active environmentalist. I learned about it. I asked experts."[1]

The actor has since used his fame to draw attention to a long list of projects and organizations. He has produced films on the environmental crisis and created the Leonardo DiCaprio Foundation to fund ecological projects.

In an interview with *USA Weekend* magazine, DiCaprio observed that it helps if kids are paying attention from an early age. "I can remember watching documentaries in which I learned about mass extinctions of species in rainforests," he said. "That emotionally engaged me as a young kid, and I said to myself, 'When I grow up, I'd love to make a difference in this field.'"[2]

DiCaprio told the *Times* that his goal is to get people to pay attention to the ecology of our planet. "We can feed all the starving people on the Earth, take care of the sick, and sustain the planet we've inherited! And live in peace. We can. Believe me, all these things are possible. And if it happens, won't it be amazing?"

like that.) He was more than a little nervous. This wasn't a public speaking contest — it was real life! He cleared his throat, shuffled his feet and prayed he wouldn't mess up. "I don't really recognize many of you. I guess you don't come to the library all that often. But my friends and I do." He went on to explain, "This is where we go after school until our parents get home. If the library closes, maybe we'll just go sit in front of the TV. Aren't adults always telling us not to do this?" The passionate appeal drew applause. The committee fighting to save the library approached Craig and asked him to address city council. He sped home with the news. Mom and Dad were surprised and supportive but they did not interfere. In fact, they didn't even attend the council meeting where Craig spoke: It was his battle. From that moment, Craig realized he had the ability to influence decisions.

A few short weeks later in April 1995, Craig reached for the newspaper at breakfast. Those of you familiar with Free The Children know that he was on his way to the comics. Craig would cut out his favorites and tape them all over the house — to the fridge, to pillows, to books. He always had a joke to tell. On this day, Craig was stopped by a headline that read "BATTLED CHILD LABOR, BOY, 12, MURDERED." The *Toronto Star* article told the story of Iqbal Masih, who was sold into slavery at the age of four for $16. The article explained that until he escaped six years later, the Pakistani boy was "shackled to a carpet-weaving loom, tying tiny knots hour after hour." Once free, Iqbal began a campaign against child labor that took him around the world. Now he was gone — shot dead.

Craig was stunned to learn that a child so young had endured so much. He interrogated Mom and Dad. They knew little about child labor but encouraged him to find out more. Off he went to the library — good thing it was still open.

Craig hadn't been looking for a cause; he'd been reaching for the comics. But he was paying attention and primed to act, in large part because Mom and Dad were also paying attention. The issue stirred his soul and inspired Free The Children. Now it is his life. In the next chapter, we will explore how he combined his gift for public speaking with his newfound passion for telling others about child labor. It would be a life-changing combination.

When Marc was thirteen, he tried not to be noticed. (This was before he started weightlifting in his bedroom to heavy metal tunes.) His ambition in life was to blend in. So he surprised Mom and Dad when he asked if he could join a school board trip to Jamaica to work with people with leprosy — a giant step out of his suburban comfort zone. Instead of throwing up obstacles, they said "Go for it" — our unofficial family motto. When Marc disembarked on the island, he headed in the opposite direction of the hundreds of tourists. He was taken to a hospital in the east Riverton slums, one of the poorest communities in the western hemisphere.

The hospital housed amputees, victims of violence and those who had lost their fingers and toes to leprosy. It was Marc's job to be friendly, make patients smile and offer basic assistance. In order to do so, he had to get over himself and his lack of maturity. For the first time, life did not revolve around him — or his feelings. During his orientation, he did not even want to look at patients. Later that day, he and the other volunteers were instructed to walk around on their own. Somehow Marc found the courage to knock on the bedroom door of Mr. Eli. The ancient man was badly disfigured and struggling to replace the batteries in his radio so he could catch the BBC news. After helping with the task, Marc accepted Mr. Eli's invitation to listen to the news, then stuck around to discuss Canadian politics. The animated exchange taught Marc an important lesson: Physical limitations don't reflect intellectual ability. It also showed him that he had the ability to help others.

In the end, Marc earned high school credits for his volunteer work. But it was never about the grades. Marc says the two-week trip showed him he could do something on his own, without Mom or Dad watching over his shoulder or classmates looking on to judge. Because most of the other students on the trip were older, Marc was exposed to role models who thought it was cool to care. Apathy was not on the agenda. Working up close with poverty inspired in him a passion to help young people — a resolve that was sustained by the discovery that he had something substantial to offer.

Step 5: When Need Arises, Help Kids Respond

Some things forever change the way a child sees the world. We think of 9/11, the deadly tsunami of 2004, the tragic Haiti earthquake, the slaughter in Darfur. In the wake of tragedy, it is only natural to want to help and hope. These wide-scale disasters with massive human loss are often the first spark for young people who become passionate about helping.

We think of Taylor Rutledge from Clarksville, Tennessee, who put together sixty backpacks and loaded each with lots of fun stuff and necessities for children displaced after Hurricane Katrina hit the Gulf Coast in 2005. We think of the students in Glen Rock, New Jersey, who raised $3,000 during a three-day bake sale. There were dance competitions and car washes organized by children from Indiana, while students in Palm Bay, Florida, sewed cloth bears for children affected by the storm.

As adults, we need to help children appreciate that large-scale issues are incredibly complex and will take months, if not years, to address. Events may be out of our control, but we can guide our response to profound and complicated moments. At the same time, we must support a child's desire to do something. For some, it could be to start a letter-writing campaign or to go door to door to collect names on a petition. Catastrophic events are confusing and frightening. Yet, with a little guidance, kids can respond in a way that makes them feel a little less helpless.

Like millions of others, our friend Terry Reeves was riveted to the television when Katrina hit the Gulf, killing almost two thousand people and displacing millions more. She and her teens, Kate and Galen, sent a monetary donation and discussed what more they could do. Before they could decide, September arrived and Galen went off to college while Terry plunged into her work as an elementary school art teacher. They moved on, but they couldn't forget.

One day, Terry called Galen to tell him

In Haiti after the earthquake

Hurricane Katrina aftermath

Habitat for Humanity was looking for volunteers in St. Bernard Parish, a community on the edge of New Orleans where twenty-five thousand homes were destroyed or damaged. Aid workers were gutting the flooded, uninhabitable homes. Terry wondered if Galen, then eighteen, might join her there during his school break. (Kate, also in university, was already signed up to work for Habitat for Humanity in Iowa.) Exhausted from midterms, Galen almost said no. He'd been fantasizing about a break on a beach or perhaps on the living room sofa watching reruns of *The Simpsons*. Although he'd never walked into the heart of a disaster, he held his breath and jumped.

Terry and Galen were shocked by what they found in St. Bernard Parish. Early each morning, they donned protective gear to enter waterlogged shells of empty houses. Their job was to salvage mementoes — baby albums, coin collections, wedding photos — before tearing out insulation, carpets and dry wall. On Day 2, mother and son were disembowelling a red-brick bungalow when the homeowner arrived with donuts and other refreshments. "I'll never forget his gratitude," Galen says. "It really made me realize how easy it was to make a difference." Terry says it was profoundly moving. "Doing hard, meaningful work together... there is nothing like it." Galen returned home determined to improve his community. At college, he has dedicated himself to student politics.

Craig and the Free The Children speakers had the opportunity to visit New Orleans recently. Addressing a young crowd of forty thousand for the Evangelical Lutheran Church in America, Craig and the team were taken aback. Set up to speak in the well-known Superdome, the exact location that thousands of the city's population was forced to harbor when Hurricane Katrina struck, the team was humbled. The stage, which had a massive cross hanging behind the speakers, literally shook when the crowd burst into applause. Craig, moved by the energetic audience, spoke about finding hope. A topic the youth in New Orleans knew all too well. Talking with the youth after the event, Craig understood that compassion wasn't just found at home with individuals like Terry and Galen, but in the youth that have faced great challenges in their lives. Compassion and hope were both running strong in New Orleans.

You can't predict what will spark passion in a child, but you can be watchful and ready. Just consider Alaina Podmorow, the inspiring kid we told you about at the start of this chapter. With a little encouragement and direction from her parents, she discovered she had a real passion for helping Afghani girls. "As a family, you're moving so fast, it's easy not to pay attention or help your kids pay attention," says her mom, Jamie, who was only too happy to support her daughter. "I felt bad that for forty years of my life I had essentially lived an apathetic life. My daughter showed me there was so much more that could be done." Jamie says she learned an important lesson from her daughter. "Always tell your children that they can do anything they dream of. Never say, 'No, you can't.' Because what if they believe you?"

SMALL ACTIONS › EVERY DAY

1. DISCUSS THE HEADLINES:
When you are reading the daily newspaper — we suggest you subscribe to one — point out stories of interest. Discuss individuals you read about. Talk about the difference they are making in the world.

2. SHAKE UP THE NEIGHBORS:
Point out growing concerns in your community. Find websites that explain.

3. DON'T PREACH:
There's a fine line. If your kids stop listening, you'll know you've crossed it.

4. TALK THE TALK:
Identify local injustices and discuss how your family might respond. Consider what the neighborhood could be doing.

5. THEN WALK THE WALK:
Take steps as a family to contribute to a solution. Budding environmentalists, for example, might decide to change energy-sucking light bulbs or to take the bus or a bike more often. They might take a garbage bag to the park on Sundays to clean up trash.

6. GO GLOBAL:
Help kids understand they are part of the world at large. Reach out to immigrants and refugees by inviting them to coffee or dinner. Write to a pen pal in a developing country.

Work Hard and Believe in Yourself

Dr. Jane Goodall is renowned for her study of chimpanzees in Gombe Stream National Park, Tanzania. The primatologist and anthropologist is a United Nations Messenger of Peace. She also founded the Jane Goodall Institute, a global non-profit that empowers people to make a difference for all living things. We consider Dr. Goodall a good friend. We spoke with her after she visited Free The Children to speak to our staff.

AS A GIRL GROWING up in Bournemouth, England, it was clear I held a special love and appreciation for animals. One of my earliest recollections is of the day I hid in a small stuffy henhouse in order to see how a hen laid an egg. I emerged after about five hours. The whole household had apparently been searching for me for hours, and mother had even called the police to report me missing. When she saw how excited I was, she didn't scold me. Instead, she sat down and listened to me tell my story of how a hen lays an egg.

My mother was an amazing listener. When my sister and I were growing up, she never tried to force us to think one way or another. She let us develop in our own way, providing only guidelines, never orders. She would never punish us for something unless she knew we understood precisely why we were being punished. If we didn't understand, she was careful to explain.

While my entire family enjoyed the presence of animals in our lives, none were nearly as passionate as I was. My mother never tried to discourage me from bringing injured animals home and taking them into my bedroom.

There is a story she told of when I was very young — less than two-years-old. Apparently I

had discovered a number of earthworms while burrowing in the soil near our home. Fascinated by these strange creatures, in my enthusiasm, I decided to take them to my room, sheltering them in my bed. When my mother discovered what I'd done, she didn't react with revulsion, but rather calmly explained the repercussions of my actions: How the earthworms needed the earth to live, and that if I kept them in my room in my bed, I'd be responsible for them dying — which, naturally, horrified me. So, very quickly, I gathered them up and she and I together put them back in the garden.

This was her way — guiding us toward understanding, rather than imposing her authority. My mother also encouraged my appreciation for and interest in animals from the beginning — particularly as I began to read. She was wise enough to realize that if she put books I wanted to read in my way, I would learn to read quicker. Looking back at my childhood books, they're all about animals. One of the books I read inspired my dream to live in Africa and write about animals. It was *The Story of Dr. Dolittle* by Hugh Lofting, about a doctor who can talk to animals and who travels to Africa. I also loved the books about Tarzan.

My mother encouraged me and told me I could make my dreams reality if I worked hard and believed in myself. Despite my passion for studying animals, when I graduated from high school my mother could not afford to send me to university. Instead, I learned to be a secretary and worked for a time at the University of Oxford typing documents. I then got a secretarial job with a company that made documentary films. I so dreamed of visiting Africa. In May 1956, a friend invited me to visit her family's farm in Kenya.

I do remember the day I received notice in the mail that I would be accomplishing my dream of traveling to Africa. The minute I received the letter, I knew I had to give my notice. I recall my mother sitting me down and methodically questioning my plan, making sure I had thought everything through. When she saw I would not be dissuaded and was able to accept the necessary responsibilities, she supported my decision.

Later, my mother came to east Africa to support me in my work observing chimpanzees. She knew nothing about Africa, and yet she accompanied me for several months, despite her fears of spiders and snakes. She supported me and developed incredible relationships with the residents of the areas in which I worked.

Looking back, it's incredible how supportive she was of my admittedly unusual ambitions. It was encouragement coupled with an intuitive way of knowing how much freedom she should grant at a given moment. I was very lucky, having the chance to grow and learn in my own way, while all the while knowing I was given such thoughtful, loving support from my mother.

My mother encouraged me and told me I could make my dreams reality if I worked hard and believed in myself."

Dr. Jane Goodall

GIFT + PASSION = BETTER WORLD

Add It Up

Gift + Passion = Better World is a universal equation. Everyone has talents to share. We all have enthusiasms. Combine the two and the world becomes a better place.

ALMOST FROM THE FIRST day of school, we are taught countless important equations. First we learn that 1 + 1 = 2. In time, we may master Pythagorean theory and $E=mc^2$. Later still, some discover that MBA = BMW. All things being equal, we'd like to share another formula for success. It's not in any textbook, but we're convinced it has the power and potential to change lives. Gift + Passion = Better World. The equation is the cornerstone of our teachings, one that sums up the philosophy of Free The Children and inspires our dedication to living *me* to *we*.

Our work takes us around the world and into the lives of hundreds of thousands of young people who are eager to make a difference. "But how?" they often say. (At this point, their enthusiastic parents usually lean in for advice: "What should they study? And where?") No matter where we are and to whom we are speaking, our answer is always the same: It doesn't matter what you study; what's crucial is that you do so with passion. If you really want to make a difference, keep your eyes open for opportunities that allow you to serve others by combining your gift with a cause. We discussed gifts in Lesson 4. (Remember? Everybody has one.) And in Lesson 5 we talked about helping kids find their passion. (Step 1: Stop, look, listen.) Perhaps our equation sounds far-fetched, a calculation worthy only of presidents, prime ministers and great leaders like Dr. Martin Luther King, Jr. Not so. Gift + Passion = Better World is a universal equation. Everyone has talents to share. We all have enthusiasms. Combine the two and the world becomes a better place.

Although shy by nature, Marc has had a

Children in Kenya making the world a better place one tree at a time

way with words almost since he learned to talk. Today he crafts them to inspire social action, but there was a time he employed them in the less noble cause of finagling his way out of work around the house! Those efforts to jabber out of chores actually led Marc to a life-defining moment back when he was twelve. In a desperate appeal to avoid cleaning the bathroom, Marc started to filibuster. With more than a little drama, he began to read aloud the ingredients in the household cleanser. When his tongue began to trip over long lists of incomprehensible print, he turned to the larger type on the bottle: EXPLODES UNDER HEAT. "Toxins could stunt my growth!" he exclaimed. "Or turn my hair orange! Or cause horrific injury! Do you really want to do this to a growing boy?" Not exactly "I Have a Dream," but a stirring oration nonetheless. (He still had to scrub the toilet.)

Not so long after this, Marc went to visit Mimi, our grandmother who lives in Windsor, across the river from Detroit. He couldn't help but notice her place was sparkling. Out of curiosity, Marc peeked in her cupboards, assuming she cleaned with the same vile stuff that Mom used. "Mimi, how do you do it?" he asked when he couldn't find a single product. She laughed at his sudden interest, then went to the fridge for lemon juice. Next, she reached into the cupboard for borax, baking soda and vinegar. Mom couldn't believe it when Marc returned home to volunteer for chores. All at once, housecleaning was a mini-science class in which he could fool around with chemical reactions. The more he experimented, the more he studied, the more he came to realize conventional cleaners were damaging the water system. He wondered why people relied on strong-smelling chemicals when they could just as effectively combine tried-and-true, non-toxic ingredients with a little bit of elbow grease.

When it came time to choose a project for the Grade 8 science fair, Marc decided to explore the issue. To kick-start his research, Mimi took Marc to visit other grandmothers who offered him lots of cookies and their homemade cleaning concoctions. He tested each one and made notes on the best. After that, he researched store-bought products and discovered many contained toxins, carcinogens and hormone disruptors. For the first time, he contemplated the ecological footprint of the Kielburger household. We were harming the planet because we'd never stopped to think about the consequences of our everyday actions. For a time, Marc became a vegetarian. (In a family that dined on a lot of take-out food, that period featured a lot of vegetarian pizza.)

In contest after contest, there was enormous interest in Marc's work. Although it was probably about a decade ahead of its time, the project was ultimately chosen as Best in Canada. In recognition of his work, Marc became the youngest person at that time to receive the Ontario Citizenship Award. As word spread, he was invited to speak in the community. Though just a kid in grade school, Craig tagged along to help his older brother collect some five thousand signatures calling for a ban on the harmful products. Reflecting back, Marc thinks his brother's presence may not have helped when he was trying to impress thirteen-year-old girls. Craig insists he was an enormous asset. He'd go up to girls and speak far too quickly. Still, they'd say, "Oh, how cute, let's sign." In all seriousness, if it had not been for Marc's example, Craig says he would never have thought to fuel his gift with his enthusiasm to take on injustice. Marc did it, so Craig felt he could do it, too.

A simple housekeeping assignment sparked in Marc a passion for protecting the environment. When this newly discovered enthusiasm inspired his science fair project, he found out he could influence thinking around an issue. Using his gift for public speaking, he started to talk to other students and community groups about the dangers of household cleaners. Just as he'd mixed vinegar and baking soda, so he combined his gift and his passion and turned it into service. Plus, our counters had never been cleaner!

When kids discover an issue, they may feel they have no option but to get involved. Others get drawn to activism before stopping to think about specifics — they're so eager to change the world that they don't take time to consider how best to do it. In such cases, we pose a single, clarifying question: "What social problem motivates and inspires you?" The sad truth is

SUPERHERO PROFILES

Name: Kyle and Ryan Szabo.
Lives: Toronto, Ontario.
Gift: Public speaking.
Passion: International charity.
Better World: At the age of eight, Kyle began to collect gently used clothing and toys for children in developing countries. Five-year-old Ryan couldn't wait to help. A Grade 8 teacher at Bloorlea Middle School in Toronto heard about Kyle and Ryan's selfless actions and invited them to speak to her class. The students were moved when Kyle shared his dream: To build a pipeline that stretches from Canada to Africa to provide the continent with clean and safe water

Name: Julie Eckstein.
Lives: Huntington, New York.
Gift: Event planning.
Passion: To raise money to alleviate hunger.
Better World: When she was ten, Julie rallied her school to hold a pajama day with a bake sale and other fundraisers. A boy in her class offered up two cents. "Every penny counts," she said. The event raised $110.02.

Name: Whitney Burton.
Lives: Kingwood, Texas.
Gift: Storytelling.
Passion: To build a school in Sierra Leone.
Better World: The teen used stories from books she had read and personal experiences to write speeches that raised more than $5,000.

Name: Maggie Lipton.
Lives: Croton-on-Hudson, New York.
Gift: Dance.
Passion: To raise money for developing countries.
Better World: Maggie, then seventeen, created a dance troupe and choreographed a huge event that raised $1,200 for Free The Children and $1,300 for Doctors Without Borders.

Name: Talia Manne.
Lives: Toronto, Ontario.
Gift: Baking and cooking with her mom.
Passion: To help kids in Africa.
Better World: When she was four, Talia put together a lemonade and cookie stand to raise money to build a school. She called each one of her relatives to ask for support. She raised $648. "Now the kids can learn and make their life better," she says.

that there's no shortage of ways to respond. We might then challenge math whizzes to come up with a fundraising formula that champions affordable housing. Or we will encourage artistic kids to design posters to raise awareness about a local issue. We invite kids like Marc to consider speaking out about something close to their heart. No matter if the young people in your life have a passion for art or athletics or God, the world needs their contributions. Remember that formula? Gift + Passion = Better World. Show your children how to take their talent, fire it with their enthusiasm and go for it!

Dream Big, Start Small

One of the greatest challenges is to help kids take on bite-sized actions. Children don't need to wait until they are older if parents, mentors and teachers help them find a place to begin. Remember your first lemonade stand? Chances are you recall the deep satisfaction of counting your earnings. What you probably don't remember is the helping hand you received buying and squeezing lemons — getting the mix just right — carrying the table to the curb, spelling L-E-M-O-N-A-D-E in poster paint. Know that your children may move on from the issue that first inspired them to act. Passions evolve. What matters is that they experience change-making triumphs — no matter how small.

So where to begin? There is an old saying that if you can find a path with no obstacles, it probably doesn't lead anywhere. Creating change is not easy. The status quo is deeply ingrained in social attitudes and practices.

Sometimes the best fundraisers start with a lemon

When kids choose their battles it requires a significant dose of bravery. Remind them that courage is something people respect, something that can inspire others to act. Craig took the first step when he summoned the will to speak to his class about child labor. Next, he recruited volunteers and started to build a team. When you are sincere about your concerns, like-minded individuals will want to get involved. In Craig's case, those volunteers spoke to other classes and, in turn, recruited more volunteers. Soon they'd mobilized a young and eager army. In the same way, Marc organized a team to help him raise awareness about the environment.

Just Say Know: Research is Key

Once a child picks his battle — remember, you

can't pick it for him — the next step is research. If he wants to convince or persuade others to embrace his concerns, he will need to find out as much as he can about the scale and scope of the problem. Fieldwork and research can help make sense of a devastating hurricane or a merciless plague or a shocking loss of lives. If children can sort through the facts, they may be able to determine what action to take. When kids know their stuff, people are more likely to pay attention.

When Craig first uncovered Iqbal's story, he made haste for the library. He dug through newspapers and magazines and found articles about children who spent hours in dimly lit rooms making carpets. He discovered stories about kids who slaved in underground pits to bring coal to the surface. He didn't yet know the next step, but things became clearer as he continued to learn more. Kids these days turn immediately to the Internet. The challenge today has less to do with finding information and more to do with putting it all into context. Parents can help to provide nuance that might otherwise go missing. Marc's research revealed all the bad — toxins and carcinogens — in cleaning products at the same time it led him to cleaner alternatives. Without facts or details, Marc's project would not have been effective. Thanks to his passion for research, he found the confidence and conviction that swayed others to clean up their acts.

Devoting time to research creates emotional buy-in. The more would-be activists learn, the greater the odds they will take on long-term projects and the less likely they'll lose hope when they encounter resistance. Having a command of the facts helps to ensure an action helps instead of hurts. (There's no avoiding what they say about the best intentions, unfortunately.) And, of course, the more deeply a young person commits to service, the more likely he or she is to come across others equally committed to their cause.

Parents and mentors can point kids to the world beyond the Internet. Talk about individuals you admire — world leaders and close friends. Discuss what actions they have taken that reveal their character. Seek out documentaries on the environment or poverty or any issue at all. Point out examples of courage and compassion both locally and in the wider world. Describe a time when you demonstrated global character — either when no one was watching or when everyone was watching. Using small steps, guide your charge into the community. Find experts who put a human face on an issue. Take your kid to a town hall meeting or an all-candidates' debate or to the screening of a documentary at a repertory cinema. Make a field trip to the museum so they can see how a story evolved. Show them how to write a letter to the editor. Brainstorm courageous ways to make a difference. Commit to an item on that list and go for it.

Baby Steps and Eleven Hands

When Craig won his first public speaking trophy, he was deeply satisfied but slightly less thrilled than he'd anticipated. Winning, he discovered, is not the only thing, which was actually the topic of his speech. (We marvel at how many clichés our work has revealed to be true.) It was only after taking a stand to defend the local library that he discovered he

SEVEN STEPS TO SOCIAL INVOLVEMENT

When kids decide to get involved, it helps to help them break things down into manageable stages:

1 Choose an issue: Ask yourself: What social problem motivates and inspires me? Try to find a topic you would like to research in order to learn as much as you can. Consider how your skills and gifts can make a difference.

2 Do your research: Learn more about the problems that prevent millions of people around the world from reaching their full potential. If you want to help them have a better life, you have to know what you are fighting for.

3 Build a team: Tell others about your issue. When people see you are sincere and hear you explain why it is important to help, some will want to get involved. As teammates, inspire and encourage one another. Friends are one of the gifts you give yourself when you get involved in a cause.

4 Call a meeting: Once you have a group of interested people, hold a formal meeting. You may find that the first one is difficult, but take heart. Organizing effective and efficient meetings takes a lot of practice.

5 Make an action plan: Come up with creative, crazy and fun ways to influence your issue.

6 Take action and then review: This is key to turning your ideas into reality. If you are planning a Human Rights Awareness Day, make certain you follow through. If you are collecting school and health kits for children in developing countries, do your best to collect as many kits as you can. It is action that creates real and lasting change in the world.

7 Have fun! Stay motivated. At times, you may feel overwhelmed and may even run into some opposition. When this happens, try to remember why you got involved. Your goal is to help others make a difference. Once you have finished your campaign, be sure to celebrate.

Craig, his Grade 7 friends and one giant petition

could use his abilities to speak up for others. It wasn't public speaking that was important, he realized, it was doing so on an issue he cared about and persuading others to feel the same way.

Not so long after, Craig surprised even himself when he walked into his Grade 7 classroom with that crumpled clipping about Iqbal, the child slave. Craig asked his teacher, Mr. Fedrigoni, if he could address the class — a huge step for a kid who had long been teased about his speech impediment. Although sweating and nervous, he shared what he'd learned. At the end of his talk, Craig asked if anyone wanted to join his fight against child slavery. Eleven hands went

up. In the months that followed, Craig and his friends told class after class in school after school about Iqbal. In this way, they discovered Gift + Passion = Better World.

At the same time, Craig was wrestling with his confidence; he was finding himself in situations in which adults would express skepticism that kids had anything to offer. Others — even other young people — accused him of being naïve and ignorant. On one occasion, Craig and his Grade 7 chums went to speak at an all boys' high school. They were armed with posters and facts, but unprepared for the barrage of questions: If the kids didn't work, how would their family eat? Would they have to beg? Craig was flustered and embarrassed. He left determined to find out more, which brings us back to a crucial step: Research.

Two-for-One: Passion and Pizza

Mom and Dad will attest that our house was always crowded with kids brainstorming crazy and creative action plans. Mom would order pizza as we discussed ways to turn ideas into action. We'd be lying if we didn't confess that Mom and Dad thought we went over the top on more than one occasion. In the early days of Free The Children, Craig wrote letters and sent faxes to anyone he thought might share his concerns. Phones rang with news of protests led by children. Our fax machine churned out shocking stories from Brazil, India, Nigeria. The mail brought envelopes from human rights organizations all over the world. In no time, our house in the suburbs became a kind of flophouse for pint-sized activists — Mom would come down for breakfast and find Free

When you are inspired by some great purpose, some extraordinary project, all your thoughts break their bonds: Your mind transcends limitations... you find yourself in a new, great and wonderful world."

Patanjali
Indian sage

The Children volunteers asleep on her couch, posters glued to her kitchen table. She had become de facto den mother to a small army of activists.

To be honest, it frequently drove her crazy. More than once Mom and Dad sat down with Craig and urged him to spend more time on his schoolwork. Of course it's important to encourage kids to balance their passion with their academic and family commitments. At this point, it may be reassuring to note that studies have found that pro-social behaviors — co-operating, helping, sharing — have been found to be a predictor of academic and social success.[1] While Craig appreciated their concerns, he was convinced he'd found his passion. (At age twelve, yes. It seems preposterously young but he was right.) Craig was quick to remind Mom and Dad of their own advice. "Go for it!" they had always said. "The only failure in life is not trying."

Kids find new interests all the time. It's often too hard to keep up with the shifts in attention, swells in enthusiasm and constant questions. With the hectic lives we lead, it's especially easy to miss cues from your kids when they try to express interest in social issues. Yet, as our friend Shelley learned, even kids in kindergarten can pair emerging gifts with a passion for tackling problems. (We have learned that early childhood educators can go a far way to help.) That said, she confesses she was almost too busy to notice.

Shelley's youngest daughter, Scarlet, loves to help in the kitchen, whether it's baking cookies or Rice Krispie squares or chopping red peppers and onions to help her dad make

nachos. She even makes a mean Caesar salad dressing with freshly grated cheese. She sits on a stool at the counter with her own cutting board. Her enthusiasm for cooking isn't exactly a gift, at least not yet, but it's a huge interest. At four, Scarlet was hungry to use her emerging skills for a cause. Shelley is embarrassed to admit she wasn't paying attention.

As a journalist, Shelley spends a lot of time on her laptop. Her kids have accused her of loving Google more than her own family. That's not true, of course, although Google almost always does what she asks. But sometimes she's distracted. A while back, she spent several nights sending out e-mails to raise money to bring Hoang Son Pham, a Vietnamese boy with a severe facial deformity, to North America for life-saving surgery. Scarlet was drawn to the boy's picture. "Is he in pain? Can he smile? Where is his mommy? Can I help?"

Scarlet is an empathetic kid who cries when she sees others in pain and is quick to hug a friend who has fallen down. But Shelley didn't notice her daughter's concern. Scarlet persisted, asking if she could bring a picture of Son Pham to show her kindergarten class. "Maybe we could help." Shelley agreed but didn't follow through. One night, Shelley woke up — a guilty subconscious at work? — and realized she'd been shrugging off her daughter's interest. She was especially horrified because she was in the midst of doing research on this book. The next morning, she printed out a picture for Scarlet to take to school. She included information about the boy and his special needs. She was doubtful a bunch of four- and five-year-olds would be that interested. Scarlet, however, had faith that her teacher (if not her mother) would know

WHAT ARE YOUR GIFTS?

Help your child to complete the following exercise:

1. Finish these sentences:

    - People always say to me, you are so good at:

      _____

    - When I have spare time, I love to:

      _____
      _____

2. Write down as many of your gifts as you can:

    _____
    _____
    _____
    _____

3. Write down the issues you care about:

    _____
    _____
    _____
    _____

4. Now come up with a way that you can use your gifts and passions to make a difference in your community:

    _____
    _____
    _____
    _____

Little Scarlet is always ready to help out with a smile

how they could help. True enough, the teacher put a donation jar with Son Pham's picture at the entrance to the classroom. Scarlet was happy enough with this effort until a few days later when she discovered that not a single cent had been collected.

"We have to do more," Scarlet told her teacher. "Let's make cookies. And sell them for millions of dollars." That afternoon, when parents picked up their kids, Scarlet's teacher had a handout with the date and details of the bake sale. For the next week, Scarlet baked (with mom at her side instead of staring

deeply into the computer). The other kids in her class persuaded their parents to help them make goodies, too. On the day of the sale, the kindergarteners arrived with misshapen shortbread and sloppily but lovingly iced cupcakes. They worked in shifts, selling over-priced brownies and using their charm to peel twenty-dollar bills out of people's pockets. By the end of the day, almost $300 was raised.

Scarlet's persistence and culinary skill paid off, with at least one unfortunate result. She now thinks she can charge money for all her cooking. Shelley learned an important lesson, too. Children, even the very young, want to help out all of the time, but we have to listen to what they are saying and realize they are capable of making a meaningful difference.

One more time: Gift + Passion = Better World. Still stumped as to how to help your children match their gifts with an issue or passion? Give us a call. Getting kids involved is our specialty. It's not always easy to live *me* to *we*, but the benefits of doing so ripple. Once kids experience what it's like to step up, they'll feel more confident when they take a stand.

SMALL ACTIONS › EVERY DAY

1. LEAD, THEN GET OUT OF THE WAY:
When children are young they especially need the support of a trusted adult — parent, teacher or mentor. There are many ways to help children as they take their first steps. Children learn by example, of course. But they are also usually open to guidance that helps them on their way.

2. CHARITY BEGINS AT HOME:
Give them a corner of the basement to work on their project. Show your support by stocking the "office" with supplies.

3. BE A CHEERLEADER:
Be sensitive to the fact kids may feel overwhelmed at times, especially if they run into opposition. In such moments, remind would-be activists why they got involved in the first place — and act.

4. BUY THE PIZZA:
Never underestimate its importance to eager volunteers, hungry for change.

5. IDENTIFY TARGETS:
Help your young activists establish achievable actions. Break large goals into smaller pieces. Make sure the action is both fun — though not superficial — and do-able.

6. LET THINGS GO WRONG:
Allow them to make mistakes. Don't always clean up their messes.

7. FREQUENTLY ASKED QUESTIONS:
Aspire to be your child's go-to person for answers. Be honest when you don't know the answers — find them together.

Use Your Talent to Make the World a Better Place

Monica Yunus, *one of America's most promising young soprano stars, is using her celebrity power to raise money for a number of causes. Monica is the daughter of Nobel Prize winner Muhammad Yunus, the founder of the Grameen Bank. She talked to us about Sing for Hope, which has grown to include five hundred artists, dancers, actors and performers.*

GROWING UP, MY HOME was filled with song. While my mother, a teacher, was at work, my grandmother would sing me Russian hymns and folk songs. In her lovely, clear voice she sang Russian lullabies. Soon I was singing, too. I joined my grandmother in the choir of our Russian Orthodox Church. The liturgy, sung in Slavonic, was dramatic and operatic. I couldn't help but tip back my head and sing at the top of my lungs. But I reserved my best singing for the back seat of our car — to and from grandma's house. My mom had no choice but to notice I had a "voice."

By the time I was eleven, she had me in singing lessons. That same year, I landed a spot in the Metropolitan Opera Children's Chorus. I dreamed of becoming a professional opera singer but I also had a sense that my voice was a gift to be shared. Mom used to take me to seniors' homes to sing Christmas carols together. It was amazing to see the smiles on the people's faces when we sang "Silent Night." Afterward, we'd have a chat and share tea. I loved it. I understood at a young age that I could use my talent to make the world a better place.

I also learned this from my father. A few years ago, after I had graduated from the Juilliard School, my father invited me back to Bangladesh, the country where I was born. I had last been there as a four-month-old, so to say this trip was an education is an understatement. I got a chance to see his humanitarian work, as well as truly understand the poverty and happiness of the people of my homeland. It was a life-changing trip. I stepped off the plane to a red-carpet welcome. It seemed like the whole country was waiting for my arrival. Yes, they were curious about the eldest daughter of Muhammad Yunus, but they were also proud of my accomplishments — a Bangladeshi girl making a name for herself.

I finally went to see a village where microcredit was operating. The women's faces were shining. They told me that before they got their loans from Grameen, they had to beg to sleep under someone's little piece of roof overhang. Now they had cows, rickshaws — and most importantly, dignity. All of this because of a fifteen-dollar loan.

Back in the United States, I too wanted to make a difference. I just wasn't sure how. Then Hurricane Katrina struck.

Like everyone, I watched television and felt really depressed. The mass displacement of people who lost their homes was devastating. I felt sick to my stomach. How could this be happening in my country? I wanted to raise funds for those affected by the hurricane, and also create a space for people to come together to grieve.

I called several singer friends and asked if they would be willing to sing in a concert to benefit victims of Katrina. Two weeks later, in Huguenot Memorial Church in Pelham, New York, more than one hundred people gathered for the concert. Each performer poured their gift and their heart into their performance. We raised $2,500 to help victims of Katrina. I never imagined how easy it would be to call on friends for a cause, and how good it would feel to stand together and lift our voices for a common purpose.

My friend and fellow Juilliard alumna, Camille Zamora, sang that evening, and was instrumental in helping me organize the event. A decade ago, after the loss of a dear friend to AIDS, she founded a benefit concert called Sing for Hope in her hometown of Houston. The annual event has raised more than one million dollars for men and women living with HIV/AIDS. Using her concert as a model for our programming and rehearsal methods (the latter jokingly referred to by us as "kamikaze opera" for the breakneck speed at which we prepared), we put together the Katrina event with an ease that surprised even us. When it came time to give the concert a name, Camille offered her simple, universally applicable Houston title: "Why don't you call it Sing for Hope?"

Later that fall, Camille and I decided to create

an organization that would unite and support artists who wish to create events that benefit humanitarian causes: Sing for Hope. We now have five hundred artists, dancers, actors and performers who donate their time to charitable events. It's amazing how willing so many artists are to help out, and how quickly we have grown.

It's been gratifying to have my father join the board of Sing for Hope and become one of our most enthusiastic supporters. He helped us raise $250,000.

People ask me all of the time how my father influenced my efforts to help others. I tell them how he inspired me. I also tell them that it was also my mother who showed me I could use my own talents in my own unique way to contribute to the world. And that's what I hope for everyone.

Back in the United States, I too wanted to make a difference. I just wasn't sure how. Then Hurricane Katrina struck."

Monica Yunus

THE SECOND C
Courage

In the second section of this book, we will show you how to teach your kids to step up, speak out and stand tall.

It takes courage to step up, to speak out, to stand tall. It takes courage to begin.

It's hard to get up in front of the class for the very first time. We know because we've been there. It takes gumption to rally friends, to raise rafters, to refuse to go away.

It takes nerve to dare to be different — to define yourself not by what you own or buy, but by what you say and do. It takes pluck to distinguish between the short-lived thrill that possessions can bring and the profound contentment that comes from living a life of meaning and purpose — aligning one's goals with one's values.

"What have they got that I ain't got?" the Cowardly Lion so famously asked in the Land of Oz. The answer? Courage, of course. It was in him all the time.

It's our responsibility as parents, teachers, pastors and mentors to model integrity and courage. It is our job to help children discover the strength of their convictions.

When people ask us where to begin, we tell them about *me* to *we*. Instead of asking

"What's in it for me?" we encourage them to ask "What's in it for my family? My community? My world?"

These are daring questions. In the next section of this book, we will show you how to raise participants in a world of bystanders. And we'll encourage you to consider what real success might mean to you and your children. Maybe the success you seek doesn't require having the most of everything — stuff, money, cars, gadgets — but instead the best of other things: togetherness, generosity and a sense of community. That, too, takes courage.

Courage might be slowing down to engage with the world, instead of racing your children from one lesson to another. It might mean raising children who are comfortable being different from their friends. One by one, we can teach our kids to step up, speak out, stand tall. Knowing that there is strength in numbers, they will find the courage to begin.

Raising Participants in a World of Bystanders

The world needs more kids primed to take action. But how? Remember that empathetic kids are caring kids. It takes courage to act on your beliefs. We can help our young people to take a stand.

HOW CAN YOU NOT LOVE a story in which boys in pink triumph over bullies with raised dukes? That's exactly what happened at a high school in rural Nova Scotia when a student showed up on the first day of school wearing a pink polo shirt. It proved an unwise fashion choice for a Grade 9 kid eager to make a good impression. Bullies taunted the boy and called him a "fag." Word spread quickly that there was going to be a rumble — another new kid knocked off the block.

But this story doesn't end with a bloody nose.

In a twist of fate, two boys who had never found the courage to stand up for themselves decided to stick up for the little guy. Eighteen-year-old David Shepherd told us he was astonished when he heard the new boy was going to be flattened for wearing pink. David had never really taken on injustices — although

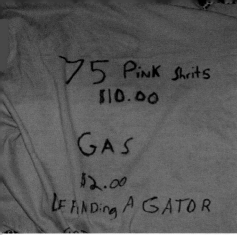

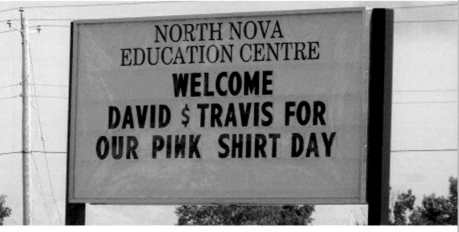

he thought a lot about it. "It was his first day ever of high school," the high school senior later explained to us. "I felt bad for him. I felt like I should do something." The Grade 12 student enlisted the help of his seventeen-year-old buddy Travis Price, who couldn't help but identify with the boy. Travis had been bullied throughout grade school because he couldn't afford name-brand clothing. "Kids look for reasons to pick on others. They target kids who can't defend themselves. I was that kid growing up," Travis told us. He faked sick to avoid school. On one occasion, someone punched him in the face and broke his glasses. Nobody had his back.

Travis and David held an impromptu meeting of about a dozen Grade 12 students. Everyone agreed enough was enough. "Guys are usually all hardcore," Travis says. "They say, 'Oh you're getting picked on, suck it up!' There are lots of stereotypes. If guys are compassionate or sensitive, then they are gay. It's just the way the world works. But you can't let stereotypes run your life. You have to go with what you feel." The group came up with an audacious plan. David was dispatched to a discount store where he wheeled and dealed for dozens of

Travis and David standing proud in pink

FIND YOUR INNER PRINCESS

In the late-1980s, patients with HIV and AIDS were treated like pariahs. There were so many unknowns, so much to fear. It took the quiet courage of a determined princess to blast away the stigma. In 1987, Princess Diana was photographed — gloveless and without protection — holding the hand of a man with AIDS. It was the smallest of gestures that had the greatest of influence as the image was flashed around the world. "When she stroked the limbs of someone with leprosy, or sat on the bed of a man with HIV/AIDS and held his hand, she transformed public attitudes and improved the life chances of such people," Nelson Mandela would later say. "People felt if a British princess can go to a ward with HIV patients, then there's nothing to be superstitious about."[15]

pink T-shirts. That night, the boys sent messages on Facebook and MSN Messenger, urging classmates to wear pink to school the next day. At the very least, they knew their small group would do so.

It was like something out of a Hallmark special when they arrived at school the next day. Everywhere they looked, kids were sporting pink. And those who weren't eagerly snapped up a tank top from the team. In the end, about seven hundred of the school's eight hundred students joined the action. When the new kid arrived, he seemed shocked, then relieved. It looked like a huge weight was lifted off his shoulders. He pulled on a pink shirt and joined the protest.

The bullies fled.

You'd think that would be the end of the story. In fact, it was only the start.

Sea of Pink made headlines. After NBC News ran with the story of student action, pink washed over schools across Canada and the United States. E-mails and Facebook messages from Germany and Japan swamped David and Travis; they also heard from high school principals from Arizona to Wyoming. Amazing, but also a little depressing: Why is it front-page news when a school stands up to bullies? It's newsworthy, of course, because it doesn't happen all that often.

'It Was Little Things, But They Were Big'

We were curious to find out what role upbringing played in the Sea of Pink. As we suspected, Travis had been raised to care about other people. "We didn't emphasize that macho thing," says his mother, Patsy. He was a helpful kid. "If someone wasn't feeling good, he'd call and ask how they were doing," Patsy says. "It was little things, but they were big things." Unfortunately, it made him a target. Patsy says she cried for days when bullies started to pick on her son. "We just kept telling him, 'we are on your side!'" She is immensely proud of her son for finding the courage to stand up for someone else — an action that inspired a Sea of Pink.

David also learned empathy and courage as a kid. When he was eight, his mother, Sherry, almost died from an unexplained illness. She thinks that difficult time made her son more sensitive to others. She talked to her kids about responsibility, telling them, "It's very important you think about it not only from your perspective but from the other person, too." All credit goes to her kids, she says. "I just guide them. They pick their life journey."

On September 11, 2008, students in Nova Scotia celebrated the first Stand Up Against Bullying Day. High school kids across the province were asked to wear pink to school. In proclaiming the day, the premier of Nova Scotia praised Travis and David. "It is an honor to acknowledge their creative and selfless efforts," he said.

Few kids are like David and Travis. In fact, 85 percent of bullying takes place in front of other students and few bother to intervene. We live in a world of bystanders unwilling to take on global warming, genocide in Darfur or conflict at the neighborhood hockey rink. Most young people — like most adults — are afraid to take a risk. It's much easier to blend into the background. Researchers have found that when push comes to shove, we prefer to sit squarely on the fence. They've also found that only subtle differences separate adults — and kids — who sit on the sidelines and those who possess the moral courage to take a stand.

The world needs more adults — and kids — primed to take action. But how? Once again, it's worth remembering that empathetic kids are caring kids. Beyond empathy, courage is also important. We can prime young people to take a stand.

Fear Factor and the Status Quo

Charles Smith, a psychologist, has written extensively about raising courageous kids. By his definition, courage is "gumption, grit and the capacity to get up after a setback with one's heart on fire."[1] The word comes from the French "curage" for "putting one's heart into action." He calls courage an essential virtue, "a source of strength that contributes to all significant human endeavors."[2] Kids are capable of dramatic and newsworthy acts of courage. We've read remarkable stories — death-defying, headline-making stuff. And there's David and Travis, who rallied classmates and dispensed with bullies. Yet, just as noble are smaller acts of persistent courage. Dr. Smith describes a child with cystic fibrosis, for example, who lives with constant fear and pain while struggling with physical therapy.[3]

As you can probably guess we'd say, it takes courage to challenge the status quo. We can't help but admire a kid who musters the nerve to knock on doors to ask neighbors to support a walk-a-thon. We know it's hard to get up in front of the class for the first time. It takes gumption to rally friends, to raise rafters, to refuse to go away. The truth is that the world is in desperate need of all these forms of courage. It needs more "hearts on fire." If our goal is to raise socially responsible young people, we need to nurture

Science may have found a cure for most evils; but it has found no remedy for the worst of them all — the apathy of human beings."

Helen Keller
Activist and lecturer

this intrepid spirit. The problem is that it's hard to stand up when there's so much bringing us down. We're afraid of an endless list of threats — starting with bullying, road rage and amber alerts, and ending with strangers, the homeless and people who don't look like us. Politicians and the media play on our fears, which are brought to life in primetime and on the big screen. It is scary when you think about it.

Although fear was no stranger before 9/11, it's been present ever since. Parents whisper about the Homeland Security Terrorism Threat Advisory Scale: Is it orange or is it red? Loud speakers in airports warn travelers to be vigilant. Grade schools lead children in lockdown drills. Even if we're not discussing our apprehension, children know it's there. They absorb horrific headlines before we can turn down the radio or click off the TV. And they spot when you cross the street to avoid helping a street person. If we ever mention we were at Mom's side as she talked to the homeless, people express disbelief. "We would never do that with our children," they say. "What if... ?" Yet here's the real cause for concern: The more insecurity we pass on to our children, the more vulnerable they become to fear. We're afraid to be different, to stand up, to speak out. Know what else we're afraid of? (Told you, the list is endless.) We're afraid we won't make a difference, even if we try.

But there is much about which to be hopeful. We may be scaredy-cats, but we also are capable of great courage. The tragedy of 9/11 fuelled fear 24/7, but it also showed us what is possible. On that devastating day in New York, Welles Crowther, a twenty-four-year-old volunteer firefighter, helped dozens of people to safety. His body was found six months later, alongside several firefighters and emergency workers bunched in the South Tower lobby. "I see this incredible hero, running back and forth and saving the day," said Judy Wein, one of the people he saved. "People can live one hundred years and not have the compassion, the wherewithal to do what he did."[4] On that same day, in the final moments of United Airlines Flight 93, passengers attempted to take back the plane from the hijackers. Sandy Dahl, the wife of Captain Jason Dahl, says a "wave of courage made its way from the cockpit to the rear of the aircraft and back again, with all persevering to the end."[5]

These heroic moments remind us of why we must teach our children to stand tall. Fear can't be their fallback, nor should it be ours. Dr. Smith has observed that there's no such thing as courage on demand. Instead, he writes, it arrives gradually, "beginning with the baby who defies gravity to sit up and the preschooler who dares to climb a playground slide for the first time."[6] Learning to remain calm in the face of fear — "a first grader jumping off a diving board" — is a building block. Step by baby step, children learn to cope.

Not all fear is unwelcome, of course. We teach kids to watch for cars, to avoid rushing rivers, to steer clear of a growling dog. "When we comfort a frightened child, neural pathways for managing fear are strengthened in the child's brain," Dr. Smith explains. "The repeated experience of comfort, in moving from alarm to calm, enables children to manage fear on their own."[7] With our encouragement — "Keep trying, I know you can do it!" — children learn to persevere even when they're anxious. The ability to keep at it prepares a child to keep moving in the face of fear.

Dr. Smith has observed that love inspires courage. A child raised in a caring home absorbs what it means to consider others. From this comes empathy, which, as we write in Chapter 2, prompts a kid to think about others and to extend compassion when required. In this way, a child develops valor, integrity and a moral foundation.

Between Us and Them

It's human nature to hang in the background: Wait long enough and someone else will step up. Tragically, though, that is not always the case. In 1964, Kitty Genovese was sexually assaulted and murdered in Queens, New York. Initial reports suggested thirty-eight people witnessed the random attack. Subsequent investigation suggests this number may be an exaggeration, but the point remains: The attack lasted more than half an hour and no one went to her aid or called for help. Everyone thought someone else would do it. As one sheepish neighbor told police, "I didn't want to get involved."[8] On the fortieth anniversary of that tragic day, Genovese's roommate and partner gave an interview. "I still have a lot of anger toward people because they could have saved her life," Mary Ann Zielonko said. "You look out the window and you see this happening and you don't help? How do you live with yourself knowing you didn't do anything?"[9]

John Darley, a psychologist who studied the Genovese case, says it wasn't fear that stopped people from intervening but rather the assumption that someone else would do so.[10] Darley teamed up with psychologist, Bibb Latané, to determine what prevents witnesses from helping. In one study, they invited participants to a lab to discuss "personal problems."[11] Because of the nature of the discussion, study subjects were told the conversation would take place over an intercom so they wouldn't see to whom they were talking. They were told that one to five others might be involved in the discussion. In truth, the sole person on the intercom was working with the researchers. As the study got underway, the researcher mentioned that he suffered from seizures. During the staged discussion, he became loud and incoherent. He choked and gasped. Before falling silent, he stammered: "I could really, er, use some help... I'm gonna die, er, er, I'm gonna die, er, help, er, er, seizure, er…"

Eighty-five percent of the participants who believed they were the lone witness to the seizure left their cubicles to help. Participants were significantly less likely to intervene if they thought there were other witnesses. It's believed this is why those who watched the Genovese murder didn't act — witnesses assumed someone else would step in.

In a subsequent study with psychologist Daniel Batson Darley, he studied seminary students at Princeton who were asked to walk across campus to give a talk. Along the way, each passed someone slumped and groaning in a passageway. Whether or not the students stopped to help depended on if they were running late. Only 10 percent of those in a hurry bothered to stop. Six times that number stopped when they weren't rushed to get to their talk.

Our friend and mentor Jonathan White is an expert in genocide studies at Bridgewater State College, outside of Boston. He explained to us that responsibility for acting against injustice is diffused in sophisticated ways. For example, a North American contemplating AIDS in Africa might say, "It's horrible. Our government really ought to be doing more—it's their responsibility!" This is active bystanding: An individual acknowledges a problem but identifies why they can't do anything about it. An observer might further rationalize this inaction by deciding that "they" are not like "us." We think it's the UN's job to act but forget it is made up of member governments; that each government is made up of politicians; that we elect the politicians. When one person fails to act, it hurts us all. And this bystanding can be transferred to the schoolyard. Let's consider all of this as it might go down on the schoolyard. When it comes to child's play, we urge parents not to bystand when kids are bystanding. If, for example, they return home with a story about a schoolyard bully or an unreasonable teacher or someone telling racist or sexist jokes, ask your children three questions: How did you deal with the situation? What did you do? How did you help?

"You Poor Boy, I Will Help"

We were lucky to speak to a man who has spent his life trying to figure out the difference between bystanders and the morally courageous. Samuel Oliner is the founder of the Altruistic Personality and Prosocial Behaviour Institute at Humboldt State University. In June of 1942, when he was twelve, Samuel and his family were forced by the Nazis to move to a Jewish ghetto from their village in southern Poland. Samuel and his family lived with two others in a small room. He would sneak away to nearby villages to trade watches, pens and other personal belongings for potatoes, fruit, eggs and bread. Early one August morning, Nazi soldiers surrounded the ghetto and loaded the Jewish families onto trucks. Samuel watched from the attic, where he hid. Later in a nearby forest, almost one thousand Jews, including his parents, were executed. Samuel had no choice but to run. For three days, he wandered the countryside, sleeping in barns and fields and surviving on carrots and apples. Desperate, he crossed the hills to a nearby village to seek help from a family friend, a Catholic woman named Balwina Piecuch. He had nowhere else to go. "You poor boy, I will help," she said. "You must live." Oliner recalls her heroic efforts in *Do Unto Others: Extraordinary Acts of Ordinary People*. Despite the danger of being found by the Nazis, Balwina did all she could to help Samuel pass himself off as a Catholic.[12]

This deliberate act of life-saving kindness inspired Oliner to devote his life's work to understanding why certain people will take risks to help others, even strangers. He headed a team that included his wife, Pearl, a professor of education. They interviewed fifteen hundred people who had helped others, including non-Jewish and Jewish rescuers in Nazi-occupied Europe, hospice volunteers, philanthropists and people who make a difference in their communities. The team discovered that those willing to assume great risk to help others were generally brought up by parents who nurtured caring and social responsibility. The rescuers were found to share a strong sense of attachment to others and a feeling of responsibility for their welfare. They learned from parents that people of all spiritual beliefs are "children of the same God, worthy of protection and love."[13]

It is also important to teach your child to be a good witness. Not exactly a starring role in a schoolyard drama but a crucial one all the same. Kids stand by bullying events because they are afraid or curious or worried about what might happen if they intervene. "Helpful witnesses understand the difference between tattling and reporting," write SuEllen and Paula Fried in their book *Bullies, Targets & Witnesses: Helping Children Break the Pain Chain.* "As many bright students have said: 'Tattling is when you're trying to get someone in trouble. Reporting is when you're trying to get someone out of trouble.'"[14]

Our parents helped us through our share of schoolyard scraps. More than that, they showed us how to possess the courage of our convictions. The Frieds and other bullying experts say parents and educators can persuade kids that they do have power to respond to bullies. Here are just a few strategies:

1. Find an adult. If your child is worried about payback, help him figure out how to do so discretely.

2. Find safety in numbers. Mobilize a group of kids to challenge the bully.

3. Don't just stick up for the target, stick with the target. Invite the child to join your group on the playground.

4. Support the victim in private.

Mr. Clean and the Mean Teens

Adults thought it was impressive — or at least cute — when Marc started to raise awareness about the harmful chemicals in cleaning supplies. He received a rougher reception in the world of preteens where standing out is so not cool.

Shortly after an article about his campaign appeared in a Toronto newspaper, Marc arrived at school to the cold shoulder. Classmates pretended he didn't exist. If he spoke, they pretended not to hear. If they deemed to notice him, it was only to body check him into a locker. It was a small school and the behavior was difficult to avoid. Marc was devastated. It was little consolation that the campaign was attracting girls to his side. At the time, Marc didn't understand that he was being punished for breaking out of the mold. It was the first time he'd encountered pushback for taking action in the face of injustice. (But, then again... girls!)

In hindsight, it wasn't surprising that Marc encountered bullies. Kids in their early teens are under intense pressure to conform. That's why they often remain bystanders on the playground and the world at large. Although he excelled at public speaking and was athletic, it was not in Marc's nature to fight back. As a result, he endured rumors, taunting and assaults. Mom and Dad encouraged him to walk away, but he couldn't ignore what was said and done. Our parents had numerous meetings with school administrators and asked

Our lives begin to end the day we become silent about things that matter."

Dr. Martin Luther King, Jr.
Civil rights leader

**This is where
Marc got his start**

them to clamp down, of course. Mom and Dad wanted Marc to find a way to cope. They urged him to share his vision, hoping he'd coax friends and allies from the sidelines to join his environmental campaign.

We were always encouraged to recruit others to our efforts. Mom and Dad believed — and still believe — that when children discover a social issue, they need a helping hand. So Marc tried to enlist a team. He approached recruits

and told them he needed their assistance, their enthusiasm, their ideas. Soon others had joined his little brother to collect signatures on his petition to ban harmful cleaning supplies. At the invitation of the federal government, Marc and his team presented their ideas. Bringing along friends — and others — helped quiet the static around his efforts. The team unfurled a petition, signed by thousands, calling on the government to ban dangerous chemicals and to put ingredient labels on cleaning products.

Mom says that from an early age she reminded us that not everyone would agree with our opinions, decisions or actions. "We encouraged you to be true to yourselves," she told us as we discussed those distant but distressing days. "We reminded you that great people often stand alone, take difficult stands against injustices. It is not unusual for people to criticize, or state opposing views when individuals challenge the norm." What Mom taught us then, and reminded us of all these years later, is that it takes courage to act on your beliefs.

SMALL ACTIONS › EVERY DAY

1. START SMALL:
Model small actions for your children. Smile at the people you pass on the street. Strike up a conversation with a stranger. Do a favor for a friend.

2. CONVERSATION STARTERS:
Young people crave stories of emotional courage. Draw examples from the civil rights movement, the Holocaust, the suffrage movement. Take stories from newspapers and books and movies. And, of course, tell stories from your own life.

3. WHERE IN THE WORLD?
Hang a map of the world on a wall in your kitchen, family room or your child's bedroom. When you discuss issues with your kids, help them to locate the country you are discussing.

4. TO WHOM IT MAY CONCERN:
Help your child write a letter to tell others what they think about an issue. It could be a note to request information, a thank-you card or a letter to a politician or an editor.

5. BE A FRIEND:
Suggest that your child offer to show a new student around — introducing them to friends and teachers.

6. DEFEND A FRIEND — OR A STRANGER:
Teach your kids to stand up to bullies, or protect those who are being bullied.

Of Loss and Legacy

Eva Haller *is a Holocaust survivor, long-time activist and chair of the U.S. board of Free The Children. She and her husband, Yoel, a physician, are dedicated to humanitarian and environmental causes. Here Eva tells us about her true hero, her brother, John.*

WHEN MY GRANDSON, ELIAS, was ten, he was given a school assignment to write a story about his favorite hero. He wrote about me. He told of how I had survived the Holocaust in Hungary and came to America and remained as an illegal alien. How I cleaned houses and then began to collect art. He skipped over important details but captured the main sequence of events that shaped my life. Each year, he added more to his story. He told of how I inspired each of my grandchildren to build schools in Africa, often participating with them to raise funds for Free The Children. And he proudly told of how his own grandmother could do fifty push-ups.

I, in turn, told my grandchildren stories of my parents. I explained that my mother and father sold their furniture and other belongings to buy flour and bake bread to feed the starving people fleeing the Nazis. When asked about the origins of my social conscience, I remember their efforts to keep others alive in Budapest during the war. I think especially of John, the younger of my two brothers. He was my true hero.

John was seven years my senior. Whatever he did, I tried to emulate. He played the accordion. I played the accordion. When he began to sneak out during the night to participate in the resistance movement, I insisted on following.

My brothers and I were raised primarily by governesses. Although we were descendents of Hungarian Jewish aristocracy, we were raised as Christians. My father, a wealthy businessman, had

lived through the first pogrom in Budapest in 1919, and he worried about our future. He fought in the First World War, was an ardent patriot and hoped he and his family would be accepted and safe by embracing the Catholic faith.

Jews in the countryside of Hungary were the first to be sent to Auschwitz. By 1942, it became obvious we would have to leave Hungary if we wanted to survive. My parents began to prepare us for a new life in the United States. My mother learned to make artificial flowers for ladies' hats, while John apprenticed as a baker. The bakeries were unionized and John became involved with anti-fascist workers. It was through the connection he made with these bakers that, at nineteen, he joined the underground movement.

John began to disappear during the nights. I was only twelve, but after nagging him incessantly, he allowed me to help him print anti-Nazi leaflets and post them around the city. One morning, John did not return. After a long and arduous search, my father discovered he had been sent to prison. The court ordered John's death by hanging. My father used his social influence and wealth to try to save his son. John spent almost a year on death row. Finally, after tremendous effort, my parents managed to have him freed. He returned home with his head shaved, his prison uniform hanging loosely on his body. I thought him to be the most courageous person I'd ever known. Once he'd eaten a decent meal and settled in, he picked up the accordion so we could make music together, but his fingers were too stiff to play.

By March 1944, the Jews of Budapest, who had once been protected, were no longer safe. We were forced to give up our clothing and jewelry, our radios and finally our homes. We were shuttled into a ghetto and ordered to wear a large Star of David, so everybody would know we were Jews. In October, the Nazis took away my brothers. I was sick with worry but had faith they would survive.

My parents secured false identity papers and went into hiding. They left me at the Scottish Mission, where they hoped I would remain safely until the end of the war. In December, all the Jews hiding at the Mission were discovered and deported. The policeman guarding us was a teenager. I stepped out of line, approached him and said: "I am much too young to die." He let me go. I still wonder what made him become so lenient. Maybe he was simply too tired of the war and its cruelty. I didn't know where to go, so I walked for miles through the snow to our home and knocked on the door of our closest family friends, who were not Jewish. They gave me a sandwich and sent me on my way. I often wonder if they ever felt any remorse at turning away a fourteen-year-old girl to face her death?

Through a bit of luck and detective work, I found my parents on the outskirts of the city. Together we spent the final days of the war in an air raid shelter. My mother snuck out routinely to steal food for all of us from the army depot. Without her bravery, we would have starved.

Then the Russians arrived and occupied our country. We returned to our apartment. My mother baked bread from dried peas and beans to share with our neighbors; my father carried the heavy loaves on his back, up and down the stairs. Life was hard. The Soviet troops were hungry and very cruel.

All the while, we wondered what had happened to my brothers. We learned that George had died but that John had escaped to Yugoslavia to join Tito and the Partisans. When my mother wasn't scavenging for food or baking bread, she was searching for John. She traveled to villages near the Yugoslavian border approaching anyone who might have seen her son. At last, she located four men who had been with my brother, trying to flee. They had escaped the Nazis and sought shelter in a hut. When John and the others heard dogs barking, John told his friends to go out the backdoor while he covered them at the front. They never saw him again. My mother rode the train to that village, hoping beyond hope John was somehow alive. When she arrived, she saw my brother's shirt flapping on a clothesline. She knew she had found the place where he had died.

After the war, we were left with almost nothing, and barely a remnant of John's belongings. My mother took his old brown suit to a tailor, so it could be made into an outfit for me. I wore it until it was threadbare, hoping somehow I could absorb his courage.

"

I wore it until it was threadbare, hoping somehow I could absorb his courage."

Eva Haller

How to Live in a Material World

"Materialistic" kids are not "giving" kids. The more youngsters focus on acquiring stuff, the less likely they are to care about others. Let's turn this on its head.

WHEN MARC WAS ABOUT eleven, Mom picked him up at school to take him to tennis practice. En route she made a pit stop at Bi-Way, a discount store that sold the kind of no-name clothing that sends self-conscious tweens running to the nearest Gap. One minute Marc was sitting contentedly beside Mom in the car, the next he'd slipped down to hide below the dashboard. The store was near school, so he was worried he'd be spotted by classmates. Until that day, Marc had assumed only welfare moms and struggling new immigrants shopped at the bargain shop. Not him. No way.

"Don't buy me anything here," he grumbled from his hiding spot. "I won't wear it!"

Mom was taken aback. She let him stay in the car. "It was hard to concentrate on my shopping," she recalls. "My son was turning into a snob."

Back home after tennis, she sat Marc down for a chat. He explained why he wanted a "cool" T-shirt — one with a logo — not one from the discount rack. "All my friends wear 'em." Mom was disappointed, but she wasn't angry. "It really wasn't his fault, nor was it the fault of his friends," she recalls. "It was the fault of advertisers who were brainwashing kids into thinking they needed the latest T-shirt to

Students sporting sweatshop-free, socially conscious clothing at school

be "cool." It was our fault as parents for being sucked in. Marc wanted to be accepted and feel good about himself among his friends. We just wanted him to be happy. That day I realized I didn't like what it was doing to my son."

Mom and Dad provided us with more than they'd ever dreamed of having when they were kids. Mom's family had been homeless for a time; we lived in a spacious home in suburbia. Both Mom and Dad had been forced to work from an early age; we devoted our free time to video games, TV and hanging with friends. They'd worn hand-me-down sneakers; we

laced up in the best money could buy. Neither of them ever imagined they'd go to university (although they did), but they expected their kids to attend and to excel. And though they both became teachers, they hoped Marc would grow up to be a lawyer, and Craig to be a doctor.

We appeared to be on the path to success. Question was, at what cost? Mom was worried that if we lacked for nothing, we'd never become sensitive to poverty or to the needs of others. Clothing, credit cards and consumerism: These seemed to be our Three Cs at that time. The Bi-Way excursion forced

MADE IN CHINA: THE REAL TOY STORY

"On the night she died, Li Chunmei must have been exhausted." We were devastated by the first line of story but kept reading. The *Washington Post* story, which appeared in 2002, goes on: "Co-workers said she had been on her feet for nearly sixteen hours, running back and forth inside the Bainan Toy Factory, carrying toy parts from machine to machine. When the quitting bell rang shortly after midnight, her young face was covered with sweat. This was the busy season, before Christmas, when long hours were mandatory. At least two months had passed since Li and the other workers had enjoyed even a Sunday off."[7]

That night in her dormitory, the slight nineteen-year-old started to cough up blood. She was found curled up on the bathroom floor. Family, friends and co-workers said she died from guolaosi, a phrase that means "worked to death." In China, where almost all of the world's toys are made, such deaths are talked about in hushed tones.

Eric Clark, author of *The Real Toy Story: Inside the Ruthless Battle for America's Youth,* describes the approximately three million Chinese workers in eight thousand factories, mostly identical concrete boxes with "swirling red dust, toxic rivers and thick, choking smog that hovers everywhere, stinging eyes and throats." Chinese law stipulates that assembly-line workers should toil for fifty-three hours a week, though eighty hours is common. The average workday lasts eleven to twelve hours. Without these places, he writes, "the modern toy industry would not exist."

We should care about these young people, mostly women, who work to exhaustion to ensure toy store shelves in North America are filled with cheap and plentiful toys. Without taking the joy out of childhood, we must make our children aware that toys, clothes and gadgets come from somewhere, and there isn't an unlimited supply.

Mom and Dad to ask tough questions. They wanted us to have the best of everything, of course. But in that moment, they decided to redefine their definition of success — no easy task in a society that measures achievement in dollars and degrees. While athletics and public speaking would continue to have a place in our lives, from that moment so would service to the community.

Toys Are Us

Nobody buys more toys than Americans. Author Eric Clark has noted that although fewer than 4 percent of the world's children are American, they own 40 percent of the world's toys — most of which are produced in Asia, many in sweatshop conditions. Clark is the author of *The Real Toy Story: Inside the Ruthless Battle for America's Youth.* He says many of us are shopping addicts — brand junkies with more disposable income than earlier generations. Hard-working parents — and grandparents — want children to have the best and the latest. Ours certainly did. The catch is that many times the harder parents work to provide, the less time they spend with their children. In lieu of presence? Presents. Unfortunately, this exchange teaches kids that work is more important than family. In the same way, children who receive money or rewards for good behavior and achievement miss out on the intrinsic satisfaction of a job well done.

When materialism becomes a dominant value in a household, kids are shortchanged of the opportunity to learn healthy buying habits. In fact, research hints that materialistic

Tim Kasser, author and leading expert on materialism

twenty-four-hour lipstick rivets them to the screen, as do commercials for high-tech gadgets and age-defying wrinkle cream. But Shelley has taught her kids to "ad bust" — to pick apart the advertisements. Every time a commercial comes on, the kids consider three questions:

1. What are they selling me?
2. Why are they selling it to me?
3. What do they claim it will do for me?

Kids hate to be duped, so it's constructive to point out that commercials are designed to trick them into buying stuff that they often don't need or want. Thanks to the ad busting, commercials seem to have no influence on Cleo or Scarlet. This is not to say they don't ask for things, but they've learned to be much more discriminating in their desires.

The $100 Question

Studies show that the more materialistic an individual—adult or child—the less happy they are. For the purposes of this book, we wanted to find out if materialism affects a young person's ability to be generous. We discovered emerging research that shows that "materialistic" kids are not "giving" kids. The more youngsters focus on acquiring stuff, in fact, the less likely they are to care about others.

Tim Kasser is a leading scholar on materialism and the author of *The High Price of Materialism*. The professor told us that kids learn early in life that what they have is more important than who they are. In 2005, Kasser, who teaches at Knox College in Galesburg, Illinois, asked two hundred and six middle-

teenagers are in danger of becoming future shopaholics.[1]

If parents can't say no to advertisers, how ever will their children? Media Smart is an organization set up by advertisers in the United Kingdom to educate children about commercials. The organization urges parents to watch TV with their kids, to deconstruct ads — "What do you suppose they're trying to sell? And to whom?" — and to help children become informed consumers.

Shelley's girls love commercials. An ad for

DID YOU KNOW?

- Approximately half of the world's population lives on $2 a day and more than 100 million people are homeless.
- 800 million people go hungry every day.
- Two billion people suffer from chronic malnutrition.
- Eighteen million people die each year from hunger-related diseases. Around half of the deaths of children under the age of five — ten million each year — are associated with malnutrition.

IN ONE YEAR...

- North America will spend $17 billion on cat and dog food. (It would cost $15 billion to provide clean drinking water for all.)
- The world will spend more than $1 trillion on the global military.
- Europe will spend more than $11 billion on ice cream. (It would cost $10 billion to stop the spread of AIDS in Africa.)

MORE THAN 100 MILLION PEOPLE WORLDWIDE

WHAT ARE THE MILLENNIUM DEVELOPMENT GOALS?

The Millennium Development Goals are eight goals to be achieved by 2015 that respond to the world's main development challenges. The goals are drawn from the actions and targets contained in the Millennium Declaration that was adopted by 189 nations and signed by 147 heads of state and governments during the UN Millennium Summit in September 2000.

Goal 1: Eradicate extreme poverty and hunger.
Goal 2: Achieve universal primary education.
Goal 3: Promote gender equality and empower women.
Goal 4: Reduce child mortality.
Goal 5: Improve maternal health.
Goal 6: Combat HIV/AIDS, malaria and other diseases.
Goal 7: Ensure environmental sustainability.
Goal 8: Develop a global partnership for development.

and high-school students in small-town Illinois what they would do with a $100 windfall. Would they go shopping? Donate it to a charity? Deposit it in the bank? Using a battery of tests, he measured each kid's self-esteem, generosity, happiness, anxiety, environmental concern and risk-taking behaviors (smoking, drinking alcohol, fighting). He found that the frugal kids tended to spend little, save more and engage in positive environmental behaviors. These same kids had high self-esteem and didn't smoke. Those who donated more to charity were found to be happier; they were less likely to smoke, use alcohol or get into trouble. Those who would spend more on themselves were found to have lower self-esteem and greater anxiety. Kasser discovered that these kids were less likely to recycle, turn off lights in unused rooms or take their bikes instead of a car.

The professor and others have shown that across cultures, materialistic values conflict with generosity and community involvement.[2] In fact, when plotted on a circumplex, materialism and generosity are polar opposites.[3] "There is something about the way these values and goals are structured in the human mind that makes it psychologically difficult to care about the world and also care about things," Kasser explains. The findings took us aback. We couldn't help but extrapolate to the many wealthy individuals known for their charitable causes. "Wealth is about what you have," Kasser explained. "Materialism is about what you want." Many wealthy people are generous, he says, but they are not exactly giving away their fortunes. "While I appreciate and applaud their charitable actions, all of them still live a very high consumption lifestyle." It's not all or

nothing, of course. You can have materialistic tendencies and still be generous. "It's just that materialism tends to diminish the likelihood that one will be generous and generosity tends to diminish the likelihood one will be materialistic."

Enough is Enough

We asked Tim Kasser how his family copes with materialism. It turns out they've gone farther than most on their farm in rural Illinois. They don't eat meat and, as much as possible, they consume fresh food from their farm and the surrounding area. Each day their tween boys are allowed thirty minutes "screen time" — TV or video games. The professor and his wife, also a psychologist at Knox College, encourage their kids to express intrinsic values — happiness, caring and community involvement, for example — instead of focusing on extrinsic values. Family members make gifts for each other on birthdays or at Christmas. When his wife turned forty, Kasser gave her forty I'll Wash the Dishes For You coupons. All she had to do was slap down a coupon and he'd grab a dishrag. "Trust me, it's more of a hassle to spend time doing the stuff," says Kasser. "It's an expensive gift in that sense. But it's a real gift." The boys also receive coupons as presents: Skip Your Vegetables and Still Get Dessert; Clean Up a Mess, No Questions Asked; Thirty More Minutes of TV.

The Kassers are also convinced that collecting experience is more valuable than accumulating stuff. One year, Kasser taught psychology with Semester At Sea — the study abroad program — so that his kids could see

GIMMIE, GIMMIE NEVER GETS

If you are a parent, then you know it's not always easy to say no — especially when you're faced with a child with a bad case of the gimmies. John de Graaf, co-author of *Affluenza: The All-Consuming Epidemic*, suggests the following coping strategies:

1. Instill media literacy: Talk to your children about the purpose of commercials and teach them to be savvy to marketer's intentions.

2. Don't comfort your child with material goods. Instead, offer a listening ear and ready shoulder.

3. Turn off the TV or limit your child's viewing.

4. Advocate keeping advertising out of your child's school.

5. Support legislation to restrict advertising that targets children.

6. Find time for meaningful one-on-one conversations.

7. Eat together at least five times a week.

8. When your kids are bored, don't let them turn to a screen.

9. Don't give in to pestering.

10. Model non-materialism.

the world. The voyage took them from Mexico to Japan, China, Vietnam, Burma, Egypt, Turkey, Croatia, Spain and finally to Florida. "They have seen poverty and know what real poverty is," he says of the journey. "They truly understand how privileged they are. What they want isn't really what they need." When they returned, his eldest son raised $600 for a new roof at an orphanage they'd visited in India. We're certainly not suggesting you move to a farm and raise goats. (Then again, why the heck not?) But we do recommend you break it to your kids that acquiring stuff will not make them happy.

Buy Buy Love, Buy Buy Happiness

When kids are suffering from "the gimmies," Kasser tells parents to try to figure out what void the child is trying to fill by shopping. When young people — or adults, for that matter — feel insecure, some pursue materialistic goals in a bid to feel better. It only makes sense. Advertisers deluge us with promises of products that guarantee security, happiness, coolness and status. "If a young person is driven by insecurity, they will shop," he explains. "They are doing the best they can to meet their needs." He urges parents to help their children understand that buying stuff doesn't solve problems.

Tweens are a target because advertisers know that there's no more awkward age on the planet. Children between eight and twelve are insecure and self-conscious. Just how susceptible tweens are to consumption was the subject of a study by marketing professors Lan Nguyen Chaplin and Deborah Roedder John. The researchers considered three age groups: eight- and nine-year-olds; twelve- and thirteen-year olds; sixteen- to eighteen-year-olds. Using collages, the researchers studied the value each kid placed on such items as "stuffed animals," "money" and "sports equipment." They did the same with such non-materialistic sentiments as "being with friends," "being good at sports" and "helping others." They asked the participants which objects or sentiments made them happy. The study determined that materialism increased between the eight- and nine-year-old group and the twelve- and thirteen-year-olds. However, it dropped between the twelve- and thirteen-year-old participants and the next group up. In a second study, the researchers showed that children with lower self-esteem valued possessions significantly more than children with higher self-esteem. Moreover, they found heightened materialistic values related directly to "a severe drop in self-esteem that occurs around twelve to thirteen years of age." These researchers believe that priming a child's self-esteem might offset the steep rise in materialism among this age group.[4]

Small Change and Big Ideas

Teach your kids to save, spend and give. Helping them to develop the habit of giving to charity will make them happy! Research from the University of British Columbia and the Harvard Business School suggests those who spend their money "pro-socially" —on gifts for others or charitable donations—report significantly greater happiness. The researchers considered a nationally representative sample of some 630-plus Americans. Participants were asked to rate their happiness, report their income and provide a breakdown of their monthly spending, including bills, gifts for themselves, gifts for others and donations to charity.[5] "Regardless of income," says researcher Elizabeth Dunn, "Those who spent

CELEBRATING FOR CHANGE

By Galen Woods

"On my twelfth birthday, I decided to raise money for Free The Children. I wanted to help others who don't have simple, everyday, necessary things in life — like water. I held my party in a ravine near my house. Holding the party outside meant there was no end of space, so I could invite lots of people. More people equals more donations. We played lots of games including football and Capture the Flag. We ended up laughing so hard that people fell on the ground. In the end, I was able to donate $400, which made me feel both great and proud."

money on others reported greater happiness, while those who spent more on themselves did not."

The researchers also studied the measured happiness of employees at a Boston firm who received a profit-sharing bonus between $3,000 and $5,000. The study found it was not the size of the bonus that made employees happy but rather if they devoted any of it to gifts for others or to charity. "These findings suggest that very minor alterations in spending allocations — as little as $5 — may be enough to produce real gains in happiness on a given day," Dunn said.[6]

Remember that ill-fated shopping expedition to the discount store? The outing embarrassed Marc and worried Mom, who fretted she was raising a spoiled and entitled teen. From that day on, Mom dragged us to garage sales and second-hand stores. We'd tag along with her to volunteer at the food bank and to places where she thought we'd come to appreciate how few possessions some people have. And when we just *had* to have new jeans, Mom gave us money and left it to us to decide if our shopping expedition was truly necessary. Sometimes we bought designer denim, other times we'd wind up donating the money.

We discovered that it's easy to ask for things. Left to our own spending decisions, fulfilling our material desires became significantly more complicated. To this day, we give a lot of thought to what we do with our money. We don't mean to suggest that we're never materialistic, but we do work to balance our needs with those of others.

Mrs. Chan and the Gift of Presence

Shortly after that Bi-Way incident, life changed at our house. Mom was eager for Marc to see that we were very lucky. She dragged him along when she visited the immigrant families whom she supported with small gifts and random acts of kindness. One of these homes belonged to the Chan Family from China.

Mrs. Chan had four children. She spoke little English, so Mom was never sure what happened to the husband. Mrs. Chan's daughter was in Mom's class. All of the children were very thin, almost certainly malnourished. Aware they were struggling, Mom got to know the family and did what she could. From time to time, the Chans joined us for dinner and on family outings. We took them gifts at Christmas, likely the only ones they received. One Christmas, Mom asked Marc to accompany her on the gift run. The Chans lived in a rundown building, the kind where the elevators stink of urine. The family's two-bedroom apartment was dingy and furnished with what seemed to be curbside castoffs. The boys slept on the floor of a closet-sized room, while the mother and daughter shared a bed. It was a world away from our comfortable bungalow. Marc was miserable and uncomfortable. He thought the plan was to drop off presents and be gone. Instead, they were invited for tea.

As Marc sat there, he started to pay closer attention. He noticed that the children were in their fanciest clothing and on their best behavior. And it occurred to him that though the apartment was unadorned, it was also spotless. The cookies before him were clearly a luxury. It dawned on him that the visit that seemed meaningless to him was of great importance to Mrs. Chan. Mom presented the gifts, which were accepted gratefully. Then Mrs. Chan handed a small present to Marc. "You are our best friends," she said in broken English. "And best friends are so important to us. Thank you." The words, which Marc will never forget, cut through his cool veneer. He realized Mom's kindness, time and caring meant the world to these isolated and impoverished newcomers. No one else had been as kind. The visit stuck with Marc for days and weeks. He marveled at how easy it had been to make a difference. It changed the way he viewed those who had less than he had. His desire for new possessions began to wane.

Mom still visits the Chans. Not so long ago, they bought a house with a small yard on a quiet street. The kids all work — one became a teacher. One of the sons reminds Mom often that it was her encouragement that helped him get to university. Mom certainly never "preached" her values to the Chans or to us. But in her quiet way, she guided us. We took note and followed.

SMALL ACTIONS › EVERY DAY

1. BUY NOTHING:
Get your kids to commit to going a week without buying anything that they don't need. See if they can rely on their own resources.

2. CLEAN HOUSE FOR A CAUSE:
Collect things your family no longer uses. Ask the kids to find clothes and toys that they've outgrown. Donate them to a local women's shelter or another service organization.

3. PUT THE FUN IN FUNDRAISING:
Hold a garage sale and donate profits to charity. Ask family members, including relatives, for donations. Think about having other events at your garage sale such as face painting or a lemonade stand.

4. GIVE A GIFT THAT KEEPS ON GIVING:
Next time you're trying to find that special something for someone who has everything, consider making a donation to an international charity in his or her name.

5. BUST AN AD:
Talk to your kids about advertising. Discuss what an ad is trying to sell — and to whom. In no time, your kids will be deconstructing messages and talking about products in a different way. It won't always work, of course, but it will be a start.

6. GO BEHIND THE SEAMS:
Learn about the people who make the products you purchase. Let your conscience guide your purchases. Shop fair trade.

We Are Each Other's Hope

*Holocaust survivor, Nobel laureate, journalist and professor, **Elie Wiesel** is the author of more than 40 books, including the award-winning* Night. *He is the founder of The Elie Wiesel Foundation for Humanity which fights indifference, intolerance and injustice. Wiesel has doggedly defended the causes of Nicaragua's Miskito Indians, Argentina's Desaparecidos, Cambodian refugees and victims of war in the former Yugoslavia, to name a few. Elie Wiesel recently sat down for a one-on-one with Craig. He spoke about his influences and the importance of education.*

DURING ONE YEAR I witnessed and experienced more atrocity and terror than I have in all my life. One year. Almost everyone I meet has asked me, "Do you hate?" and my response is always "No. How can I?" Hate is the seed of all conflict. To hate is to reduce myself, to lower myself to the level of the perpetrators of the world's deadliest horrors. Hating one group results in hating everyone — and ultimately leads to hating oneself. I was angry, naturally, but in the end I used my anger as a catalyst to help and act, not hate.

For many years I refused to talk about my experiences. I thought that not thinking or talking about what took place meant that it didn't happen. I was wrong.

Remaining silent and forgetting is just as terrible as committing evil acts. To forget is almost to accept. If we forget, we are guilty, we are accomplices. To forget is to remain passive and indifferent, and indifference is not an option. The opposite of knowledge is not ignorance, but indifference. The opposite of beauty is not ugly, but indifference. The opposite of life is not death, but indifference.

Ultimately, I had to choose. And in order to save myself and even attempt to do something about the world's suffering, I had to choose knowledge, beauty and life. I made a vow to myself never to be silent whenever human beings endure suffering and humiliation.

Action is the only remedy to indifference.

This became all the more clear in the late 1940s. While I was studying in France, I met a scholar by the name of Mordechai Shushani, a mysterious man who knew thirty languages and could quote several religious texts purely from memory. I eventually became his student, and, as a result, he had a deep and profound influence on me. He taught me many things. But, most importantly, he taught me how naïve I was, how to question and how little I actually knew.

It was he, more than any other teacher, who was responsible for making me into the man I am today. He left an imprint not only on my thoughts but also on the language I use and the manner in which I feel. He made me realize how important education truly is.

Our children are the future. Their education is our greatest assurance for a better world. That is why I pour my heart and my soul into teaching and into my students. Today's youth seem to want to rise above what the generation before them has not prevented and help as much as they can. They can do it.

This generation has given me great hope. I am surrounded by students and I truly love them. I enter classrooms with palpitations because I love them so much. I want to sensitize my students to the pain and joy of others. The only kind of education is global education. Education must be for humanity, not against it.

Children see hypocrisy, and they don't

respect it. That is why education must rise above boundaries and nationalities. We must teach all children the universality of their condition, that they—we—are all part of humanity. Curriculum should teach the absurdity of war, the ugliness of fanaticism and bigotry and the inhumanity of terror.

If we taught in such a manner students would learn that there are no winners in war, only victims. They would learn that every person, regardless of ethnic background, race or religion, deserves basic human respect. Because what might happen to one community will ultimately affect all communities. Therefore, global education is becoming more and more imperative and terribly urgent.

When I look back on my life and my experiences, I see God, family and teachers; not war, terror and inhumanity. Despite everything, my childhood was blessed with love, hope, faith and prayer. I spent most of my time talking to God more than to people. He was my partner, my friend and my teacher. My father taught me how to reason, how to reach my mind. My soul belonged to my grandfather and mother. They influenced me profoundly. To this day when I write I have the feeling literally, physically, that one of them is standing behind me, looking over my shoulder, reading what I'm writing. That is a reward. All children should have such a blessing, whether it is faith, a friend or teacher.

In the end, it was my teachers, family and God who influenced, motivated and inspired me. My only wish now is to have the same influence on my family and my students; to convey to them how important it is to act, to question, not to remain indifferent and never to forget.

Years ago, a student of mine asked what his class could take away with them after spending so many years together with me. I told him, "Think higher and feel deeper." Whatever you do in life, whatever endeavor you undertake, wherever the road of destiny takes you, remember these words.

Our children are the future. Their education is our greatest assurance for a better world."

Elie Wiesel

What Do You Want to be as Your Kids Grow Up?

If you don't stand for something, you'll fall for anything, or so the saying goes. Define the values you hold most dear. As you hold onto those values, lead by them every day.

WHEN MARC WAS EIGHTEEN, he worked as a page in the Canadian House of Commons, while attending his first year of university. For the most part, he delivered water and — in those primitive days before the BlackBerry — messages. One day he delivered a note to a formidable gentleman who stopped him with an odd query. "What kind of legacy do you want to leave?" Mildly baffled, Marc still managed a snappy reply. "Sir," he said, "I intend to study hard and deliver water with ever greater efficiency." The man was unimpressed but nevertheless went on to tell Marc about his work with a charity in the slums of Thailand. He asked if Marc was interested. Uh, no. Each day the man called him over to ask: "What kind of legacy do you want to leave?" The question haunted Marc long after he left the House of Commons.

Marc wasn't sure what he wanted to do

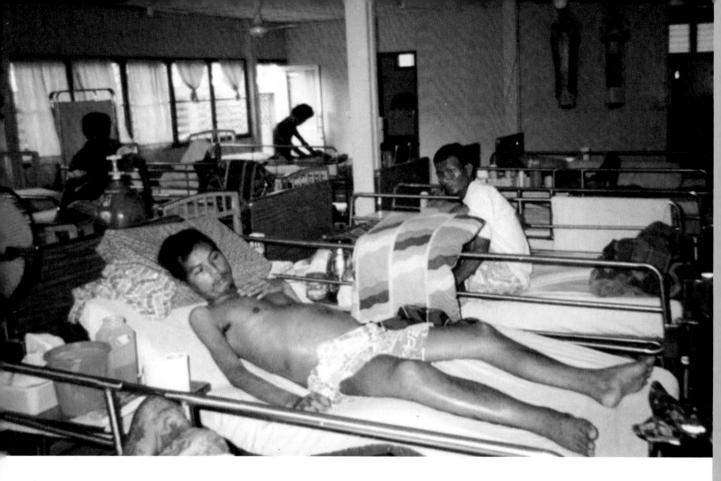

AIDS patients in a Klong Toey hospital in Thailand

with his life. He'd earned a full scholarship to Harvard but wasn't certain what he wanted to study. The politician's question seemed like a dare: "What kind of legacy do you want to leave?" Marc wanted to change the world, but he didn't know if that meant he should be at school or in the slums of Thailand. After some soul searching, he deferred his scholarship, drained his bank account and bought a ticket to Bangkok. It was a shock to Mom and Dad but not entirely a surprise. After all, they'd raised him to define success on his own terms.

Klong Toey was worse than Marc could ever have imagined. He tried to stay calm as he navigated a sprawling sea of corrugated tin, mud and cement bricks, zinc roofing, open sewers and garbage heaps. Inside, he was panicking. After dropping his bags at a small apartment next to a pig slaughterhouse, he was taken to the AIDS ward of a primitive hospice. The Thai nurses were relieved. They were short a doctor and he would do. When Marc started to protest, the nurses gave him a crash course on cleaning wounds, administering IVs, treating bedsores and dispensing medicine. With that, they were gone.

Marc worked the next shift alone, caring for twenty-four patients, many near death. He was reassuring himself that all would be fine when he heard a patient choking. Although Marc was terrified, he administered some medicine. The man continued to fight for breath. Not knowing what else to do, Marc ran to the street to enlist help. Passersby refused — they were afraid they'd get AIDS if they entered the hospice. With nothing more to offer, Marc sat down and held the man's hand as he died. When the nurses returned and found Marc crying, they ordered him back to work. Later, when he was finally alone, he acknowledged that he was in way over his head.

He made a phone call home.

"I can't take it anymore," he told Mom, who asked how she could help.

"Change my ticket," he urged.

Marc started to repack. Until that point, he'd been a cocky teen who was convinced he could accomplish anything. Although he imagined people back home asking why he'd left so quickly, he didn't care. As he was organizing his belongings, there was a knock at the door.

"What are you doing?" asked a young boy in a yellow T-shirt and shorts. Marc explained.

"You can't leave!" the boy insisted. "You need to stay for our birthday party."

The boy explained that as street kids, he and his friends did not know their parents, their ages or their birth dates. Every year, they pooled loose coins and crumpled bills earned from shining shoes to hold a single, massive birthday party. The celebration was days away. Without thinking, Marc called Mom back.

"Don't change my ticket. I've decided to stay."

Mom was confused.

"I need to go to the street kids' birthday party," he explained.

This didn't help.

"Marc, are you using drugs?" she asked — only half joking. (Three-quarters joking, she now claims.)

On the day of the party, Marc followed the sound of laughter to a feast of peanuts and watermelon. It was a remarkable gathering hosted by kids too poor to buy shoes, yet generous enough to share what little they had. After the food, there was singing, dancing and storytelling. It was so different from birthday parties in North America where there are often mountains of presents, hired clowns and over-the-top loot bags. These children had found a way to celebrate despite their circumstances. Mom and Dad had taught us that the best things in life are neither bought nor sold. Now, in that spare but joyous tableau, the message hit home.

Time Out for Good Behavior

Kids take their cues from parents, teachers and mentors. When they are shuffled from soccer to piano to drama to language classes, they learn to value the importance of being busy. When they are given time for lazy afternoon picnics and long family bike rides, they come to appreciate togetherness. In the same way, when they work with parents to clean up a river or to flip pancakes at a breakfast fundraiser, they learn to contribute to the community. When they can sample from all these activities, they experience the richness and diversity of a balanced life.

Kids exit the womb into a world of

EXTREME PARENTING

Real titles of real books available on Amazon.com. (*Really!*):

- *How To Multiply Your Baby's Intelligence*
- *Learning Before Birth: Every Child Deserves Giftedness*
- *Raise a Smarter Child by Kindergarten*
- *How to Have a Smarter Baby*
- *How to Raise a Brighter Child*
- *Smart-Wiring Your Baby's Brain*

Competition starts early in the Parenting Olympics. A British website, www.raisingkids.co.uk, documents Competitive Sleep Syndrome, "where parents argue with each other over who has less sleep." On the flip side? The website reports that one in five parents is guilty of bragging about how their baby sleeps through the night.

Aware of how life experience plays on résumés, parents are now reported to be padding children's passports with power trips. In April 2007, the *Wall Street Journal* reported that at one school in Grosse Pointe Woods, Michigan, a fifth-grader did a show-and-tell of more than five hundred pictures from his family trip to China; it ran for an hour — so long, the teacher had to cancel math.

Moms and dads are calling their children's prospective employers to discuss salaries and benefits. "Parents are contacting us directly," Betty Smith, a university recruiting manager at Hewlett-Packard, told *USA Today*. Recruiters at the company have actually been trained in parent wrangling.

Doctors in pediatric sports medicine say they are seeing more and more cases of overuse injuries in young children. "You get a kid on the operating table and you say to yourself, 'It's impossible for a thirteen-year-old to have this kind of wear and tear.' We've got an epidemic going on," sports orthopedist, Dr. James Andrews told the *New York Times* in February 2005.

scheduled activity. Almost from Day 1, we bounce them from Water Babies to Gymboree to Kindermusik. We used to think that kids involved in two or three extracurricular activities were overscheduled. Today they'd be considered slackers. These days, moms with MBAs taxi small passengers across the city initiating conversation and doling out Ziplocked snacks while zigzagging through traffic. Parents are part social convenor, part chauffeur, part sherpa. Studies confirm what we know anecdotally. Sandra Hofferth and John Sandberg at the Institute for Social Research at the University of Michigan studied how kids spent their time during a sixteen-year period. Here is just some of what they found when they considered kids aged three to eleven between 1981 and 1997:

- Playtime decreased 25 percent.
- Television viewing decreased 13 percent.
- Church attendance dropped 40 percent.
- Outdoor activities such as walking, hiking and biking dropped 50 percent.
- Household work, including accompanying parents on errands and shopping trips, more than doubled.
- Time in passive leisure activities like going to a movie or watching a sports event increased five-fold.
- Time spent in organized sports almost doubled.[1]

Cultural observers suggest after-school activities emerged as a form of child care during the 1980s. Why the overcrowded Day-Timers? More mothers were working, for starters. At the same time, cities were gripped by stranger danger, so it seemed safer to put a kid in Tae Kwon Do than to allow him to play at the neighborhood park.

Renowned child psychiatrist, Dr. Alvin Rosenfeld, coined a term that describes this pervasive phenomenon when he wrote *Hyper-Parenting: Are You Hurting Your Child By Trying Too Hard?* "Parents become relentlessly self-sacrificing, enrolling children in activities so early so they can excel at academics, athletics or specialties," he explained. Each scheduled activity is thought to be critical, he explains. "Make all the right moves, your child will get into a top-name university and be a winner at life."[2]

Dr. Rosenfeld confessed that he's a recovering hyper-parent. "Except when I'm not," he quipped. His kids were raised on music lessons and competitive sports. His eldest daughter Lisa was in competitive gymnastics — one of the biggest time investments for girls, he says. He finally convinced her to quit in Grade 9. "Hyper-parenting is seductive," he says. "None of us want our kids to fail."

The father of three gave his head a shake and then worked hard to teach his children that traditional success isn't everything. "I care way more that they are good people." Lisa is now at Harvard in part thanks to a very funny, completely authentic application essay that included a section in which she described teaching a four-year-old boy to fart. "This sad little boy had had bowel surgery and was having all sorts of problems. She used a Whoopee cushion and they played a farting game," Dr.

INTO THE FIRE

In the dying hours of our overseas school-building trips, on the eve before the tired teens board a plane for home, we set a bonfire and gather around. It is time to reflect on lessons learned after long hours in the hot sun — or driving rain — digging holes, laying bricks, hauling water and helping impoverished but happy children gain a place to study. It is time to prepare teens for the transition back to their lives of wealth and privilege.

Life involves choices, we say at the start. One choice affects every other. We encourage the teens to consider their choices.

And then the hard work begins: We pass each teen a piece of paper, which they rip into ten squares. On each, they identify a Most Important Thing in their lives. And so they write: Family. Friends. Boyfriend. Girlfriend. Bestfriend. Grades. Car. Prom. iPod. Sports. Scholarships.

We move clockwise around the circle and ask each teen to toss into the fire the piece of paper that represents the least important of the ten. Before they do so, they're invited — though not required — to explain their choice. Cars, iPods, laptops and prom are usually the first to go. Boyfriends and girlfriends rarely make it past round five. By the time they get to the top three, most are left holding parents, siblings and, maybe, faith.

At this point, we ask them to consider how much effort or time they devote to the top three. Kids are stunned.

We participate, too. Craig once tossed "be a doctor" into the fire. He had realized he didn't have to be a medical doctor to help people, which to him was what was really important. Marc set "Harvard" alight. Although he was accepted, he chose instead to volunteer in the slums of Thailand before deciding to study international development.

Before the young people leave, we ask them to commit to the people on the final slips of paper. We encourage them to express feelings, resolve relationships and to find a way to spend more time together. The teens jot down their priorities in a letter, which we seal in an envelope and bring back to Toronto. Every week, a staff member pulls out a handful to drop in the mail. Each letter reminds its recipient of values, priorities and commitment.

Rosenfeld says with pride. "I think it told Harvard that she was a good person."

It's hard not to marvel at the stories of child prodigies — an eleven-year-old math whiz at Princeton, a young Picasso painting *Picador* at eight-years-old, the Williams sisters tearing up the court. But hold on, says Dr. Rosenfeld, who offers ample examples of individuals who achieved greatness on their own sweet time. Michael Jordan? Cut from the junior varsity basketball team. Mickey Mantle? Couldn't hit as a kid. Leonard Bernstein? Started piano at age ten. So why hurry?

Dr. Rosenfeld, who has taught both at Harvard and Stanford, now has a private practice in New York. He speaks frequently to moms and dads about the sufferings of the "hyper-parented." For starters, studies show that affluent youth in their final year of high school report the highest rates of marijuana, inhalant and tranquilizer use — substance abuse linked to an "overemphasis on achievement" and, unfortunately, "isolation from parents." Dr. Rosenfeld and child psychiatrist Bruno Bettelheim observe that some parents focus on the accomplishments of their kids without taking time to know them as individuals. "As a result of pressure and absence of deeper values, parents often suffer from the same anxiety and depressive disorders as their children."[3]

Children need time to reflect on their own sense of being in order to appreciate that they're valued for more than just doing. We must give them freedom to nurture their imaginations. If we give them time and the opportunity to make choices, they'll learn that we trust them to live their lives.

Unfortunately "busy" does not necessarily

mean "happy." Consider the statistics: More than 50 percent of children today will spend some time living with just one parent by the time they reach age eighteen. David Popenoe, a sociology professor at Rutgers University, notes that some 40 percent of children live apart from their natural fathers. Many of these kids seldom see their fathers. "Once children were beaten, now they are neglected," Popenoe writes. "Once they went hungry, now they are materially spoiled; once they lived in over crowded conditions, now they sometimes live in virtual isolation. The most consequential change, particularly in recent decades, is the deterioration of the bond between parents and children. No longer can children count on what they need most — loving parents devoted to their well-being who act as good role models and protect them from harm."[4]

So how do we nurture values? How do we give kids the courage to reject the dominant messages of our culture that tell them to be busy, to shop, to build résumés?

Keeping Up with the Junior Joneses

From time to time we're asked to hold workshops for parents. If we're speaking in front of a well-off audience, the folding chairs are generally occupied by hypercompetitive, Type-A moms and dads. Their kids don't listen, they're spoiled or in trouble. We always begin by asking about their kids. Dads stand up to boast of academic awards, double-A hockey trophies and debating plaques. When one dad sits, another stands to talk up his championship skier or class president. And so it goes, around the room. (Our parents were known to boast, too!) Next we ask parents to consider the values they hope to nurture. Here it's the moms who rise to talk about love and kindness and caring and passion. We ask parents to contemplate all of this in the context of how their children spend their time. If the goal is to raise caring and compassionate children, the question becomes: What is best? Do jam-packed schedules nurture souls and spirits? Do they leave time for family? Or volunteer work? Or goofing around with friends? At this point, the room usually falls silent.

We believe there's a disconnect between the qualities parents hope to nurture and the time they devote to doing so. A mom says she wants to raise a compassionate, caring son but will note that his free time is consumed by sports. A dad agrees that community service is key but confesses he can't get his son to clean up his bedroom. For many, this is when the light bulb goes off. When prodded, even the most defensive parents acknowledge that what they say they want for their kids is much different from what their kids are actually doing.

Parents invest heavily in their children, and understandably they hope that investment pays dividends. Many will brag about a son or daughter getting into a great college or landing a job on Wall Street. But what would they say about a child who delays school to help rebuild a parish in a hurricane-ravaged city? It definitely takes courage to stand up at the water cooler to boast about a kid who is compassionate and dedicated to service. Just as there are MY KID IS ON THE HONOR ROLL bumper stickers, we think there should be ones that proclaim MY KID CARES.

We wish parents would dare to step back.

WHAT'S IMPORTANT TO YOU?
INTO THE FIRE: THE PARENTS' EDITION

1. On the lines below, write down the Ten Most Important Things in your life:
    _____
    _____
    _____
    _____
    _____

2. Now, like the kids around our campfire, choose three of these items that you could live without. What does your list look like now?
    _____
    _____
    _____
    _____
    _____

3. Decision time again. Time to list your Top Three:
    _____
    _____
    _____

    Now consider how much effort and time you devote to the most important things in your life.

    Consider how you might change your life so that you can commit to your Top Three.

    While this exercise is fresh, why not write yourself a letter? Decide what, if anything, you need to do to restructure your priorities.

Scarlet at soccer

One father who dares to put down his BlackBerry may inspire another to eliminate an extracurricular activity from an overloaded schedule. If more parents follow suit, perhaps fewer will worry that their kids will fall behind. We're all for extracurricular activities, we just want parents to be realistic about what their kids are doing and why. We ask our workshop parents to talk to their kids about their activities. We give them a few questions to get the conversation started: Are you having fun? Do you feel pressured to participate? Are you tired? Overworked? Happy?

Shelley confesses that she signed up four-year-old Scarlet for soccer because everyone else seemed to be doing it. Although her daughter was suited up in professional-looking soccer kit, it was pretty clear all she wanted to do was pick dandelions and hug the boys on her team. Shelley had been convinced her daughter would miss future opportunities if she didn't start young. The truth is, Shelley didn't even know

if Scarlet liked soccer. Shelley and her husband decided to put soccer on hold until Scarlet asks to play. Instead, they've put a priority on gentle, unstructured activities in which Scarlet contributes to family or community. She joined Sparks, (the precursor to Brownies). And they've set dates so Scarlet can help her ailing grandparents walk their dogs. And since one of Scarlet's favorite activities is skipping stones in the nearby river, they signed up as a family for the bi-annual river cleanup.

Time for Soul Searching

When Craig was in Grade 8 and just back from his first trip to South Asia, he received an invitation from Upper Canada College, one of the most prestigious boys' schools in Canada. Craig and Dad chatted about what was in store as they walked into the old stone buildings. There, the headmaster thanked Craig for being an outstanding role model and then offered him a full scholarship. It was the opportunity of a lifetime. Attending the elite school was almost certain to lead him to a top-tier university, then on to medical school.

Craig was flattered, of course, but he had an awful lot to think about. He wondered how the new arrangement would affect his Free The Children work. Teachers at his current school tried to be accommodating when FTC work took Craig away from school for days or even weeks. UCC administrators promised to be supportive to a point: Craig could miss no more than three days of school each month. Craig's head was swimming. He thought about his upcoming schedule, which even back then was busy. He'd been invited to meet U.S. politicians and to appear on a national TV program to talk about child labor. Plus he wanted to travel to Brazil to meet child workers.

Mom and Dad listened as Craig went over the pros and cons. UCC would set him on the path to med school. He'd meet some influential families and have contacts for life. But it might mean he'd have to turn his back on the fledgling FTC. Back and forth he went. Although Craig was only thirteen, Mom and Dad entrusted him with the decision. They didn't hide the fact they hoped he'd accept the scholarship, but they didn't object when he turned it down. In the end, he decided to enroll in an alternative high school where he could study independently around his FTC schedule. Craig visited the headmaster at UCC to inform him in person of his difficult decision. Thinking back, the most amazing part of it all is that though Craig was so young, the choice was his alone. Once made, that decision gave him the confidence to make others that took him down a road less trampled.

In the late 1990s, Craig was invited to serve as a children's ambassador in Belgrade and was asked to speak on behalf of war-affected children. His local hosts took him to meet people who shared first hand reports of people fleeing Kosovo. Along the way, Craig's delegation delivered small boxes to refugee camps — gifts for the children, mostly. Unloading a truck at one stop, he started to chat with a thirteen-year-old boy. As the conversation unfolded, Craig realized that conflict was all the boy knew of life. He'd lost his parents to the first Bosnian war. Then, as the fighting progressed, he and his uncle had been forced to leave Kosovo. Now they were in a refugee camp outside of Belgrade. Shifting the conversation to the future, Craig asked the boy what he hoped to grow up to be. The question was met with a blank stare. In the silence, Craig offered that he wanted to be a doctor like those with Doctors Without Borders. The boy was familiar with the group from the refugee camps. After a very long silence, the boy spoke. "You know what would be nice," he said. "It would be nice if we didn't need the doctors anymore because the bombs wouldn't fall in the first place."

All his young life, Craig had wanted to study medicine. No matter who asked, his answer was the same: Doctor. But in that moment, Craig realized there was more than one way to heal and to help. When he thought about it, Free The Children was doing just that. Med school had been his destination — an aspiration Mom and Dad were never shy to champion. Inspired by that young boy, Craig went on to take peace and conflict studies in his undergraduate years. And, as before, he was left to his own decision.

If you don't stand for something, you'll fall for anything, or so the saying goes. During our workshops, we encourage parents to define the values they hold most dear. In our household, it was the Three Cs: Courage, Compassion and Community. Choosing priorities helps inform tough decisions, like the ones Craig was fortunate to have the chance to make. Harvard University child psychologist Dan Kindlon told us it's difficult for parents to convey values if they've never stopped to figure out what they are. "Parents have to make up some for the kids' sake. Come up with a couple of things so the kids know, 'We feel this is important.'" Parents do a great service any time they can be concrete about what they stand for, he says. "There are so many gray areas in life, it's important to have black and white." Kindlon told us that values can be as simple as: "We don't hit. We don't swear. We don't make fun of these kinds of people." No exceptions. Adults, he says, must live up to the same expectations. "When a child points out, 'You laughed at that person,' you say, 'You're right, I was wrong.'"

If you're not sure about your family's values, ask your kids. It might be sobering to hear them say, "We can't fail. We must get into the best schools." Or it might be deeply moving if they say, "We believe in helping people. We put people first. We try to lighten our load on the environment. We always do our best."

When Marc returned to North America from Thailand, he enrolled in Harvard with new priorities. He was eager to study international relations and to shape his legacy in honor of the children he had met in Klong Toey. After Harvard, his volunteer work helped earn him a scholarship to Oxford. In no time, he realized that Rhodes Scholars were in high demand among top-name companies. Marc received unbelievable offers with jaw-dropping bonuses — not bad for a kid whose only official job experience was delivering water in the House of Commons for $12 an hour. It was tempting to go the big-money route, but Marc's work and travels had led him to a different path. He decided he already had everything that mattered.

SMALL ACTIONS › EVERY DAY

1. WHERE DO YOU SEE YOURSELF IN FIVE YEARS?
Take the proverbial question and apply it to your family. Consider how you can achieve a goal.

2. POLL THE FAMILY:
Ask your kids how they define success. Their answers may surprise you.

3. TALK AMONGST YOURSELVES:
When you see an example of someone who has achieved success on their own terms, point it out to your kids. Discuss how the individual's actions differed from the more traditional path.

4. HAPPILY EVER AFTER:
In the same way, find movies — both fictional and not — that highlight a similar message.

5. WATCH YOUR BALANCE:
Help kids see that there's more to life than marks. Show them that it takes more than money to make the world go around.

6. TAKE A STEP BACK:
From time to time, try to see the bigger picture. It was Marc's hide-and-seek act that gave Mom pause to see that her eldest son was suffering from affluenza.

Doing the Right Thing

*Within the music industry, **Sol Guy** is known for his work with such artists as Lauryn Hill, OutKast and P. Diddy. He is also host and co-creator of the MTV series 4REAL, which takes celebrities around the world to connect with young leaders in extreme circumstances who are solving pressing social issues.*

TWO MOMENTS IN MY LIFE caused me to change the focus of my work and passion. One was a visit to Sierra Leone, the other was the death of my father.

We grew up in Grand Forks in the interior of British Columbia — the only black people in the community. My dad, originally from Kansas City, Missouri, met my mom in the late-'60s when he was just out of the service and working at the Pentagon. My mom was a Jewish secretary from upstate New York. Martin Luther King, Jr. had just been killed. It was a heavy time. My parents decided to leave it all behind, move to Canada and essentially become back-to-the-land hippies. They were quite the sight. My dad was a huge, six-foot-

four, dark-skinned black man and my mom was a small Jewish woman. They found themselves in a new world. My sisters and I are the products of that ideal.

My mom is an activist. She would ship farming supplies and clothes by rail to South America. My dad and I were really close. He helped me understand that I was different and what racism was. When I was twelve, he gave me the book *Roots* and had me write a project on it — not for a class assignment but for life.

It was probably natural that as the only black guy in my high school I gravitated toward hip-hop. The movement was as beautiful as it was ugly. It took me awhile to define what I would and would

not accept within the culture. At the outset, I wanted to be down — to be accepted.

I did really well, made a gold record and ended up working at a record company in New York. I was flirting with the upper echelons of the culture on both an artistic and business level as hip-hop was breaking out globally. I found myself in all the right places, doing all the things I wanted to do. There is no doubt if I stayed on that path, I'd be running a record label now. Then those two life-changing moments arrived.

In 1998, when I was in New York, my dad died. He'd been bedridden with cancer for the last six months of his life. I was twenty-four and didn't have much context for how to cope. I was sad and angry. I didn't really process what his values and beliefs meant for my legacy.

In 2000, I accompanied a rap group called the Rascalz to Sierra Leone for a War Child/MuchMusic documentary. A truce had just happened after a ten-year war over diamonds and natural resources. I was totally unprepared. Suddenly I was standing there on that soil, the first person of my family to go to Africa since slavery.

We found ourselves in child soldier camps talking to kids, five- to fifteen-years-old who had fought in the war. One ten-year-old was marching the others in soldier formation, yelling out commands. When he pulled down his dark aviator sunglasses, I found myself looking into the eyes of a killer. The next day we visited a rehab camp for people missing arms, legs and ears. I held a six-month-old baby who had her arm chopped off. I saw both sides of the impact of war. I also saw a beautiful country filled with people willing to forgive and wanting to move forward. I met people willing to share their last bowl of rice. It made me think of the men I knew in New York, who'd walk over a man on the street without giving a dime.

Back in New York, I knew something had to change, I just didn't know what. It dawned on me that if what I was doing wasn't good for people, and if my father wouldn't have been proud of me, I didn't want anything to do with it. I committed career suicide, gave my company to my business partners and spent the next six months sitting and wondering what I was going to do. Everyone thought I'd been fired or gone crazy. In hindsight I was going through a depression. I tried to get a construction job but no one would hire me because I had no experience.

Truth is, I got rocked. My dad's death and that trip made me question who I was. It forced me to ask whether I could do something that would have an impact on the planet. What did I want to be known for? Now I know. I started working with my friend, Josh Thome, who grew up with the same values I did. I'm using my skills and talents to tell stories about social justice. By using celebrities, we're putting those stories in front of young people in a big way. I finally feel like I'm doing the right thing with my time. It took me half my life to find the space to hold on to what my parents gave me.

It forced me to ask whether I could do something that would have an impact on the planet. What did I want to be known for?"

Sol Guy

Helping Kids Overcome Adversity

Finding the motivation to contribute in large and small ways is one "secret ingredient" to survival. And when passion is found, when kids stand out to pursue their dreams, they are a force to be reckoned with.

YOU CAN NEVER ANTICIPATE a "Do Something" moment. Nor can you ignore one when it arrives. For Oprah Winfrey, such a moment presented itself when she traveled to South Africa in 2003 on a mission to bring Christmas joy to AIDS orphans. "I realized in those moments why I was born, why I am not married and do not have children of my own," the talk-show host told viewers. "These are my children." In an interview with CNN host Larry King, Oprah explained the inspiration for her mission. "I remembered in my life there were times when people did that for me,

so I wanted to be able to extend myself and kindness." On that trip, Winfrey pledged to be a voice for those children, "to empower them, to help educate them, so the spirit that burns alive inside of them does not die." The story of Oprah's journey — one she would later call the single greatest experience of her life — was televised in December of 2003.

Watching that show in Wheaton, Illinois, was ten-year-old Kendall Ciesemier. "Eleven- and twelve-year-old kids — kids my age — were taking care of two- and three-year-old kids because their parents had died of AIDS,"

Kendall recalls. "Kids, I realized, were caring for kids! I knew then that I wanted to do something to help." And so in another "Do Something" moment, Kendall raced to her computer to research "AIDS" and "orphans in Africa." When Google turned up a Christian relief agency, she clicked to read more. Just a kid herself, Kendall decided she had to sponsor a child. "I went to my room and stuffed $360 that I had saved into an envelope." Around 10 p.m., she emerged in search of a stamp. "My mother was like, 'Kendall, what are you doing? Go to bed!'"

That was almost six years and many hundreds of thousands of dollars ago. It was also several transplants ago. Kendall's story is remarkable and inspiring when you alone consider her fundraising prowess. It is all the more amazing when you realize what she is up against. Kendall has a rare disease that affects the duct between her liver and small intestine. She was also born with a congenital condition in which the major organs are reversed. In her short life, she's endured five major surgeries and has fought for her life on several occasions.

Soon after that *Oprah* show, Kendall began to support an eight-year-old Mauritanian

Kendall is a true inspiration to youth everywhere

foster child named Benite. "It made me feel so empowered," she told *Chicago Magazine*, which in 2007 named her a Chicagoan of the Year. "I thought I could change more kids' lives with a little help."[1]

At the same time that she was plotting to change the world, Kendall was preparing for a liver transplant. Anticipating that friends and family might soon be buying her flowers and get-well gifts, she set up Kids Caring 4 Kids and instead politely requested donations. "It started with a bunch of little things that people would do while I was in the hospital," she says. "They had bake sales. They made movies and charged people admission to screenings. Others donated money from chores or garage sales or lemonade stands." During her recovery, Kendall started to make Bow Wow Bling Bling — dog necklaces — to raise money to help the AIDS orphans.

From Oprah Winfrey's journey of a lifetime to Kendall Ciesemier's "Do Something" moment arrived another instance that neither is likely to forget. On September 4, 2007, Kendall showed up at her high school and discovered Bill Clinton was there for an apparently impromptu assembly. The former president was in town to promote the release of his new book, *Giving: How Each of Us Can Change the World.* He talked to the students at Wheaton North High about making a difference. Then he called Kendall to the stage. It was, in her words: "Crazy!" In fact, it was only the start. "I'm going into Chicago to talk more about giving with a friend of mine who wants to meet you, Kendall," Clinton told her as she stood in front of her school. With that, she was whisked to the set of *Oprah*. "I wanted you here today to say that you are the shining light for the rest of the world," the talk-

Bill Clinton made a surprise visit to Kendall's school

show host told Kendall. "President Clinton has written a whole book about giving, but you are the prime example of what one person can do."

Kendall's family has tried to understand why she works so tirelessly to help others, even while she is suffering. Kendall's dad, Michael, says his daughter has long been filled with a huge sense of purpose. "She's always demonstrated care and love." Ellery, Kendall's mom, thinks her daughter's illness has made her sensitive to the needs of others. She knows what it is like to walk in the shoes of someone who is struggling. It is this heightened sense of empathy that inspires her to work on behalf of others. Although Kendall's health challenges are far from over, Michael says the family draws sustenance from her mission to help children in Africa. "It's been positive for us to turn our attention to others in need." Kendall often reminds her family, "We can't choose, this is our life." So the Ciesemiers take things day by day. "We've stopped postponing things," Michael says. When we last spoke to the family,

Michael and Kendall had recently completed a five-mile charity run. "We no longer just take a walk around the block for granted, we revel in it. We've chosen to strive to cherish every moment to even out all the horrible ones. That is our way of coping with uncertainty."

By absolutely no means are we suggesting Kendall's compassion sets the standard for children dealing with adversity. This is only one way of coping. Everyone is different. There are no "shoulds." In our work, we've encountered many memorable kids like Kendall who responded to adversity by helping others. Some explain that it makes them feel good. Others say their circumstances made them aware of the suffering of others. These young people have been challenged by extreme poverty, depression, eating disorders, war, displacement, serious illnesses or loss of loved ones, yet they've found ways to help others in profound ways.

If helping out can bring a bit of happiness to the most challenging of circumstances, we think it makes sense that it could be a healthy coping strategy for everybody. First a disclaimer: We know this is a sensitive subject, especially because many children face real and often insurmountable challenges. It is well documented, for example, that poverty can increase teen pregnancy, high school drop-out rates, drug and alcohol use and delinquency. Recent research indicates that poverty and family breakdown make it less likely a teenager will volunteer.[2] And yet when it's possible for a child to lend a hand—to help someone else or to join a fundraising campaign, for example — it's possible they'll draw strength from their efforts.

Bring on the Helper's High!

You may have heard of the "runner's high" — that burst of energy followed by calm that comes from physical exertion. Volunteers have actually reported the same euphoria from helping others. Allan Luks, long-time executive director of Big Brothers Big Sisters of New York City, coined the term "helper's high" after surveying 3,300 volunteers and finding that many reported feelings of exhilaration when they helped out. Luks documented the effect in the book *The Healing Power of Doing Good* with writer Peggy Payne. Subjects of his study reported that this "high" lasted several weeks and returned when individuals simply reflected on what it felt like to help others. Ninety percent of those surveyed reported that volunteering lessened stress, chronic pain and insomnia. Luks theorized that helpers replaced stressful thoughts — perhaps about work or relationships — with self-enhancing good feelings drawn from personal contact with those they help regularly.[3]

Eleven- and twelve-year-old kids — kids my age — were taking care of two- and three-year-old kids because their parents had died of AIDS."

Kendall Ciesemier

NEVER GIVE UP, AND LAUGH A LOT

Spencer West joined Free The Children on a school building project in Kenya. He is now one of our speakers who tours schools and helps young people to believe in themselves. Here is part of the message he often shares:

I thought I would start by answering the question that I'm sure you all have in your minds right now, and that is "where are my legs?" Well, when I was a kid, I went to a magic show and they asked for a volunteer from the audience to get sawed in half and then put back together again by the magician. I raised my hand ... obviously the magician got fired. And my legs are still in the box. For those of you who laughed, that's awesome and for those of you who didn't that's okay, too. I want you all to be comfortable with me — not afraid to ask questions or laugh, because we always need more laughter in the world.

In all seriousness, the reason I don't have legs is because I was born with a genetic disease called sacral agenesis, which caused the muscles in my legs to not work. At the age of five, they were amputated just below my pelvis so I could get around better. I was told I would never walk by myself, sit up by myself or be a functioning member of society. But my parents and I set out to prove to ourselves and the rest of the world that I could be just like everyone else.

Because I looked different than other people, I was singled out a lot. Most people were just curious and wanted to understand me. But, being different meant I was bullied. As I got older, the boys in my school started to play sports. I not only couldn't, but I didn't really want to either, so I hung out with the girls. Because of this, I was called names like "faggot," "gay," or "queer," insults thrown at me to make me feel bad about myself. Whether I was gay or not was irrelevant, they called me names because I was hanging out with the girls.

When I was in high school, I became a cheerleader and I'm sure some of you are thinking, "If I didn't have any legs I'd be a cheerleader, too." One day at a game, I overhead a girl in the crowd say, "What's he doing out there? This isn't a handicapped team!" Again, this was another label used to describe me that I knew was untrue.

After I finished school, I moved to Arizona and started working at a job I didn't really like. I knew I had the potential to do more. One day, my dear friend Reed Cowan invited me to go to Kenya where he had been building schools with Free The Children in the name of his son who had tragically passed away. After a lot of thought, I accepted, embarking on the trip that changed me forever.

The minute I got to Kenya I felt peace and clarity. I also felt excitement as the first day I arrived at a Free The Children school I was instantly surrounded by swarms of school kids, laughing and pointing and speaking a mile a minute in a language I didn't understand. When we finished a tour of their school, they all sat around me in the grass and asked me every question under the sun about my life.

Then, at the very end of this conversation, one of the girls raised her hand and she said, "I didn't know this sort of thing happened to white people, too." Up until this point I had been trying to prove that I was like everyone else. At this moment, I realized I was different and I was different for a reason. I was different because I needed to show others, like these kids in Kenya, that it doesn't matter what your abilities are, where you are from in the world, what color you skin is, what your gender or sexual orientation is. If you work hard with others, never give up and laugh a lot, you can achieve anything.

I'm different. We're all different. And with our differences, together we can achieve greatness, as long as we aren't afraid to walk our own path.

Another interesting study showed how the chronically ill benefit when called on to volunteer. In 1999, researchers C. Schwartz and R. Sender had multiple sclerosis patients provide telephone support to others with the same debilitating disease. Three years later, the helpers reported less depression and fatigue and greater self-esteem than those who did not volunteer.[4] Since then, numerous studies have shown that helping does indeed make us healthier and happier (See sidebar).[5] This is good news for those of you watching your children take tentative steps into the world of helping others.

Earlier, we introduced you to Dr. Samuel Oliner, the sociologist who has spent his life trying to figure out why some people will assist others while most will not. He's observed that it is not unusual for those who experience trauma to turn into helpers. "The experience of being sick sensitizes you to others' suffering," Dr. Oliner told us. From his research and observations in Humboldt and Boston hospices, Dr. Oliner has noted that it is a reciprocal kind of helping: "Somebody helped me, somebody cared for me, and I would also now like to help others." Dr. Oliner says he's a living example of this point. "People ask me why I do all this crazy research. Well, I became sensitized to people's suffering. I lost my entire family in the Holocaust. That's immense suffering and guilt. And then somebody risked her life to save me. I was just a boy, but it sensitized me to other people's troubles perhaps more than others."

To further understand what motivates people to help after personal tragedy, we turned to Jerry White. In 1984, Jerry lost his leg — and almost his life — in a landmine accident. After overcoming pain and loss, he went on to lead the International Campaign to Ban Landmines. The father of four is co-recipient of the Nobel Peace Prize. After meeting thousands of landmine survivors from Vietnam, Ethiopia, Columbia, El Salvador and Bosnia, he wondered why some people emerge from tough times stronger than they were before. He shared his conclusions in the inspiring and poignant book *I Will Not Be Broken: Five Steps to Overcoming a Life Crisis*.

Jerry argues that finding the motivation to contribute in large and small ways is the "secret ingredient" to survival. "Until we reach a point where we can be grateful for our life experience, we are at risk of sliding back into victimhood. We won't cross the finish line until we rediscover gratitude and learn to give again. Only then will we thrive." He cautions that you can't force someone to do what they are not ready to do.[6]

Jerry spoke to us about resilience in childhood and emphasized that giving back is essential to healthy survival. "Some of us are concerned that we are raising the least resilient generation of all time," he said. "Children are not used to having to overcome. Children are used to having their parents step in and take away the pain and suffering because they are worried Little Jimmy is going to be tested too far." No one wishes harm on anyone, but Jerry says it can be reassuring to know that children can overcome hardship and thrive. "Sacrifice can be good. Loss and learning at an early age is exactly what will teach young people coping skills and the resilience they need to survive." Parents can help create opportunities for their children to grow. Our conversation with Jerry made us think of the lessons we've learned from two young men who found a way to help others despite poverty, illness and loss.

Cody Clark and The Three Cs

Cody Clark lost his father to cancer when he was just a boy. During his father's illness, Cody experienced first hand the potency of kindness and compassion. Money had always been tight for the Clarks. As his dad grew sicker, times got tougher. Yet as they did, friends and neighbors organized "food, funds and hugs," quietly paying an electric bill or delivering hampers of food. The helping gestures buoyed the Clarks and laid the groundwork for Cody.

When the freckle-faced boy entered Grade 2, he learned that his classmate Brenna needed a new heart. Everyone was concerned, of course, but Cody was moved to act. The seven-year-old launched a campaign to "buy" Brenna a new heart. He rallied hundreds of sponsors in Jump Rope for Heart and was thrilled to raise $2,500. But on the heels of his success came news that the cardiac unit was closing at the hospital where the girl was to be treated. Undaunted, Cody regrouped. "What do adults do when they want to get things done?" the grade school kid asked his mom. Having no idea what the spark would ignite, Jan advised him to start a petition. Cody scrawled a sentence atop a sheet of lined paper and took it to school. Then he took it to eleven others where he spoke at assemblies and over the school public announcement systems. More than two thousand signatures later, the cardiac unit was saved. The best part of the story? Brenna is doing OK.

Shortly after his campaign, Cody ended

VOLUNTEER AND THE FEEL-GOOD FACTOR

Findings from the 2007 report "Health Benefits of Volunteering."

Researchers with the U.S. Corporation for National and Community Service reviewed more than thirty studies that examined the relationship between health and volunteering. Here is some of what they found:

A study of adults sixty-five and older found that the positive effect of volunteering on physical and mental health is due to the personal sense of accomplishment individuals gain from volunteer activities.

Another study found that volunteering led to lower rates of depression in individuals sixty-five and older.

A Duke University study found that individuals who volunteered after experiencing heart attacks reported reductions in despair and depression — two factors that have been linked to mortality in post-coronary artery disease patients.

Two studies found that the volunteering threshold is about one hundred hours per year, or about two hours a week. Individuals who reached the threshold enjoyed significant health benefits, although there were not additional benefits beyond the one hundred-hour mark.

Cody and a few friends

of kits to appreciative kids. The bears have even been dispatched to soldiers wounded on duty in Afghanistan. Cody has organized fundraising dinners to raise money for hospital equipment. He has even delivered Grandma and Grandpa Kits to hospitals and nursing homes, "because sometimes they have nobody."

Cody's mom says her son's determination kept her going during the darkest of days. Jan is also a cancer patient, though hers was in remission. She emphasized that Cody's work was a distraction, but it was never a shield. And even as she helped her son to channel his pain, Jan made sure he received the emotional support he needed to grieve. "He is my inspiration," she says. "His sweet heart is in the right place. He is just brimming with empathy."

When the boy reached out, his mom was there to support him and to nourish his spirit. "I applaud Mrs. Clark's effort and support for her son," wrote one letter writer in response to a front page story about the family. "It would have been simple and quite frankly acceptable for her to say there is nothing to give right now. Despite her present health condition and financial situation, she continues to fuel Cody's spirit of generosity and raise one incredible young man. Mrs. Clark might not have the monetary wealth, but with her amazing child of endless potential, she surely has a richer life than many others."[7]

When such life-changing moments are thrust upon a child, the care and support of an adult is critical. Robert Brooks and Sam Goldstein are the authors of *Raising Resilient Children: Fostering Strength, Hope and Optimism in Your Child*. In their work, the therapists cite the research of the late Dr. Julius Segal, who

up in the hospital with a minor ear infection. Bored silly, he appealed to his mom to bring toys from home. It got him thinking: If he was restless, surely so were the other kids stuck on the ward. Another spark. Cody told his mom of his idea. Like before, she was encouraging, though she cautioned him that he'd have to find a way to finance his mission. Just as soon as he was out of the hospital, Cody was on the case. One day he stood at a grocery store for eight hours collecting coins. "I knew then how dedicated he was," Jan recalls. The result? Cody's Comfort Kits: Backpacks stuffed with books, puzzles, cars, crafts and — always — a teddy bear. Cody has since delivered hundreds

SEE GOOD, FEEL GOOD

In 1988, Harvard researchers coined the term "Mother Teresa Effect" to describe how just watching an act of altruism can be good for you and bolster your immune system. Subjects were shown a film of the famed nun caring for orphans in Calcutta. Researchers then measured the viewers' saliva and found increases in immunoglobulin A, which fights the cold virus.[9]

DID YOU KNOW?

A study of 1,106 high school students born during the late-1970s to disproportionately young, socially-economically challenged single mothers found that only one-third had engaged in some volunteer work in the previous two years. This is compared to a 1995 study of a broader cross-section of teenagers that reported 70 percent of high school seniors had volunteered in the past year. It is particularly important that family members, educators and mentors actively provide volunteer opportunities for children from single parent families.[10]

observed that the key ingredient in nurturing hope and resilience in children is a connection with at least one significant adult "with whom they identify and from whom they gather strength." The authors say this is a common factor cited in individuals all over the world who have risen above adversity. Brooks and Goldstein suggest the image of "gathering strength" raises questions for us all: "When you interact with your children, do you ask yourself if they are gathering strength from your words and actions? When you put your children to bed at night, do you think whether they are stronger people because of the things you have said or done that day? Have they gathered strength from you that will reinforce their sense of self-worth and resilience?"[8]

The Measure of a Man

By the age of thirteen, Michel Chikwanine had lost his father, watched gunmen ransack his hometown and witnessed the rape of his mother and sisters. In time, he would go on to use these devastating events to unsettle and challenge others.

Michel grew up in the Democratic Republic of the Congo, a former Belgian colony in Central Africa. In his hometown of Beni, the scent of forests filled the air each morning under the

hot African sun. Michel's father, a politician, provided very well for his family. They enjoyed a quiet life in an upscale home where Michel and his sisters were raised with strong values of integrity and compassion. "I was always told, 'It's not always about you, it's about the other person,'" he says. "When you help someone else, you help yourself." Meanwhile, war had broken out between Kabila and Mobutu civil armies. Rwandese and Ugandan forces were entering the Congo in droves. Insurgent armies banded together in rebellion of the government, the intensity of their war crimes escalating with each passing day. This was the beginning of a five-year conflict later known as the Great War of Africa. It would claim 3.8 million lives.

As the rebel foot soldiers descended, Michel's quiet hometown became the epicenter of the conflict. As the weeks and months passed, rebel war tactics intensified into all-out acts of genocide. So many were killed. Young Michel, just five, could not escape the unrest. "I was abducted by rebels to become a child soldier. It was the end of a school day, and I was playing soccer with my friends when I saw fifteen armed men coming out of trucks with the intent to kidnap us all." It didn't matter that Michel was so young. "I yelled, 'I am five, and if you don't let me go, my father will kill you.' They hit me with the butt of a gun, picked me up and threw me in the back of a truck."

Michel was taken to a camp in the jungle along with his buddies, including his best friend, Kevin. Soldiers cut the boys' wrists and rubbed a mixture of cocaine and gunpowder into their wounds. "I felt pain like a million drums being pounded in my head and my eyes. I started sweating as if I just came out of the swimming pool. I felt like I was going to fall over and throw up." The soldiers then lined up Michel and the others, blindfolded them, placed guns in their hands and then yelled "Shoot! Shoot!" Michel and the others did not dare disobey. When they took off their blindfolds, they found Kevin on the ground filled with bullets. "It was the worst day of my life." For two weeks, Michel trained with the rebels while plotting his escape. When the child army was taken to a village with orders to take it over, Michel slipped away. He ran for three days and nights and was eventually reunited with his family.

Soon after the rebel invasion, Michel's father took a job with the United Nations Human Rights Commission. He spoke out against the rebel invaders and unearthed their secret war tactics. In response, the rebels kidnapped Michel's father and five of his colleagues. Seven months later, Michel traveled with his family and a visiting priest to infiltrate an enemy prison, a filthy underground lair, where naked corpses lay one on top of the other amid rats, maggots and human waste. Of the six activists kidnapped, only Michel's father and two others were alive. Miraculously, with the help of the priest, they escaped to Uganda.

When the rebel soldiers learned of the escape, they descended on ten-year-old Michel's home. "It was a Friday afternoon. I had just finished my homework and was taking a nap when I heard gunshots and women screaming. I dove under my bed. Then I remembered telling my father that I would protect my family if he had ever left." Michel went downstairs where a rebel forced him at gunpoint to watch as rebels raped his mother and two older sisters. When he jumped at a rebel, he was slashed across

It was a Friday afternoon. I had just finished my homework and was taking a nap when I heard gunshots and women screaming."

Michel Chikwanine

Michel was a former child soldier in the Congo

the cheek with a machete and then knocked unconscious. Months later, in 1999, Michel, his mother and younger sister fled to a Ugandan refugee camp for a tearful reunion with their father. Two years later, Michel's dad died from the kidney damage and concussions he'd suffered during his confinement. "He was my hero, he was everything I wanted to be," Michel says. "I wanted to take revenge." But every time he thought of retribution, he thought of his father's words: "Great men are not described by their size, but rather by their heart."

In 2004 — after five years of hiding in Uganda — the UN granted Michel, his mother and younger sister a one-way ticket to Canada. They have since made their home in Ottawa, while Michel's two eldest sisters remain in Uganda. Michel's "Do Something" moment came soon after he'd arrived in his new home. He encountered many students who were preoccupied by such issues as what to wear on dress-down Fridays. "I heard a lot of students complaining about classes and being in school. I thought of my four cousins and six nephews and nieces in Africa who *loved* to go to school but didn't have any money to go."

Michel felt compelled to share his story. "It was the first time I saw what an impact my story could have. So I kept on telling it." These days Michel travels around North America working as a motivational speaker for Free The Children. "I especially love when hundreds of students come up to me afterward and tell me how my story motivated them to tell their own stories and motivated them to want to make a difference."

He graduated from high school in June 2007 and plans to study international development,

children's rights and African politics. He thinks often of his father's words. "I finally realized I have to be the person that can give hope to the world, which is what my father did." Inspiring others has given his difficult life new meaning.

Never Say Never

We can't help but be amazed by Kendall, Cody and Michel who remain hopeful that a better world is possible. To help us comprehend the compassion of these astonishing children, we consulted our friend, Dorothea Gaither, a registered clinical psychologist in Toronto. She is also the wife of John Gaither, our long-time volunteer, so she knows our work and our young people well. She emphasizes, as do we, that every family is unique. "Not all children, not all teenagers, not all adults will have an altruistic response to suffering," she says. "But the ones who do, transform their suffering or pain into something good." Compassion often begets compassion, she explains. "When one person has suffered and had someone reach out to them, they're much more likely to recognize suffering and want to return the favor or be that person for others."

Dr. Gaither told us that when a child steps away from being the center of attention because of a circumstance such as illness or other traumatic life challenges, he or she can become a world citizen who sees other kids suffering and will want to help. "They might have a sense that there's something they can do, which is pretty remarkable for a sick or traumatized child to feel." With this sense of agency, kids feel they can make a contribution. In doing so, they claim their connection to humanity.

Acknowledging again that each family is unique, we discussed with Dr. Gaither how parents and mentors might respond when they find their child up against a huge challenge but are determined to reach out. "If the parents have any energy left, they may be able to connect with the child and say, 'That's a great idea. How can we make this happen?'" Certainly the parents of Kendall, Cody and Michel were amazed and worried and awestruck when their children sought ways to help others.

Support is crucial, Dr. Gaither says, even if nothing else happens. Parents can help children articulate that they care about other people. "Before you do anything else, say, 'How did you come up with that?'" Next, perhaps, parents might suggest an action plan. "Never discourage the bigness of the idea," she advises. "Having a dream could prove the difference in quality of life for the child or even outcome." Rather than bogging down in practicalities, say instead, "We might be able to begin." Help the child share the idea with people who will be encouraging. Dr. Gaither says that assuming the child and the parents have the emotional energy, it can be healthy to work toward a goal.

"It's good for us to think about others. Our brain chemistry changes. The chemical soup changes when our thoughts turn to being creative and wanting to help others." Even if the idea doesn't get far off the ground, recognize that the child is trying to make a contribution. "They have received love and they are trying to give love back. That, in and of itself, should be recognized as valuable." Bottom line? Never say never.

SMALL ACTIONS › EVERY DAY

1. LEND A HAND:
Help someone who is dealing with hardship in life. Encourage your child to write a letter to an elderly relative.

2. ... OR AN EAR:
Arrange for you and your child to visit a nursing home and spend time with someone who has no family nearby. Listen closely — storytelling is therapy for the loneliest soul.

3. FILL A POCKET WITH LOVE:
If you are a poet, a teller of jokes or simply a kind-hearted soul, sneak a note into the pocket or lunch of a loved one who hasn't been feeling well lately. It is guaranteed to bring a smile to his or her face.

4. SHOW THEM THE BIG PICTURE:
Help kids to overcome smaller obstacles and to cope with larger problems that they must confront.

5. DO A GOOD DEED:
With your child, help elderly neighbors with chores. Make sure to reflect how they feel at the end of the task. More than likely, you will all be inspired.

You Are One of Us

*After losing his leg in a landmine accident, **Jerry White** led the historic International Campaign to Ban Landmines and was the co-recipient of the 1997 Nobel Peace Prize. He founded Survivor Corps, the first international organization created by and for survivors to help victims of war rebuild their lives. His life's work — transforming victims into survivors — is fired by the belief that with the right tools everyone can rise above tragedy and give back to their communities. He told us his passion for helping others is rooted in the lessons of his mother.*

IT WAS THANKSGIVING and I was just eleven when I learned that my friend's father had killed himself. I struggled to understand what would drive anyone to take his own life, and for the first time heard the terms suicide and manic depression. I was also horrified on behalf of my friend, Katie. I had no idea what to say. My mother had no such hesitation. She said, "You have to go see Katie and simply tell her you're sorry about her Dad." I wanted to pretend it hadn't happened, but my mom insisted. "You will learn this when you

are older, but all you have to do is show up. You don't have to say anything but 'I'm sorry.'" When I resisted, my mom offered to drive me. That meant pulling out of our driveway and into the driveway next door.

As I went inside Mom waited. "All you have to do is go find Katie, give her a hug and come back. I will be right here." I remember knocking on the door, feeling pained and sick and furious at my mother for some seemingly random lesson she was trying to teach. I approached the house

*It's not a
parent's
duty to
protect
children
from
everything.
Instead,
we have to
prepare our
children."*

Jerry White

and opened the door. The house was eerily silent. I called up to Katie. I can remember to this day what she looked like when I first saw her. I blurted out, "Katie, I'm sorry about your Dad." And then I gave her a hug. And she looked down and sheepishly said, "Thanks." Then I fled, my assignment complete.

Only recently did I understand why my mother made me do that. When she was thirteen she had lost her father to pneumonia. Not one of her friends acknowledged this horrible and lonely loss. She wanted to make sure her kids knew how to express condolences. My Mom, my parents, didn't protect us from pain. They helped us learn to deal with it, and offer our support to others.

Parents have this impulse of wanting to protect their kids — from viruses and colds and bullies at school. And pain. I understand. I am a father of four. We have to balance that impulse with the need to push children into the world. We have to remember it's OK to be exposed to germs — we're supposed to get colds because we're building up immunity. This is an analogy for building up resilience. It's not a parent's duty to protect children from everything. Instead, we have to prepare our children.

We grew up in a large, affluent Irish Catholic family, playing tennis and racing sailboats, but also understanding that it was our "duty" to serve and give to others. My mother told us not to pay attention to people above us on the ladder, but to those who are struggling below us. As a kid, when Christmas was coming, I took the business of making a wish list pretty seriously. I'd consider all the games, cars and toys I wanted before committing them to paper. Just when I had the perfect list, my mother would insist that my siblings and I pick the toys we most wanted. Then we would go to the store and

buy that toy. But we didn't get to keep it. Instead we would go and give that toy to the children at the Home for Little Wanderers, an orphanage in nearby Boston. I remember hating giving up my coveted toy, even though I still got most of the other toys on my list. One year, I had to give away this pogo stick that looked like a pony. My mother wanted us to see, meet, feel and enact some level of sacrifice, of giving, of volunteering at an early age. It wasn't guilt she was trying to induce. She wanted me to understand that as much as I would enjoy this pogo stick, so would another kid my age who didn't have the same opportunities. She was teaching me to take another's perspective.

It is no surprise, then, that I ended up in a job trying in my own small way to make the world a better place. I committed myself to stopping nuclear proliferation. Even after I lost my leg, I continued in that work. Nearly ten years after my accident, I met a man whose simple request changed my life. Ken Rutherford lost his legs in a landmine accident in Somalia. He knew I was an amputee and wanted to find a local prosthetist. We went for lunch and we chatted. "Jerry, don't you know that landmines are called weapons of mass destruction in slow motion?" he said. "They've killed more people than nuclear, chemical and biological weapons combined. With your personal and professional experience why don't you join this campaign that's starting up to ban landmines?" It was like a light bulb going on. How could I say "No" to this invitation?

Other invitations would come. Ken and I went to Cambodia, one of the most heavily mined countries in the world, to meet landmine survivors. You see them on every street corner in Phnom Phen. Many of them beg to survive. One afternoon I sat at the side of the road to take off

my artificial leg and adjust my stump sock. A little girl, maybe ten or eleven, came hobbling across the street on one leg and one crutch. I thought she was coming to ask me for money, but instead she blurted something in Khmer. My translator explained that she had just said, "You are one of us." My first reaction was to distance myself: I'm not a Cambodian beggar; I'm an American with a $17,000 prosthesis. But, my Grinch-like heart grew two sizes that day and I suddenly realized that this girl was my Cindy Lou Who. She stirred a real connection in me. How dare I separate myself from this child in need? It was an invitation to acknowledge that I was connected with, and equal to, landmine survivors around the world, including this Cambodian child. I realized I didn't want to "rescue" people but share our strengths and offer tools and support so people like her could recover and reclaim their lives.

I want my children to learn the same lessons my parents taught me. I try not to sound too preachy because I don't want them to roll their eyes. I have taken them to meet survivors without eyes and limbs. They have met people with disabilities from all walks of life. I try to show not tell. I hope when they are older they will reflect almost as I did, asking, "What was my father trying to teach me back then?"

The "Right" Rites of Passage

Without formalized rites, children create their own because they want to prove they can take on the world. Life experience is a powerful and necessary teacher to help kids grow and develop.

BY THE TIME OUR FRIEND Naabala was twelve, the schoolboy and budding Maasai warrior had been entrusted to protect his family's cattle against predators. When he'd proven he could contribute to his family's welfare, his father and the village elders determined it was time for his initiation into manhood. Once a man, he'd be granted warrior status and would be considered a defender of all — there was no greater achievement in his community. First, though, he faced a series of brutal rituals.

One afternoon, while sitting in the shade of a gnarled acacia tree, Naabala told us about this journey. He confessed he'd been filled with dread and pride. His first task had been to clear a spot on his father's land to build a hut where he'd live after his initiation. Imagine asking the twelve-year-old in your life to build a tree fort on his own, never mind a home. In fact, this was the easy part. Next, the boy was instructed to scour the savannah for a mound of stinging fire ants. Under the watch of village elders, he jammed a stick into the anthill, removed his clothes and lay down so that the feast could begin. The angry ants began to bite,

leaving behind stinging venom. Even a flinch of discomfort would bring shame. In the same way, Naabala was also expected to be still when hot embers were placed on his skin. Looking down at his scars, we felt completely inadequate. At the end of these silent assaults, Naabala was deemed ready for the greatest test.

One morning after taking the cows to pasture, he went to the river to wash away his sins. Then he turned his back on his boyhood chores, leaving the cows in the field and his clothing by the river. He returned to his mother's home, where she shaved his head.

When he emerged from her hut for the last time, the men of the community sang songs of encouragement. Still naked, Naabala lay down. The men formed a tight circle. The circumcision took about ten minutes. It involved no Tylenol or Xanax or the Maasai equivalent. Just a dull knife. The pain was excruciating but Naabala did not move. When it was done, he was given a spear, a few cattle, a baton-like weapon and the woven red cloth of a warrior. (The equivalent here of getting an electric guitar, leather jacket and a RAV4 from mom and pop.) Then he and other teenagers on the cusp of manhood were

Naabala's rite of passage differs from those practiced in North America

sent to live in a cave where they had to forage for food, eat their own oxen and learn to hunt. Only after killing a lion could Naabala and the others return to the village. Some adolescents stay in the wilderness for months, some for years, too afraid or too unlucky.

Neither Here Nor There

Meeting Naabala proved as confusing as it was instructive. We had many questions. How does a community help a child become an adult? Is it appropriate to give a youngster challenges and responsibilities beyond her years? Is it right to encourage young people to fight — even metaphorically — for their beliefs? Naabala's journey from boyhood to adulthood took months. By comparison, some adolescents in North America meander for years. We're obviously not advocating that you send your teen to the Maasai Mara to endure ritual circumcision or a date with the stinging ants. And yet Naabala's story offers valuable lessons about stepping up when the time is right.

It's actually strange how few formalized rites of passage there are in North America. The period of adolescence in the west can last as long as fifteen years — age thirty is the new fifteen! The transformation to adulthood is defined in the Jewish faith by a bar or bat mitzvah. In other traditions, it may be loosely marked by menstruation, obtaining a driver's license, attending a Sweet Sixteen party or debutante ball or earning a high school diploma. "As a culture, we could use more wholesome rituals for coming of age," anthropologist and psychologist Mary Pipher observed in *Reviving Ophelia*, her searing book on adolescent girls.

"Too many of our current rituals involve sex, drugs, alcohol and rebellion. We need more positive ways to acknowledge growth, more ceremonies and graduations. It's good to have toasts, celebrations and markers for teens that tell them, 'You are growing up and we're proud of you.'"[1]

We talked to many experts about this disparity. In our conversations, they observed

that without formalized rites, children create their own because they want to prove they can take on the world. This struggle for self-definition leads some kids to rebel against parents, shoplift for kicks, engage in early sex, joy ride and perhaps even engage in violence or gang activity. David Baum, a psychologist who specializes in life transitions, helped us to understand why many youth struggle with identity. Teens crave responsibility but are treated like "grown-ups in waiting," too young for challenges or to fight for their beliefs. Baum points out that such kids are on the receiving end of everything — homework from teachers, instructions from parents, pressure from peers.

We work with many high school students who are convinced they could make a difference if people would just take them seriously. One of Craig's biggest challenges was to get people to listen to a twelve-year-old kid talk about child rights. Someone once advised him to be seen and not heard. We were lucky, though. Mom and Dad let us make life-changing decisions early on and allowed us to assume responsibilities that most would have assumed were beyond our capabilities. Thanks to their endorsement, we grew into mature young adults convinced we had something valuable to contribute.

Naabala endured circumcision to prove he can withstand pain — a source of pride for his family and his village. Naabala's success was the community's success. He was ready to protect the village. Here in North America, for the most part, growing up has little to do with giving back.

MIND THE GAP

The gap year is a rite of passage for adolescents in the U.K. In the year between high school and university, "gappers" work or travel or volunteer — or a combination of all three.

Most famously, Prince William spent a year working on a British dairy farm and visiting countries in Africa before returning to study at St. Andrews University in Scotland. In turn, Prince Harry spent part of his year in Africa, where he made a documentary about the plight of orphans in Lesotho.

Administrators in charge of admissions at Harvard have urged North American kids to take a similar "time out." In fact, they recommend it when they send out letters of admission.

"Regardless of why they took the year off or what they did, students are effusive in their praise," the educators write in an article titled "Time Out or Burn Out for the Next Generation" posted on the university's website. "Many speak of their year away as a 'life-altering' experience or a 'turning point,' and most feel that its full value can never be measured and will pay dividends the rest of their lives. Many come to college with new visions of their academic plans, their extracurricular pursuits, the intangibles they hoped to gain in college and the career possibilities they observed in their year away. Virtually all would do it again." That's certainly the case with Marc, who spent a "gap year" in Thailand after leaving high school.

From Boys to Men

When Craig was a Scout, he once hiked into the winter wilderness with a knapsack on his back to carve out a snow cave where he spent the night. He wasn't asked to return with a cougar's tail or a moose on his back, but the challenge definitely symbolized his transition from childhood. It was just one of the rites of passage he faced during his Scouting days. Some of Craig's favorite memories are of canoeing excursions through uninhabited country, rain or shine. In fact, countless experiences toughened Craig up, filled him with confidence and nurtured his leadership abilities. Those skills still come in handy every single day — except the carving of the snow cave, at least not yet!

Shortly after creating Free The Children, Craig and the other members of the new group spoke to dozens of schools about child labor. Lots of kids supported their efforts with enthusiasm. Others, though, questioned their right to speak. At one meeting, a man urged Craig to step aside to let Dad talk. Dad's response? "Everything I've ever read on the subject was handed to me by Craig." It dawned on Craig that in order for Free The Children to be taken seriously, he would need to go on a fact-finding mission — not to the library, but to India. He confided this hunch to Alam Rahman, a university graduate and human rights activist who had become an invaluable mentor to the FTC gang.

Not too long after, Craig was at the food bank when he got to talking about his fantasy trip. Mom and Dad were so sick of the pestering that they'd banned the word "Asia" from the house. Alam listened with a mischievous grin before announcing that he was heading away to tour South Asia, starting in Bangladesh. Next he floored Craig with a question: "Do you want to come?"

"Uh. Yes!"

Of course, Craig was pretty sure he'd never be able to convince Mom and Dad. After all, he was only twelve! Still, he strategized. "Dad?" he ventured. "Mom? … I want to take two months off school and go investigate child labor in India and Bangladesh."

Mom's answer was short and swift. ("No.")

Dad took time to explain that, as teachers, they could not head away in the middle of the school year. He suggested we could travel as a family the next summer.

"I want to go with Alam," Craig clarified.

Again, Mom and Dad were quick to reply. ("NO!")

Craig has always had a talent for getting what he wants. (Though he'd never admit it, it really is a gift.) He continued to hound Mom and Dad at the same time that he started to contact children's rights groups in Bangladesh and India and Thailand. For months, he raked leaves and mowed lawns to earn travel money. At the same time, he invited Alam around so that Mom and Dad might grow to trust the young mathematician. One day when Craig boldly presented a detailed itinerary and the names of the adult human rights workers he hoped to meet, resistance gave way.

"Mom, what do I have to do to change your mind?" Craig asked.

"Convince me that you would be safe," came the reply.

On December 11, 1995, Craig stepped off a KLM flight in Bangladesh and into the unknown. Why did Mom let Craig go? It's a question she's been asked hundreds of times since that day. It was truly a remarkable decision. But rather than nominating her for Parent of the Year, some people suggested she was nothing short of negligent. But Mom observes that Craig seemed stuck — he was passionate about an important issue but at a loss to act without more information and experience. He craved the credibility that the experiences of this trip had to offer. Mom and Dad acknowledged quickly that they could not give Craig what he needed. Thanks to Scouts,

they trusted Craig was equipped with survival skills, maturity and a sense of responsibility. "Alam was someone from whom Craig could learn, someone who could help him reflect upon the situations, people and places he would encounter and someone whose strong sense of social justice was compatible with Craig's growing interest," Mom reflects.

Looking back at it now in the context of this chapter, we see that the trip had all the makings of a coming of age ritual. Craig, twelve, had to make sacrifices and fight hard to get what he wanted. In order to achieve his goals, he had to leave behind his parents. In Alam, he discovered a guide and a mentor.

Without a doubt, Craig relied on Alam's wisdom during a journey filled with twists and turns. Everywhere Craig went, he found kids working. In one market, he asked a child what he wanted to do in the future. The boy only stared — the question was strange to him and unanswerable. It was Alam who helped Craig put the life-changing trip in perspective. "Your greatest teacher is the world around you," he advised as his young friend prepared to return to North America. "Take time to look at it. Don't just accept it for what it seems on the surface. Look at all the angles."

While Craig came of age on the other side of the world, it can happen anywhere — even in a shopping mall.

Identity Crisis in Aisle Six

Long before his last year in high school, Marc dreamed of being student council president.

ANATOMY OF AN ADVENTURE

Our overseas school building trips didn't start out as rites of passage, but during the past decade that's what they've become for thousands of teens, aged thirteen to seventeen, who have joined us in India, Ecuador and Kenya, among other places. Teens arrive eager to help. They depart a little more mature and equipped to inspire change in their communities.

When they get on the plane, they leave behind their families — not to mention TVs, daily showers and iPods. When they disembark, they are at once immersed in the language, traditions, foods and expectations of a foreign land.

The work is hard. So is the earth. Yet the kids find a way to dig six-foot holes for the support beams. Some kids, especially the boys, pick up an axe to break the earth only to discover they can't do it alone. They must work as a team. Boys are forced to reassess their roles in the group. Girls, accustomed to co-operating, emerge as leaders.

It is a journey of exploration. Friends are made with the children of the community. Teenage volunteers meet women who spend hours each day hauling water and tending to their families. The kids are forced to question what it means to be a woman in the world.

Many mentors guide the young people along the way. Village elders. Warriors. Mothers. Me to We facilitators. Usually about three-quarters of the way through the trip, the work seems insurmountable and everyone is exhausted. On a race against time, the teens are forced to make key decisions.

When they step off the plane back home they are taller, thinner, wiser, sadder and surrounded by many more friends. All at once, they are capable of making change — first in a strange land and soon, we hope, in their own.

More information at: www.metowe.com

He even took extra courses the year before so that he might take fewer during his tenure. It was a three-candidate race. Marc came up with slogans — "Not just a burger, but a Kielburger!" — and recruited campaign workers from a nearby all-girls school to help sway his all-boy electorate. Although he campaigned tirelessly, he lost by a handful of votes.

At the time, it seemed like a major setback. Marc had fast-tracked so many courses that he couldn't imagine what he'd do with his time. He wasn't exactly the loitering type. Lifting weights to Metallica at top volume held only so much appeal. He had so much to give but didn't know where to begin. It's not always easy for teens to see beyond the schoolyard, but Marc knew he was ready for something new. A few weeks into his final school year, he told Mom and Dad that he wanted to find another way to graduate. (In other words, he wanted to quit school.) At this point, most parents would exclaim, "Are you crazy?" In fact, Marc expected three different words from Dad: "Tough it out." Dad, the son of immigrants, had high expectations for our academic success. Still, he and Mom did their best not to freak out as Marc explained his unorthodox plan. Mom and Dad contemplated Marc's wishes. Deciding it would be a character-building experience, they told him he could leave as long as he met certain expectations: He couldn't just hang out, he had to volunteer and he had to finish his diploma at night school.

Mom had heard about a school board program run out of a shopping mall in one of the tougher areas of the city. It was a last-chance program for high-school dropouts and, for some kids, a parole obligation. Students attended class in the morning, then worked in the afternoon. In this way, they graduated while gaining valuable work experience. She suggested Marc volunteer there three days a week while completing his two high school credits at night school.

Around the same time, she noticed a newspaper ad for a leadership course designed to help business leaders identify strengths, set goals and motivate others. Marc's crash course in running a company and working with people would later prove invaluable.

One minute Marc was ready to make the leap, the next he was consumed by indecision. He worried it was a mistake to give up classes, homework, varsity bragging rights and invitations to the best parties. He was scared to leave his comfort zone. It didn't help that many teachers he respected attributed his decision to his election loss and sour grapes. Still, with the support of Mom and Dad, he decided to go for it. Marc still talks about the first time he arrived to volunteer at that alternative school in the mall. He was accustomed to classmates in uniforms; here kids wore bandanas and jean jackets — not to mention a veneer of toughness. Many of the girls had children. None of the kids demonstrated any respect for the teacher.

Marc couldn't have felt more out of place. It didn't help that the head teacher introduced Marc as an overachiever — "someone younger who finished high school early." Everyone sneered when they learned he was to be their tutor. Marc wanted to raise a white flag, surrender and leave. Instinctively he knew to keep his mouth shut. Rather than teach, he listened. Amanda had fled home because of an abusive stepfather and was living on her own. Michel confessed to a number of wrong

THE HERO'S JOURNEY

Joseph Campbell has observed that almost all rites of passage include separation, initiation and return. Bret Stephenson, a noted authority in adolescent male development, helped us take a closer look at some of the steps he's noticed in that journey.

CONVENTIONAL SLUMBER: The adult-to-be is "asleep," reluctant or not ready to confront any problems — injustice, family dysfunction, apathy, immaturity.

THE CALL TO ADVENTURE: The teen is presented with a problem or a challenge or an adventure. The challenge might be to win a spot in an elite orchestra, to make the varsity basketball team, to embark on a wilderness adventure. It could be to clean up one's act, improve marks or assume new responsibilities in the home.

THE THRESHOLD OF DIFFICULTY: A teen accepts the call to adventure but encounters significant obstacles. He might be paralyzed by the fear of not making the orchestra or the basketball team. She could sense she does not have the knowledge or skills to answer the call. Young people without family support, or the guidance of a mentor, might give up when the going gets tough.

DISCIPLINE AND TRAINING: Early in the journey, the teen realizes he does not know everything. It's easy for teens to get stuck here if they don't ask an adult for help — or if there is no adult to ask. At one time, older men and women guided boys and girls through coming-of-age rituals. Stephenson says today teens choose to bond with their peers. If a teen doesn't make the basketball team, she might attend basketball camp or spend a year in her driveway practicing shots. A boy looking for a job might ask a neighbor for help practicing interviews. A teen might accept a tutor in algebra; or could take karate to learn self-defense.

CULMINATION OF THE QUEST: The teen finishes the task. A weak student graduates from high school, a bullied teenager earns a black belt, a promising but impoverished scholar finds money to attend university.

RETURN AND CONTRIBUTION: The focus turns from *me* to *we*. A basketball player might volunteer to help coach a team or help the young girl down the block perfect her free throw. The boy who got a job might help a friend create his own résumé. A boy who struggled with a bully before learning self-defense could help a younger neighbor in the same boat. This stage is crucial if the journey or rite of passage is to have any meaning.

choices, including joining a gang. Most of the kids resisted Marc's help.

It was not easy, but with each passing day, he gained their trust. Over time, a few welcomed his efforts. Eventually, they even became friends. Marc taught lessons in math, science and English. He learned lessons in social reality and the failures of our education system. The kids gave names and faces to issues we had previously only read about. They were good people who had difficult lives. Away from high school, Marc gained perspective, leadership experience, a sense of purpose and an education in life.

We asked Mom recently why she didn't force Marc to finish at his high school. "Life is too short," she replied. She observes that it's awful to feel "unhappy, restless or bored" when you have so much to give. "It's not healthy for a young person," she told us. "It is not healthy for any of us, at any age, especially when there are alternatives." As teachers, Mom and Dad were well aware of the importance of an education. "We also understood that life experience is a powerful and necessary teacher to help kids grow and develop."

The Hero's Journey

Bret Stephenson has spent two decades counseling at-risk and high-risk youth in Lake Tahoe, Nevada. He is also the author of *From Boys to Men: Spiritual Rites of Passage in an Indulgent Age.*[2] His organization, aptly titled Rite of Passage, treats twelve hundred adolescents in twenty facilities in four states. "Sadly, business is booming," he quipped when we spoke. The young people he works with are "incorrigible, gang-affiliated, addicted." Stephenson's program is their last chance. Kids in his program came from homes divided by divorce. Fathers were absent without leave — a disaster for teenagers on the verge of adulthood. "I started to see these kids as not so much the cause of all the societal ills, but more the symptom or result."

Stephenson's study of traditional rites of passage revealed that no matter the culture, rites follow similar steps. It's known as the "Hero's Journey," based on the work of Joseph Campbell. In the course of reading mythological stories from diverse cultures, Campbell noticed almost all rites of passage include separation, initiation and return. The journey is the stuff of blockbuster movies. In fact, *Star Wars* director George Lucas has said he is indebted to Campbell. Just consider the journey of Luke Skywalker from farm boy to hero of the galaxy.

Mom and Dad didn't know anything about the "Hero's Journey," so we're stunned at how closely our own passages match what we're talking about here. They seemed to know we needed to be tested. They had the confidence and good sense to offer guidance at a distance.

To pass successfully to adulthood from adolescence, a teen must find his or her identity. It's a painful proposition that may require a child to separate from all that is safe and familiar. It can force a teen to confront fears and temptations and to seek new experience and knowledge. In the end, with luck, the teen emerges more mature, more confident and with a sense that they are part of something larger.

Of course, one need not travel to complete a

hero's journey. We believe that introducing kids to the *me* to *we* way of life can also help during this transition. By reaching out — rather than drawing in — teens may see the world from a different perspective that might encourage them to make different decisions. It's possible they might find new measures of meaning — you know, beyond counting how many friends they have on Facebook.

The journey will be made up of many steps. When Galen Kerrick was nine, his stepdad, psychologist David Baum, took him to the forest near their home in rural New Hampshire. It was dusk. After a pep talk about bravery and courage and overcoming fears, he left Galen in the growing darkness. Baum was never really that far away. After about an hour, he rang a bell, a signal that it was time for the boy to make his way home. Baum says this simple initiation showed the boy that determination overcomes fear and anxiety. At sixteen, it was time for Galen to experience a more full-fledged rite of passage. This time they made tracks for Sandusky, Ohio: Roller Coaster Capital of the World. Strange as it sounds, Baum created a ceremony about facing one's fears. "We talked about what these roller coasters would represent in our lives, in his life. It was tremendous fun but steeped in significance."

Meanwhile, on a completely different kind of journey, Galen's sister Kate, at sixteen, went to Northwaters Wilderness School, which specializes in rites of passage. She spent three weeks paddling to remote James Bay and back. "I had no idea what to expect," says Kate.

As she canoed, portaged and canoed some more, Kate discovered she could work through pain and exhaustion to accomplish her goals.

"I could choose to be afraid or overwhelmed by something, or I could just do it." When Kate and the other teens returned to base camp, they were greeted by cheering and whooping and the sound of banging paddles. Kate felt the vibrations in her chest. No longer a child, she was filled with accomplishment. Those who make it through such a quest learn that they are strong and capable. When Kate fell in love with the wilderness, she discovered she wanted to be an outdoor education instructor to pass on her knowledge. She returned to the camp for many summers. Like so many who complete such a journey, Kate was filled with the desire to give back to the community, to the environment and to others.

Mom and Dad did not plan our rites of passage, but they paid attention to the transitions and extended support when it was required. Instead of sheltering us, they gave us room, guidance and confidence. When the calls came, we were ready. As a result of leaving high school, Marc discovered he could help others and travel his own path. It's no surprise he went on to volunteer so far off the familiar path. Marc tells people that working in the slums of Thailand changed his life. "I arrived with teenage baggage and left with the confidence to be myself."

In the same way, when Craig stepped off the plane from Asia, everyone noticed he was different. He was more confident and at once able to speak from experience. He returned with videotapes, photographs and interviews — proof that child labor was as appalling as he had said it was. He went on to speak around the world. Craig will always divide his life between pre-Asia and post-Asia. The trip inspired him at a very young age to re-evaluate his life and the contribution he hoped to make. All of this takes us back to that afternoon we spent under the tree with Naabala. We understood how proud and accomplished he must have felt when he returned to his village waving a lion's tail.

SMALL ACTIONS › EVERY DAY

1. CELEBRATE TRANSITIONS:
Honor your children as they age by marking milestones and passages in a symbolic way.

2. FIND THE RIGHT RITES:
Help your teens do what is hard, confront what they fear: Speaking in public, standing up for what they believe, fighting against the status quo.

3. REWARD WITH RESPONSIBILITY:
Make adolescence about doing, not being done for. Prepare kids for adulthood by making them take charge.

4. AROUND THE BEND:
Encourage your teens to step into the great unknown so they can test themselves and expand their horizons.

5. THEN BACK AGAIN:
Be open and attentive to what they have learned about the world. Help them share their experiences and newfound wisdom with others.

6. HIT THE ROAD:
Go on a volunteer vacation to Kenya or China or Ecuador and build a school or a well. Encourage a gap year to volunteer.

7. GIVE FREEDOM:
Give them freedom to hold down part-time jobs, earn and manage their own money.

Opportunity is Not a Chance, It's a Choice

*You should see **Robin Wiszowaty** carry water on her back while shoeing flies with a notebook. As a university student, she conducted development field research in a Maasai village and decided to stay. She now serves as Free The Children's program director in Kenya. Here she explains what led her there.*

GROWING UP IN SCHAUMBURG, Illinois, a large, middle-class suburb of Chicago, I was surrounded by a world that seemed ordinary and safe. Neighborhood kids would gather for endless games and sports, while parents watched from lawn chairs or traded gossip over barbecues and potluck dinners.

Being an athlete, a good student and a musical performer in high school earned me a label — one that felt more self-containing than self-defining. My struggle to free myself of life's monotony birthed an uncontrollable anger that threatened to tear apart my family. Dad learned through his life what success looked like for him, but when I didn't share the idea of being a rich, renowned entrepreneur driving to fancy parties in a Lexus from my two-story home in an upper-class neighborhood, we began to fight. My anger would

bubble over in an instant, turning me into a person I — nor my family — recognized. I did anything I could to rebel against the life Dad wanted for me, even when it meant giving into things my peer group agreed with more than I did. My parents — who had balanced three children and successful careers — didn't know how to care for their raging and rebellious daughter.

When I went away to university, I thought the new-found freedom would bring peace. But my dissatisfaction only continued. I needed to do something drastic. Through a university study-abroad program, I moved to a Maasai village in Kenya. The Maasai are an indigenous tribe occupying vast regions of south Kenya and north central Tanzania. A generous family welcomed me into their home. Before long, I was carrying water on my back, collecting firewood, preparing traditional meals over a fire and conversing in Swahili. Basic survival chores filled my days from sunrise to late at night.

My family and I fell in love with one another, despite backgrounds that couldn't have been more different. After a while, I became an accepted member of the community. I eventually moved into my own *manyatta* — a hut constructed with mud, sticks and cow dung. My friends were the old mamas who invited me for tea. As we sat inside their dark homes over a smoky fire, the mamas spoke freely about their fears, their struggles, their politics, their values, morals, dreams and priorities. I attended traditional ceremonies and celebrations, including the wedding of the family's father to his second wife and the circumcision of a neighboring fifteen-year-old girl.

During those twelve months in rural Kenya, my outlook began to shift. With my new Maasai name, Naserian, I staked out a new identity through which I could adopt new values and a new perspective. I came to think of family in a broader sense. Everywhere I went I encountered people working against challenges for the greater good. In areas crippled with drought, communities shared scarce resources. In regions wracked with poverty and hunger, people spearheaded initiatives to generate new sources of income. If a household ran out of food, another provided them with tea. Children crowded around elders to listen to their stories with fascination and respect. In places where it would be easy to abandon hope, I saw young people eager to attend classes at new schools — the shining promise of generations to come.

One morning, I was lucky enough to get a ride on a pickup truck to the market. I squeezed in with almost three dozen others into the truck's bed. An old Maasai grandmother, unable to stand fully erect from decades of hauling water and firewood, wedged herself next to me on my left, her wrinkled face and weathered feet telling of many years of hardship and work. As a small boy took a seat on my lap, a chicken, to be sold at market, pecked at my feet. As the pickup bumped along the rocky, craggy road, I asked myself: How did I, an ordinary American girl who grew up arguing with her parents, swimming for her high school team and playing kickball in suburban streets, end up here? And what was I even *doing* here?

During that year, I came to realize that opportunity is not a chance, it's a choice. I returned to North America with a renewed sense of purpose, knowing I was destined to give back to the people I'd grown to love.

In my current role as Free The Children's program director in Kenya, I work closely with communities in transition throughout the country.

Having lived in Kenya for several years, I now consider this adoptive country my home. My former dissatisfaction has given way to an unwavering commitment toward helping others. This life is more fulfilling than I could ever have imagined.

"

My family and I fell in love with one another, despite backgrounds that couldn't have been more different."

Robin Wiszowaty

Robin fetching water in Maasailand

THE THIRD C
Communi

In the third and final section of the book, we will discuss what it means to come together. It's in a sense of community that compassion and courage are tied together.

It takes a village to raise a child. We all know the African adage, which applies to parenting in Toronto, New York or the Maasai Mara. We Day is a great example of this thinking in action.

In October 2009, some 32,000 student leaders crowded into stadiums in Toronto and Vancouver to join the 100-School Challenge — a campaign to build that number of schools in developing countries. During the annual event, student leaders listen to inspirational speeches from actors, leading activists, experts and politicians.

"I have never stood in a room like this in my life!" actress and activist Mia Farrow told the raucous crowd. "You are the generation I've been waiting for!"

"Yes!" she said. "I believe in you."

The annual event itself was the work of many villages. Principals signed up their schools and took care of the paperwork. Teachers and parents served as chaperones. Politicians and inspirational speakers alike rallied the young audience. Singer Sarah McLachlan did, too, along with the Jonas Brothers, Justin Bieber and so many others. Michel, a former child soldier shared his harrowing life story. Cub Scouts and Girl

Guides were in the audience, along with members of the Boys and Girls Club of Canada. CTV, Canada's largest broadcaster, filmed and televised the event. So did technology whizzes who helped us to broadcast the event into school auditoriums across the country. More companies than we can name donated time, money or services. Even the government stepped up, donating free school buses so the students could attend.

The day was the work of countless individuals — a village of caring and compassionate adults. A day that we want to continue for years to come with young students and change-makers.

Already in this book, we have shown you how to nurture empathy and responsibility and passion. We've discussed how you can coach courage by daring to redefine success. We hope we've convinced you to make sure that the way you spend your time reflects your true beliefs.

In the next section, we'll look at how all of this applies to our communities. We'll see it at play in our schools, religious groups and sports programs, and we'll consider how teachers and mentors and coaches can nurture social responsibility. Caring and compassion starts at home. Once out in the community, its potential is limitless.

How to Find Your Rebel a Cause

The downsides of peer pressure have been well documented. On the upside, it can be incredibly persuasive when it's used for good.

WHEN WE MET ALEX APOSTOL, he was gluing insects to a table. To tell you the truth, we weren't sure who to rescue — the brooding teenager or the defenseless ants. The fourteen-year-old was a not-so-happy camper at one of our first leadership camps. We tried to engage him in a workshop — How to Find an Issue You're Passionate About — but he just glowered and later stomped out.

He was back the next morning, albeit not voluntarily. Public speaking was the topic that day. Kids were writing and rehearsing speeches about volunteerism, the environment and child labor. We could only imagine the topic Alex might choose: Seven Ways to Antagonize Ants. When it was his turn, Alex stood up and took aim at program facilitator Ed Gillis. He made fun of Ed's hippie clothes, joked about his Anthony Robbins delivery and mocked his do-gooder messages. The kids in the audience thought it was hilarious, though they weren't sure they should laugh. During the mid-afternoon break, Ed asked Alex to remain behind. Everyone assumed he was going to be told to pack up his gluestick and go home. Instead, in a master stroke, Ed complimented the teen on his gutsy, side-splitting speech. "I was intrigued," Alex admits. Suddenly we had his attention.

We've since met many angry and apathetic kids, most of them escorted to our workshops by parents at their wits' end. But Alex was our

first encounter with an unwilling participant who had little desire to be at camp and less respect for our work. Gradually we learned Alex's story. The Apostols had recently changed houses — a move made necessary by a new addition in the family. So after mom, Debbie, had her fourth child, the family relocated to a spacious but remote new home. They made the switch in the middle of a school year.

"There was nothing around," recalls Alex. "We had to be driven everywhere." He didn't even try to make friends. As summer approached, Alex knew his mom, a teacher, would push him to attend some lame camp or another, perhaps one devoted to computers or sports or rockets. It turned out that Debbie had picked up a brochure for our leadership academy. She liked the idea that her son might meet new friends who were interested in building the community, rather than dismantling it. She wasn't convinced she could get him to attend. "He was not exactly into organized activities," she explains with deadpan understatement. Predictably, he threw a tantrum. Alex had seen Craig on TV. "I remember thinking, 'Oh what a loser. I don't want to hang out with this guy.'"

Ed Gillis and Alex Apostol are unbeatable pals

Alex with his brothers

What's more, he adds, "I was pretty cynical."

Debbie and Alex made a deal: He would give camp a try. If he didn't like it, he could quit. "I fully expected he would walk out," she says. Fortunately, as it turned out, we weren't about to let Alex get away. Although we were young and relatively new at running leadership camps, we sensed we could win over the unwilling teen. And that's exactly what Ed did when he complimented that obnoxious but wildly funny speech. "Even though I was defiant and I was misbehaving, someone recognized my potential." Alex discovered he had a gift for making people laugh. Ed brought Alex on our side. We played our part by surrounding him with excited young people who were keen to participate in their communities.

Without question, Alex was a rebel. In no time, he was a rebel with a cause. On day three, he was hooked. By week's end, he was piling into our family van to join us on a hunt for hamburgers. That "loser" Craig was now his pal. The following week, Alex was at Free The Children offices asking how he could volunteer. Soon he was traveling with Craig and speaking to kids, parents and dignitaries. Alex has since led several volunteer trips to Kenya, India and Mexico. After finishing a degree in peace and conflict studies on a full scholarship, he's now director of special projects for Me to We. Whether on an overseas mission or in a brainstorming session, Alex still makes us laugh — not always an easy task given our line of work.

The downsides of peer pressure have been well-documented. On the upside, it can be incredibly persuasive when it's used for good. Like-minded friends can stand up to doubters and bullies. United, they can say "No" to smoking or drugs or shoplifting and "Yes" to homework. (OK, even we're not that naïve.) We realized quickly that kids who are angry or apathetic don't necessarily know they have leadership skills or anything of value to offer. Many have never been told that they do. Others, like Alex, refused to listen. Our leadership camps are a safe place where kids can explore their views and ideas. We work hard to create a place where teens can communicate their concerns. Who knows what would have happened if we'd allowed Alex to hang out at the back of the classroom scoffing at others. At our camps, kids don't win points for the clothes they wear or the playlists on their iPods. Instead, they get props for what they know about developing countries or the Millennium Development Goals.

Not every parent will choose to drop their kid with the keeners at a leadership camp. But parents still have more power than they might realize to influence their kid's posse. Debbie was determined to find a community where she had some influence over how her children might interact. She was anxious to build Alex's self-esteem and to awaken his social awareness. She hoped to ground him in a positive peer group, which is why he ended up at camp. She wanted to equip her family unit to take on societal ills. As Alex reflects, "Our society is full of hockey dads and soccer moms, families that center their lives around sports, ballet and other things that aren't really about broader issues. Mom's point was that just as we have hockey families, we need socially responsible families that, among many other things, also encourage positive activities and peer groups."

Debbie continued to guide her children long after they'd settled in their new neighborhood. In some ways, she made it easy for Alex — and eventually his brothers, Jason and Josh — to donate time to our organization.

SHARE AND SHARE ALIKE

Gandhi once said that if there is to be peace in the world, it must begin with children. We've learned our best lessons from other children. Craig often tells people this story about his friend José, a boy he met in the streets of San Salvador, Brazil:

José lived in the streets with a group of street children between the ages of eight and fourteen. He and his friends showed me the abandoned bus shelter where they slept under cardboard boxes. They had to be careful, he said, because the police might beat or shoot them if they found their hideout.

I spent the day playing soccer on the streets with José and his friends — soccer with an old plastic bottle. They were too poor to own a real soccer ball.

It got late and time for me to leave. José knew I was returning to Canada and wanted to give me a gift, but he had nothing — no home, no food, no toys, no possessions. So he took the shirt off his back and handed it to me. José didn't stop to think that he had no other shirt or that he would be cold that night. He gave me the most precious thing he owned: the jersey of his favorite soccer team.

Of course, I told José I could not accept, but he insisted. So I removed the plain white T-shirt I was wearing and gave it to him. Although José's shirt was dirty and had a few small holes, it was certainly much nicer than mine.

José grinned from ear to ear when I put it on. José taught me more about sharing that day than anyone I have ever known.

Sure, they did all the work, but she did all the driving — to and from meetings, the airport, you name it. "Don't you have anything better to do?" other parents would ask. "Actually, no," she'd respond. "This matters." She wanted to make it as easy as possible for her kids to fall in with a good crowd.

Thanks to Alex, we learned a lesson that continues to inform our work. It's something that psychologists have proven: A pro-social posse has the power to transform an angry or apathetic kid. Over and over, we've seen a lost kid find himself in a socially-minded crowd. Once found, we've watched that kid discover a passion and a cause. Surrounded by like-minded friends, supported by a network that's ready to tackle issues and challenge conventions ... well, look out!

It only makes sense to worry about the company your children keep. Friends can be enormously influential, especially when they run in packs. We've all read stories about teens and drugs and no end of other risky behaviors. Plus, as never before, children are dependent on their pals for emotional support, advice and wisdom. Parents are busy making ends meet, so kids turn to each other for support. As Gordon Neufeld and Gabor Mate pointed out in *Hold On To Your Kids*, throughout the history of the human race caring adults and mature, responsible peers have served as models to children.[1] Kids can't raise kids. The authors argue that it's crucial for parents to become the "go-to" support system for their children. Of course, it's always easier when they choose a good group of friends but what if they don't? We wondered if there is anything parents can do. To find out more about the push and pull of peer groups, we talked to Wendy Ellis, assistant professor of psychology at King's University College at the University of Western Ontario.

Ellis has done groundbreaking research on peer groups. She explained that the need to belong to a crowd seems "biologically determined" as kids separate from their parents and establish independent identities. Ellis says it's understandable that parents worry about peer groups: "They are incredibly powerful." The good news is that they are not always a negative influence. There are pro-social groups that support the values of kindness and helping.

Ellis says it's important for parents to realize that they have more power than they think, even with teens. "With older kids it's mostly what they see in their homes that matters. We tend to think modeling proper behavior is a task confined to younger childhood but adolescents still want parents' approval, even if they sometimes push them away. Just by having a certain family climate is really important. That predicts pro-social behavior." When kids are younger, parents can encourage them to participate in activities that support their values. For some that may mean joining Scouts or Guides, a church group or a socially minded after-school club. Many parents have turned to Free The Children to help guide their children: an honor, to be sure, and occasionally a challenge.

Take My Kid, Please ...

To be clear, most of the kids that go to our leadership camps or overseas school building trips want to be there. They are passionate about global issues or making a difference. But there are also purse-lipped moms and

dads with furrowed brows who drop their teens at our leadership academies. Some scrape together money to send their kids on an overseas school building trip. Many confide that their kids are stunned or stuck. In some cases, a teen has already been to boot camp — a detail left off application forms but disclosed around the campfire in Kenya. Parents ask us to transform their children. But, we wonder, to what? From surly to sanguine? Troubled to peaceful? Disobedient to helpful? Apathetic to passionate? The best we can do is help parents connect their kids to a circle of caring that we hope will encourage them to become active, engaged citizens.

We learned quickly not to make assumptions about children or presumptions about parents. Still, there are a few things we have learned over the years. Before trips or leadership camps, we like to ask parents a lot of questions: Do you volunteer with your children? Do your kids participate in other pro-social activities? Are you a part of their lives? Before trying to solve a problem by sending a child away, we encourage families to seek resolution closer to home — connecting with their kids through shared activities is ultimately the best way to guide them in their choices. When we welcome young people into our leadership camps or overseas trips, our plan is pretty simple. By

JOIN THE CLUB

Once a kid has found a few like-minded pals, gently encourage them to take on a small project. It can be hard to know where to start. Here are a few suggestions from the O Ambassadors on how classrooms can help others:

TAKE ACTION ON POVERTY

Create a package of colorful school supplies for an elementary classroom in need in your town. New crayons, markers and other goodies will help you spread community spirit and reach out as mentors to younger kids.

TAKE ACTION ON EDUCATION

Find out if your local elementary school has a mentoring/buddy program. By helping younger kids, you lead by example and make a big contribution to your community.

TAKE ACTION ON HEALTH

Malaria is one of the leading causes of death for children in developing countries, but most people don't know much about it. Research causes of malaria, then give a presentation to your class.

TAKE ACTION ON WATER

A water walk is one of the most popular awareness activities we hear about friends doing for the Adopt a Village clean water campaign. Here's how it works: Participants have to walk a certain distance carrying a typical load of water that a girl in a rural community would have to collect each day (groups usually decide on an amount between two and five liters). You can collect funds by charging people to participate or having them collect pledges. Turn it into a friendly competition by setting up races.

the time we're done, these kids will have been enveloped by a group of community-minded friends who are intent on building a better world.

During our overseas trips, for example, kids get to be who they aspire to be. It helps that they leave parents and emotional baggage at home — not to mention cell phones! Time away from boyfriends and girlfriends creates room to breathe. Distance from shopping and texting and just hanging out creates perspective. Stripped of possessions and trivial pursuits, they become who they are — not what they own. What they have in common with their new peer group is the shared experience of Africa or Ecuador or China or Arizona. These kids still want to fit in, it's just that their definition of "cool" changes. The cachet comes from being up on development issues, not down on the latest celebrity. Status is conveyed on those who pitch in and pull their weight, giving of their hearts and souls. In such an environment, posers suffer a power outage. These transformations can last a lifetime, so can the friendships.

Sending your child half a world away to make new friends is not always possible or realistic, nor is it guaranteed to be successful. For every kid who connects, there are others who just don't, no matter what we do. But, of course, it is not about sending your kids away but rather about finding them new circles of caring. So maybe you could find them an after-school "getaway" — Boys and Girls Clubs, Scouts or Guides or church, mosque or synagogue groups.

Some schools have programs to link students with positive peer groups. One Ohio-based school program called Positive Peer Groups has long helped troublesome and troubled teens.[2] The group begins with a "kick off" to attract students to tackle such school-wide issues as bullying, drug abuse or racism. Anyone can join, though some are referred by teachers, particularly those who are routinely shunned, ridiculed or rebellious. Troubled kids work with engaged youth to solve school problems. Frequently, the unsettled kids are tapped to become mentors and tutors for others, allowing them to take on leadership roles.

Studies found that participants developed new attitudes about teachers and school. Many reported higher levels of self-esteem and showed greater get up and go. Educators reported many positive changes. Some students were observed to be much more sociable.

An Open-door Policy

When Craig stood in front of his class with that crumpled clipping about a murdered child laborer, he could never have guessed that his simple question — "Who wants to join?" — would inspire a worldwide movement that now includes millions of children. At the time, he was simply following Mom and Dad's simple and intuitive advice: "Get others involved." They had suggested there might be other kids, like Craig, concerned about child slaves in Pakistan. If he could enlist some friends, they could share the work and perhaps even have some fun.

When eleven hands went up, Craig realized that friends gave power to his passion. What was true then, remains so now, more than a decade

later. At lunchtime that day, the impromptu group met to discuss what to do next. Craig suggested they meet again after school. "At my house," he said without hesitation.

Beyond encouraging Craig to enlist friends, Mom and Dad made sure our home was always welcoming. Marc's sports pals were always stomping through. Craig took advantage of Mom and Dad's goodwill. He was pretty sure they wouldn't embarrass him by hauling out his baby pictures. And he knew from experience that they'd gladly offer advice, but only if solicited. More likely, they'd try to stay out of the way until it came time to pay for the pizza.

Mom and Dad advised Craig to ensure everyone had a role, a chance to make decisions and the opportunity to speak. No matter the cause, Mom and Dad were quick to offer up their van, their house and their time. And so it was with everything in our lives. If they believed in what we were doing — Scouts or public speaking, for example — they supported it wholeheartedly. If they didn't approve — like when Marc befriended the neighborhood boy with the knife collection — they made it difficult for us. They never lectured us about poor choices or worrisome behaviors. Instead, they made it hard for us to do what they didn't want us to do. Their wallet was always open for a new book but closed for a video game. (We had to save our own money for that.) The car door was always open for volunteer activities or sports or a drive to a good friend's house. We always knew it was in our best interests to bring our friends home to hang out, not just because of the pizza but because our parents trusted us enough to let us do our thing.

Dad drove Craig and his friends to their first

Friendship is born at that moment when one person says to another: 'What! You, too? Thought I was the only one.'"

C.S. Lewis
Author

speaking engagement at a local school. Vance Ciaramella spoke about Iqbal. Ashley Stetts told the story of Easwaris, a young girl who worked at a fireworks factory loading sulphur and charcoal into tubes. She was badly scarred in an explosion that killed her eight-year-old sister. Craig told the class about the 250 million working children in the world — a number that at the time was equal to the population of the United States. The students were as shocked as we had been when we first learned the facts. We challenged them to take their first action that day by writing to a company to guarantee their products were not the result of child labor. Or to a leader to urge them to put more money into education and the protection of children. Or to the Pakistani government to demand that Iqbal's killers be brought to justice. At that school, we went from class to class telling kids about our mission. At the end of each session, we appealed for help and hands went up. By the time we'd finished with the fourth class, we returned to the first where students presented us with a pile of letters — the first of thousands we would receive. "Who wants to join?" Craig had asked. The answer was overwhelming.

The early days of Free The Children also showed us how easy it was to draw in unlikely activists. The guys on the Grade 7 soccer team — who had just discovered girls — couldn't help but notice that our mystery group had by this time fifteen girls and five guys. They asked to be included before even stopping to find out what it was they were joining.

Check Your Ego at the Door

We often meet parents who are convinced that the only way their child can make a difference is to create their own organization. They discourage their kids from recruiting help in case it dilutes the effort or threatens their child's success. We'd love your kid to earn a spot at Yale or Harvard, but that shouldn't be the be all and end all of their volunteer efforts. Plus, assuming they get in, they'll need someone to carry on their good work — another good reason to recruit friends to their cause.

We were once contacted by the mother of a budding social entrepreneur. She was worried that speaking engagements were consuming her daughter's time. They'd never thought to say "No" to demands. We reassured the mom and explained how our parents had encouraged us to share the spotlight and, thus, the load. Parents don't always understand that social issues are larger than any one child.

Just as parents get caught up in the moment and the movement, so, too, do children. We've seen compassionate kids alienate others in their zeal to change the world. Twelve-year-old Kim Plewes was riveted when her French teacher told the Grade 6 class about the suffering of millions of child slaves. Kim and two pals were swept up and moved to create a petition calling on the government to ban child labor. That action turned into a mission, which inspired an exclusive club. Although the girls had the best intentions, Kim now admits that they didn't know how to convey their compassion. "We alienated a lot of people. We'd say things like, 'We don't know if you can help us with our petition because it's our petition and our idea.'"

Tweens, more than almost any age group, are desperate to define themselves. Some identify with jocks or musicians or mall rats.

FRIENDS IN FARAWAY PLACES

Marc and Roxanne met on Parliament Hill where they both worked as parliamentary pages in the House of Commons in Ottawa, Canada. Since that time, they've grown together and worked side by side on many Free The Children projects. After Marc and Roxanne were married in Toronto, they left for a honeymoon in Kenya. Here is what Marc later wrote about what happened there:

"Sitting under the stars in the breathtaking Maasai Mara, Roxanne and I were sharing stories around a bonfire with our parents — they convinced us to take them along! Suddenly we heard rustling in the bushes. We jumped up, worried about what animal may have strayed too close to our camp.

Luckily, it wasn't a lion or zebra but a large group of warriors and elders. They had become our friends over many years of working in the region and wanted to congratulate us on being married.

The chief explained that, while we were officially married in Canada, they considered us part of their community as well and wanted to give us a traditional Maasai wedding. We were touched.

So the elders positioned Roxanne and I back to back while everyone else began singing and dancing around us. Their elaborate necklaces jangled to the sound of their chanting and their bright red garments stood out against the night sky.

When the dancing stopped, they ripped pieces of grass from the ground and gently placed them on our shoes. Then the elders blessed us by spitting fermented goat's milk at our feet — a sign of great respect!

Marc and Roxanne in Kenya for their wedding

The ceremony ended with Roxanne and I being given traditional Maasai names.

After a heated discussion with the elders, the chief declared that I would be called the Maasai word for "baobab tree" — a large, sturdy tree that lives for many generations, meaning I would live a long life.

Roxanne would be called the word for "rainmaker," meaning she would have many children. When I asked the chief how many, he said "at least twelve, maybe more." Our parents were thrilled.

We thanked our friends for the incredible ceremony, and they disappeared into the bushes just as quickly as they came. As we sat back down by the fire, Roxanne and I realized that while we received many wonderful gifts at our wedding in Toronto, this one was truly unique.

Kim Plewes and friend in Africa

Kim and her pals became do-gooders, though self-righteous ones at that. Kim couldn't let a name-brand sneaker go by without calling out the person in those shoes. She lambasted classmates, friends, family and strangers and anyone else she caught dressed in clothes made by child laborers. "I was so passionate, I couldn't help lecturing everyone I met. I couldn't understand why people wouldn't change their habits. I forced my views down everyone's throats."

Kim remembers the day in Grade 9 science where she turned into something of a social experiment. "Look at my sneakers," a classmate taunted as he plopped his shoes on a lab table.

"I can just feel the fingers of the kids that made them." He didn't have to wait long for a reaction. "I took the bait and lit into him." Nothing she said changed his views. He was laughing too hard to listen.

With time and distance — she went to Europe on a high school exchange — Kim came to realize the best way to change attitudes was to lead by example. She realized she didn't have all the answers. Instead of lecturing, she began to research and learn more about the issues. Kim's quiet dedication spoke volumes. High school classmates respected her efforts. "I realized I should not attack people for not doing what I was doing, I quietly had to show why certain choices would be beneficial."

Kim's mom, Cathy, helped her daughter to understand that the mission was more important than the messenger — a heady realization for any tween. Cathy realized parents have to help children reflect on why they're doing what they're doing. The question at hand: "Is it for the attention or the cause?" Like the parents of so many children on a mission, Cathy became a de facto recruit not to mention a dedicated driver. She supported her daughter's passions, but insisted she pursue balance. "She always said 'Yes,'" Kim recalls, "as long as school remained a priority and we were safe." In addition to her social justice projects, Kim played a sport and earned decent — if not stellar — marks. Oh, and by the way, that petition she started when she was twelve? It ended up with six thousand signatures.

We trust we've convinced you that the world needs your kids. We urge you to nurture their social consciences. We want them to lend a hand and bend an ear. Heck, we hope their deeds enhance their applications and land them scholarships to Princeton. What we really want, though, is for them to be blessed with good causes and great friends.

SMALL ACTIONS › EVERY DAY

1. ENCOURAGE YOUR KIDS TO RECRUIT:
It's easy to ask others to join. Tell new friends that your cause needs their "gift" in order to thrive.

2. BEGIN CLOSE TO HOME:
Show your child how to bring a sibling on side.

3. PUT THE "FUN" IN FUNDRAISING:
Make it easy and tempting for your teen to entertain at home.

4. SUPERVISE BUT DON'T INTERFERE:
Help them get to where they need to be.

5. STAY IN THE LOOP:
Find out what your kids are doing and why. Encourage other parents to get involved.

6. SHARE THE JOY AND THE JOBS:
Help your child ensure every pal they enlist to a cause has a job to do.

Mr. Lucky Jr.

*Two-time NBA Most Valuable Player **Steve Nash** is also a noted philanthropist. The point guard for the Phoenix Suns formed the Steve Nash Foundation in 2001. It serves children in Phoenix, Arizona and British Columbia who are affected by poverty, illness, abuse and neglect by giving them opportunities for education, play and empowerment.*

I CAME TO CANADA WHEN I was one. My parents did, too. I was born in South Africa. From such a young age, I learned that my parents didn't want me to grow up in apartheid and why. That's a lot to take in, to learn about such dividing history as a child. But to know they did this sheds light on where I come from. Those lessons start to make you realize the reach between each of us, and the reach between all of us. It's far more about connection than it is about stretch.

Right from the start there were these associations made between us as a little family and the bigger world. My parents were so happy to be living in Canada. We call my dad Mr. Lucky because he's always telling us, "I'm the luckiest guy in the world." He's extremely positive and optimistic and full of energy. My dad used to work on Operation Track Shoes, which was like a Special Olympics day in Vancouver. As a young kid, if your dad comes home and tells you that he wiped an athlete's bum all day because he couldn't do it himself, it makes an impact on you. I was twelve. At first I'm sure I thought, *Why? You're crazy.* But then you realize, well, I suppose that's really nice. And to question: Wait, why would you do that? What for? And it starts to open up your mind to the fact that not everyone is afforded the same opportunities, whether it's being able to wash himself or dress herself or live in an environment that's not abusive.

My environment, all things considered, was pristine. From a tactile sense, I was sheltered. But I'd experience things through my parents' reaction to them. My mom and dad are both very sensitive people. I would watch them get upset at the inequality in situations. I think that rubs off on you, and that I was taught to realize just how lucky we are — we lived in a safe, beautiful, over-served part of the universe. We were afforded a lot – and at the same time it didn't really matter what you had or didn't have, it's a matter of your attitude. If you *feel* lucky. And if you *feel* able and you *feel* willing, you can do so much to help. So much to help make change in young people's lives. In my life today, I'm very aware how little of it is me – people give you so much credit for having a foundation and doing all these things, but you're just a small light that helps ignite change. So many people and their stories have impacted me and made me feel even more compelled or inspired to get involved. I spend lots of my time plotting to help people now. I'm not great at it yet, but I think I'm learning.

Having kids is part of that desire to learn. My wife, Ale, and I have twin girls and we talk all the time about what we want for them. One of Ale's big goals is that she wants them to be worldly, and that's a natural thing for us because we both love to travel. We love differences in cultures. And for me, I want them to be difference makers. I want them to be individuals, to be self-thinking and to be motivated team players. In conceptualizing what we'd like our children to be, obviously we're just trying to lay the foundation for them to have those skills and tools. Then they decide what they want to be. Some nature, some nurture, I suppose.

But look at the nurture. We nurture our kids. We raise them, and we're always setting an example for them to mimic, good or bad. And in some ways, you know, our basic response is to mimic our parents. Our girls are young, and we don't force them to be involved in what we're doing. But we definitely put it in front of them. They're the first children in my family tree who have been privileged enough to have access to whatever they want. That's scary as a parent because you think well, here's one way that I can screw them up. So, it's important for us just to show them that this isn't how it is for everyone. And I think that the best way to do that is to do what my dad did and say, "I'm so lucky and here's why: Not everyone has this." We started telling them that some kids don't have food or shoes or a mother or a father, and just get their little minds thinking. And something's registering. I don't mind pointing out those differences and inequalities to them — this person over here is sick or can't walk as easily as you can or is homeless. They begin to get a realization that they should feel thankful and that they should feel concern for people. But that's really it. I don't structure it. I just take the opportunity. Instead of hiding them from the ills of the world, let them know they're out there. That there are kids out there that don't get dinner.

Not every kid, not everyone has the same things in life, but at the same time, we are all the same. At my foundation, I've started to think about this same idea — We Are One Team. We've put it on T-shirts and baby onesies (We Are Onesie). I really believe that. We all came from the same place, we're all connected. And whether you're born in Paradise Valley or Sudan, it is not something you choose. That choice is made for you. Where you grow up, whether you're physically or economically challenged, is not your fault. It is your fault if you don't make the most of each day and try your best, though, right? So that's what I'm trying to instill in my kids, to teach them the power of energy and having a great spirit about them. And that they have a decision to make every day: Is this going to be a good day or a bad day? You get to ask yourself, how lucky am I?

*If you feel lucky. And if you feel
able and you feel willing, you can
do so much to help."*
Steve Nash

BE THE CHANGE

How to Coach Kids and Modern Mentors

Young people need mentors. To be a mentor is to be a wise guide and caring confidant, someone to whom a young person might turn for advice or support as they transition to adulthood.

GREG ROGERS IS AN EXPERT in chaos control, be it on the rugby pitch or at the wheel of a minivan loaded with screaming kids. The long-time teacher and rugby coach is also a father of seven. Greg has never claimed to have all the answers when it comes to raising kids, but he's forever grateful that people trust him with their children. We know Greg well because he mentored Marc in leadership and in life.

Kids who run for class president assume they were born to lead, the rest of us don't know it or dare to think it. Jocks are usually the last to presume they have a role to play away from the basketball court or the football field. Greg helps convince athletes that they have much more to offer than a hard tackle.

Greg was Marc's Grade 9 teacher. He understood quickly that this smart kid was drawn to student council but too shy to participate. One day, Greg pulled Marc aside and challenged him to try out for the rugby team. Just to get to the tryouts, Marc trained long hours, lifting weights in his bedroom and

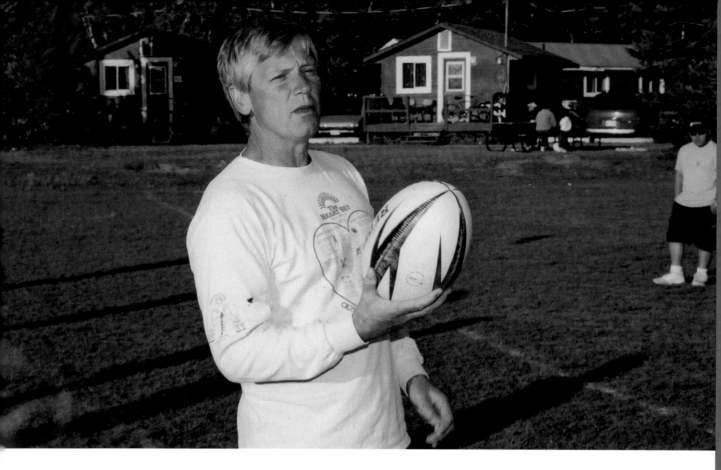

running laps in the rain. He'll never forget his first game. He'd assumed he'd be a bench warmer, but instead Greg threw him in at the start. From that day, Marc learned many lessons about sportsmanship and governance. A few years later, Marc was happy to step up when Greg called on the team to mentor a group of Grade 9 boys.

Greg had received an unusual assignment from Brother Lawrence Maher, the esteemed principal of Brebeuf College School. Brother Lawrence pointed to a disheveled group of freshman at the school. "They just don't look like Brebeuf material," he complained. "Can you do something?" Greg sized up the boys. He noticed a few untucked shirts, a couple of crooked ties and a handful of wild-looking teens. What was he to do? "Model them after your rugby team," Brother Lawrence advised. The principal was not asking Greg to turn the scrawny band into a burly squad. Instead, he wanted the coach to shape future leaders. After Greg considered the request, he advised his boss that he was taking the Grade 9s and the rugby team to a sports camp. Brother Lawrence voiced concerns about broken noses and dislocated shoulders. "Trust

Extraordinary teacher, coach and mentor, Greg Rogers

Children are likely to live up to what you believe of them."

Lady Bird Johnson

former first lady of the United States

me," Greg replied.

During the three-day, off-campus adventure, the rugby team showed the freshmen the ropes — literally! The big boys and their protégés took on the camp's climbing wall, swinging vine and high ropes. They played non-competitive soccer, football, basketball and "touch" rugby. In between the team-building activities, the seniors shared stories of history, tradition and life at Brebeuf. By the end of the expedition, the Grade 9s were friends with each other and with the older boys whom they had feared. When the boys returned to Brebeuf, the freshmen filed off the bus with their heads held high.

A few days later, Coach Greg was chatting with his rugby players about how well the Grade 9 tuneup had gone when a player raised his hand. "Anything else, coach?" As you might have guessed, the eager kid was Marc. "Absolutely," Greg replied. During the months that followed, the coach and his team leveraged their rugby-player status in an effort to give back. The players started with a bench-press contest. For every pound lifted, they collected pledges for Covenant House, a shelter for street kids. Greg helped Marc to organize Wear your Civvies Day. For $2, students could go without ties and blazers. Thanks to car washes and pizza fundraisers, the team made a mark at school and in the neighborhood.

Years later, Greg continues to play a significant role in our lives. He's now co-ordinator of student leadership for the Toronto Catholic District School Board. He also helps us lead trips of high school students to Kenya. He's showed us how young people — athletes, in particular — can contribute locally and globally. Greg was not just a mentor, he was also a role model. In turn and in time, we became mentors for others. We paid it forward, as they say. If there's one lesson we've learned in our work with Free The Children — and thanks to people like Greg — it's that young people need mentors. To be a mentor is to be a wise guide and caring confidant, someone to whom a young person might turn for advice or support. In the absence of extended families, mentors can be there to reach out. In the rush of our 24/7 world, they can dare to slow down and help.

Touchstone and Foundations

Shelley recalls making a nervous call to the Chinese Community Association looking for a Mandarin-speaker to play with her fourteen-month-old daughter, Cleo. In halting English, Bin, a twenty-seven-year-old pediatrician from Shanghai, offered her services. Twice a week, she dropped by to sing songs, play clapping games and teach the Mandarin words for cat, dog and cookie. Bin knew more about Chinese adoption than most immigrants from China. As a pediatrician, she had seen grieving parents walk away from a baby daughter at birth. Over long talks about China, she and Shelley became good friends. The strong, educated and ambitious immigrant with a kind heart and a quick laugh was a wonderful role model for Cleo. Based on this early friendship, Shelley encouraged her adoption agency to start a friendship program that pairs immigrants with adoptive families.

She continues to seek out caring mentors. Mom and daughter remember Cleo's first day at her rhythmic gymnastics club. Sing, the Chinese coach, scooped up Cleo and held her on her knee where they watched the other gymnasts. Several of the other girls were adopted from China and other countries. From Day 1, Sing has demonstrated that it's not enough to be exceptional athletes — the girls must also be good citizens. The athletes perform at nursing homes and at such community events as Asian Heritage Month and International Children's Day. Twice a year they perform for the retired nuns who live next to the gym. After a devastating earthquake in China, the girls put on a performance to raise money for the victims. Thanks to Sing's leadership, the girls have learned to give back and to take pride in their heritage.

Now that Cleo is ten, Shelley arranges "dates" with cool, older Chinese immigrants. Cleo's face lights up when Alicia — a third-year science major with great clothes, a wicked sense of humor and a passion for science — invites her out for hot chocolate. When you're a tween or teen in a mostly white world, it's a comfort to connect with someone who looks just like you.

At We Day in 2008, music guru and *Canadian Idol* judge Farley Flex asked the eight thousand kids in Ricoh Coliseum to repeat after him:

1. Find a mentor.
2. Find out what they did to get where they are.
3. Do exactly the same thing.

One good relationship with an attentive adult can dramatically and positively influence the life of a young person. A caring adult can provide a teen with a foundation on which to build. In the same way, a warm-hearted nurturer can buoy a teen's self-esteem, encourage study and discourage such diversions as crime and drugs.[1] In fact, long-term

HOW TO FIND A MENTOR

1. Sign your kids up for activities run by would-be mentors.

2. Find babysitters with great attributes to share with your kids.

3. Hire tutors who are solid role models.

4. Contact a community organization that specializes in pairing kids with caring adults.

Josh Apostol laughs with his mentor at a Take Action Academy

studies show that when a young person has a mentor, he or she will be 80 percent more likely to finish high school, 46 percent less likely to use drugs, 27 percent less likely to use alcohol and 52 percent less likely to skip school. Having a mentor is also linked to improved relationships with family and friends.[2]

You don't have to be a teacher to play a significant role in a child's life. You need few qualifications, in fact. It's not the length of your résumé that matters; it's the size of your heart and the depth of your capacity to care. Mentors come from all neighborhoods in all shapes and sizes. Coaches, counselors and faith leaders can provide guidance, so can family friends and wise peers (not all mentors have to be older).

Boys and Girls Clubs specialize in matching kids with mentors, as do Big Brothers and Big Sisters. In his younger years, Dad mentored two boys through Big Brothers. It is increasingly difficult to find guides and gurus. Families are fractured. Older generations are separate and away. Teachers are overworked and under pressure to prepare their bursting classrooms for standardized testing — there's little time for back and forth about anything but curriculum. On top of all this, many of us don't even know our neighbors.

Go-to adults are needed desperately. Little Brothers and Little Sisters today have to wait a couple of years for a match. The organizations fret about what this will mean to youngsters in limbo. In the absence of mentors, they've started "Big Bunches," so kids can go to basketball games or movies with a couple of volunteers. It's not the same as having a single special mentor, but it's a start. Craig once spoke at a celebration hosted by a Big Brothers and Big Sisters chapter. He recalls watching a middle-aged man assist an elderly gentleman into the room — father and son, he assumed. Not quite. In fact, it was a Big Brother and his Little Brother, a pair matched thirty years earlier and still in touch.

A Good Turn Every Day

We've joked that Dad has no memory for details, yet when we sat down over lunch to talk about the influence Boy Scouts had on our family, he was flooded by recollections of long ago camping trips. Craig entered Scouting at five — Beavers first, then Cubs and Scouts. The movement inspired his passion for the outdoors, leadership and service. (Full disclosure: Craig fully admits he's a walking cliché — when he sees a senior shuffling across the road, he can't help but offer to help.)

Of course Scouts wasn't just about ghost stories and collecting badges — although that part appealed to Craig's competitive streak — it was about spending time with Dad, working side by side. Although Dad wasn't sporty or outdoorsy, he volunteered as a cook and "gopher" on the camping trips. He's actually a pretty good chef. "Growing up, if I didn't cook, we wouldn't have eaten," he explains of the skills picked up after his mother's death. In a way, that's why he agreed to go camping — somebody had to do it. He

HOW TO BE A GOOD MENTOR

- **BE PATIENT:** Cultivating trust takes time. A youngster may not show it at first, but your help may be just what is needed. Keep at it.

- **TRY TO UNDERSTAND A CHILD'S VIEWPOINT:** By listening and understanding, you show you care.

- **SET BOUNDARIES:** Mentors aren't meant to replace family or social service professionals. If problems come up, a mentor can guide a young person to additional help.

- **CELEBRATE DIFFERENCES:** Working with a young person from a different background broadens a mentor's horizons and deepens understanding of other people and cultures.

- **BE HONEST:** If you make mistakes, admit it. Say you're sorry. Taking responsibility for one's actions is a skill that you can exemplify.

- **BE AVAILABLE:** Just the sound of your concerned voice can make a big difference.

- **BE POSITIVE:** Ask yourself, "What encouragement can I give if my young friend disappoints himself or herself?" Mentors are in the business of helping young people make the most of their lives. Allow the child to make a few "growing" mistakes when they learn new things.

- **BE SUPPORTIVE:** A little bit of praise in a critical world can transform a child. Your faith in them can be the greatest gift you can give.

BE THE CHANGE

We sign off every letter and every e-mail with these famous words of Mahatma Gandhi. The story at the heart of this sage advice has altered ever so slightly with each retelling. Here is our version:

A mother weighed down by worry once walked a great distance to see Gandhi. She wanted the great spiritual and political leader to order her son to stop eating sugar. The boy's addiction was endangering his health. The mom thought that if Gandhi — the boy's hero — ordered him to quit the sweet stuff, he might actually listen.

"Mahatma, out of humbleness, I ask for your help and guidance. Please talk to him. He'll listen to you."

Gandhi considered every word. Both mother and son leaned in to hear his advice.

"Come back in a month," he said. "I will have my answer."

The woman was disappointed. Mother and son made the long journey home. One month later, they returned. "Mahatma, please talk to him. He'll listen to you."

Again they leaned in to listen.

"Young man, listen to your mother," Gandhi said. "I want you to stop eating sugar."

That's it? The mom couldn't help but be a bit indignant. "Couldn't you have told him that last month?" she asked. "We wouldn't have had to make this long journey a second time."

Gandhi looked at the woman. "Madam," he replied, "last month I, too, was eating sugar."

He explained that he'd had to cut out sugar from his diet before he could ask the same of the boy.

"We must be the change we wish to see in the world," he said.

enjoyed the challenge of trying to please an army of boys armed with forks and spoons. He loved subjecting them to franks and beans. Dad delighted in time spent with his son. More than that, he welcomed the chance to mentor the young boys. Dad's commitment told the kids that they were important and that Scouts were important, too. Craig was proud of the way his friends looked up to Dad.

Step Up to the Plate

Leaders and coaches can play pivotal roles in a child's development. When Marc decided to try out for the rugby team, he shared his doubts and frustrations with Coach Rogers. Greg egged Marc on as he ran lap after lap on the rugby field. He managed to convince his team that almost anything was possible. He also persuaded Marc that he was overflowing with leadership potential. (Greg could deliver a barnburner of a pep talk!)

We may not always give much thought about coaches, but we should. After-school sports consume the lives of North American children. Some thirty million children participate in youth sports under the direction of 4.5 million coaches and 1.5 million administrators.[3] With extra-curricular practices and weekend tournaments, it's quite possible your daughter or son spends more time with a coach than with you! For many kids, coaches are larger than life. They watch and mimic. When a coach yells at the ref or at his players or encourages violence as a means to an end, young athletes soak it up. If a coach stresses competition over co-operation, the lesson endures. Not all coaches lead like Greg Rogers. Some use ridicule and anger to motivate athletes — even the novices. If for no other reason, parents need to be involved with the team. Get to know the coach beyond his or her win-loss record.

Researchers once studied the competitiveness, social hierarchies and attitudes of seventy-three athletes — between the age of five and eight — in three different after-school sports programs. These kids, most of whom were boys, were mostly white. Some of the teams studied co-operation and fair play. Others didn't. On the more competitive teams, kids often cried if they lost. On less competitive teams, kids didn't get so upset. Athletes on the less competitive bench were observed jokingly making bets about which team would win. Beyond the fun factor, how were the top athletes treated compared to those who were less skilled? Researchers found that top athletes received more attention and better treatment from coaches and players. Coaches of the competitive teams allowed their top players to form cliques and to hog the ball. Less competitive coaches included all kids, regardless of skill. The athletic kids were asked to name three people they'd pick for a team and three they'd invite to a birthday party. The jocks chose the same people in each circumstance — they did not want the clumsy kid on their team or at their party. This study shows that a coach can influence how children play — and perhaps party — for years to come.[4]

Players don't usually choose coaches, of course. But parents can seek out leagues that stress sportsmanship and co-operation and leadership skills.

In the same way, parents can model this behavior on the sidelines and in the bleachers and in the car on the way home from the game. One of the reasons for a continent-wide shortage of coaches is that there aren't enough volunteers. Coaches often remark that they can't withstand the pressure and criticism of expectant parents, who hope Johnny or Suzie will end up with an athletic scholarship. When we sign up our kids for sports, we need to consider seriously what we hope our children will gain: A killer knuckle ball? A powerful butterfly stroke? A sense of integrity, fair play and co-operation? Or, maybe, skills *and* character.

Bangladesh or Bust

As we've mentioned, Mom and Dad shy from the spotlight. When parents seek them out, it's to ask some variation on the following question: "Why in the world did you let Craig go to Asia by himself when he was twelve?" Their answer, in two words: Alam Rahman.

Craig's life has been filled with fortunate coincidences. One week after reading about Iqbal, he noticed a newspaper article about Youth Action Network, a group that was inviting organizations to participate in an information fair. Craig called their number and ended up in a long conversation with Alam, a recent university graduate whose parents were from Bangladesh. At the end of the call, Craig committed to gathering some of his Grade 7 friends to set up a booth about child labor. The next day, Craig asked his teacher for permission to address his class. The rest, as they say, is history. The founding members of Free The Children arrived at the event armed with posters and idealism. It was there that Craig met Alam face to face. In no time, the young

man became a mentor.

On the day Craig will never forget, Alam invited Craig to travel with him to South Asia. As we've mentioned, Mom and Dad set many preconditions. For starters, he had to convince them he'd be safe — arranging for trusted adults to meet him every step of the way. None of this would have went anywhere had Mom and Dad not trusted Alam. A mathematician by training, Alam would methodically explain why he had no interest in staying in North America to become a bean counter. During the trip, he and Craig discussed materialism, consumerism, wealth and happiness. During rickshaw rides, over curries in open-air markets and while traveling the back roads, they discussed books, movies, friends and family. They also talked about the meaning of life and legacy — challenging conversations for anyone, especially a twelve-year-old! Alam insisted they live on three dollars a day — food, transport and accommodation — and splurge on nothing. Together, they walked his talk.

One of the great mentors of all time is Obe Wan Kenobi, Luke Skywalker's guide in *Star Wars*. Alam was not that kind of mentor. He did not have all the answers, but he did ask lots of questions. Craig remembers one thirteen-hour journey in southern India, a region that is home to fireworks and match factories. Craig and Alam wanted to gain access to the factories and document — with a video recorder — the plight of the children inside. The bus was filled with chickens and goats and sleepy passengers who hadn't showered in days, perhaps weeks. Loud Hindi movies played overhead. When there was quiet, Alam lobbed question after question at his travel companion.

"Why do you think I don't have a TV?"

Craig was stumped: "You don't like the programming? Your parents banned it? You can't afford one? You're allergic to TV? You don't have room?"

He tried to change the topic, but Alam asked again.

After eight hours, Craig gave up. "I don't have a TV because I don't need one," Alam confessed. Craig was flummoxed. What about *The Simpsons?*

Alam then asked Craig what it meant to be "cool." Was "coolness" essential to happiness? He helped Craig recognize that you don't need "things" to be happy. He showed his young friend that being different — as long as you are true to yourself — is not just OK but ideal.

Alam talked about getting married, Craig mused about dating. Alam contemplated a career, Craig thought about high school. Alam never laughed at Craig, although on some level he must have found Craig's concerns hilarious. He didn't lead but instead followed a few steps behind as Craig made important decisions. Soon enough, like many mentors, he stepped into the background and let Craig continue his adventure alone. While they were both still in Asia, Alam told Craig that when his trip was over he planned to stay to help the child laborers they'd encountered. Back in North America, Craig would tell the world about these same children. They'd both be doing the same work, just in different ways. Of the many lessons Craig learned from Alam, perhaps the greatest was of the power of a mentor.

SMALL ACTIONS › EVERY DAY

1. JUST LIKE YOU:
Think of the mentors in your life. Ask yourself why they played a significant role in your development. Consider how you might model their actions in your own relationships with young people.

2. A WORD OF THANKS:
List the mentors in your child's life. Take the next step and thank that person for the difference they are making.

3. SEEK SUPPORT:
If your child doesn't have any mentors, find some. Look to valued coaches, community leaders, trusted teachers or faith leaders. Look for a trusted teen or a wise friend.

4. IF IT TAKES A VILLAGE ... CREATE ONE:
From time to time, find a reason to gather the people who are important in the life of your child. Throw a party on their tenth birthday, for example. Let everyone celebrate your child, not just school chums.

What My Father Gave to Me

*Two-time Grammy Award-winning singer-songwriter, **Jason Mraz** has had his international breakthrough, all the while with his chart-topping ditty, "I'm Yours" spreading a message of generosity and respect. It has become his message. Having performed at We Day and going silent with the Vow of Silence, Jason is also a heavily involved environmentalist. Here he reflects on his relationship with his father, and how a few words shaped Jason into the person he is today.*

MY LIFE IS A RESULT OF MY PARENTS. That includes all my caregivers, music teachers and mentors. Although I grew up in two different households as my parents divorced when I was young, I wouldn't be where I am today without them. My life is a result of my parents supporting my creative interests. My parents knew that I loved to bang around on the piano at home. Or to make short videos with the home video camera. They were the ones that drove me to the music rehearsals and piano lessons.

When I was sixteen, I would work with my Dad after school. He built fences for a living. In those days, I learned a lot. I learned how to drive a truck. I learned how to clean up a construction site. And, of course, I learned about the grueling nature of manual labor. But most of all, I learned to pursue my dreams. All from my father.

On one particularly sun-drenched day, I was helping my Dad drill a fresh hole. His muddy hands were gripping his posthole digger, or what he called his Ph.D. With a perfect line of fence posts standing proud behind us, we were digging the thirty or fortieth hole when he stopped to wipe the sweat from his brow. Resting against a newly-planted post, he turned to me and said, "Son, I want you to do what you love to do." He paused for a moment and sighed, exhaling a deep breath. He then continued, "And it will never feel like a job to you."

At this point in my life, I was questioning my abilities as a musician. I was questioning my future. But those few words were a moment of great clarity for me. My dad was a pretty quiet guy, so when he did speak, you listened. And as a role model to me, I wanted to emulate my father. But when he said those words, I was free to live my dreams. I remember thinking after, "Well, Dad doesn't want me to dig holes. Dad wants me to live my dream." That gave me the green light to be adventurous for the next twenty years.

And I have always done *just* that. Today, as I reflect on this, I realize how much of a greater service I am to the world by heeding that advice. It woke me up to the responsibility I have. I feel like I was raised to be me. To me, if poetry is stirring in the gut of a young child, then the universe wants that child to be a poet. That there is a voice the child needs to share with the world. It's not going to serve for this child, then, to become a bricklayer. He might serve the community, but he's not going to serve the world. And it might not serve that child's happiness and fulfillment. That's what I believe my father gave to me: The freedom to make my music. The freedom to explore and be an adventurer. I tried college twice, but both times I received opportunities for my music outside of the classroom. And during these times of uncertainty, my parents were extra supportive.

And now I'm passing on that same message that my dad gave me in my music. One of my songs called, "I'm Yours" shares a similar message of generosity. Like my dad gave me the ability to dream, I want to give others the same support. It's not like he told me what to do, he just left the door open for me to do what I love. It has sent me on with a purpose, the message entwined unconsciously. And the whole time it was fueled by the support from my father.

I couldn't have done what I loved if it weren't for my dad telling me to do what I wanted. And although I work constantly, I feel like I have been on vacation for fifteen years.

To me, if poetry is stirring in the gut of a young child, then the universe wants that child to be a poet. That there is a voice the child needs to share with the world. It's not going to serve for this child, then, to become a bricklayer. He might serve the community, but he's not going to serve the world."

Jason Mraz

LEARNING THROUGH SERVICE

From Cradle to Classroom to Community

Classrooms that encourage service help students develop a strong sense of social responsibility and citizenship skills. Community involvement increases the chances kids will volunteer when they grow up. On top of that, children who "learn" to serve usually do well academically and socially.

OLA OTUN WAS BORN in New Jersey after her parents arrived from Nigeria. She grew up to become an avid sports fan and an editor of her school paper. Ola works hard and strives to make the most of all she's been given. One day she hopes to study anthropology and public health.

Shannon Stevens has struggled on her own in a tough part of Toronto since she was sixteen. She's determined to do well in high school while caring for her sister and working at a neighborhood video store.

Then there's Jeremie Griffin from the south side of Chicago. He's a five-foot-six point guard with big dreams of scoring a basketball scholarship.

On different paths with different dreams, these students united behind a single goal when they joined nine others in a remote corner of the world. The teens were in rural

O Ambassadors
sharing the peace

Kenya to kick off O Ambassadors, a program we developed with Oprah's Angel Network. We've been working with Oprah since Craig first appeared on her show when he was sixteen. Every kid selected for that first O Ambassadors group had studied up on world affairs and global issues in East Africa. Each had organized kissing booths, dodgeball tournaments, carnivals and the like to help finance a school for the Kipsigis tribe. Once they'd collectively raised $8,500, the kids made tracks for Africa where they put their ideas into action and their sweat into construction.

The teens watched on as the Kipsigis sacrificed a goat to bless the building site, then faked sips of the animal's blood when the elders offered it around. Few of them had heaved a hammer or wielded a pick or even lifted a shovel. If they had any muscles, it was from holding cell phones to their ears. During the trip, the team learned to herd goats and fetch water and help with chores. Shannon swung from frustration to joy. Jeremie was so inspired by the Kipsigis children's ability to find happiness in adversity that he recommitted to his basketball dream — deciding that what he lacked in height he'd

WHAT DIFFERENCE WOULD ONE YEAR MAKE?

Middle school students who participated in school-based service learning for one year were found to maintain their concern for others. Grade 6, 7 and 8 students not enrolled in service learning projects actually declined in their compassion. The study included a racially diverse group of 682 students enrolled in three middle schools. All kids in this age group talked less to their parents, but girls enrolled in service learning projects were best at keeping communication lines open. Kids who clocked the most hours of caring curriculum also came to believe in the importance of helping others, pursued better grades and believed their school was filled with opportunities.[5]

make up for with determination. One day after helping the Kipsigis girls, Ola hid in the bushes to sob. It had dawned on her that this might have been her life had her parents not left Nigeria. After a few days of bickering and floundering, things got easier — especially when the slightly skeptical Kipsigis pitched in. Mamas prepared food, dads left their fields to help, future students showed up to lend a hand. Brick by brick, the school went up.

There was a lot riding on our dozen do-gooders. Every minute of the journey was documented by a video crew and later edited for broadcast to millions on *Oprah*. We hoped the program might motivate the moms and dads and teachers and administrators in the TV audience. We dared to imagine it could inspire the creation of O Ambassador chapters across North America. Our trailblazers were transformed, so were *Oprah's* viewers when they met the teens on a show in spring 2008. It was an awesome debut. The show demonstrated why schools are the perfect place to introduce global issues. Since that program, two thousand O Ambassadors clubs have been created. The groups explore United Nations' Millennium Development Goals — tackling poverty, education, health and sustainable development — and educate classmates to help communities overseas.

One club in Fort Collins, Colorado, was started by a passionate mom in search of a purpose. Shana Stegner Bode, a mother of three children — ten, eight and five at the time — was living a crazy-busy life. On the rare occasion she had to reflect, she worried she was not making a difference. She tried to follow Oprah's advice: "Get out of bed each morning and ask yourself how you can serve." When she heard about O Ambassadors, it occurred to her that such a club would encourage kids at Shepardson Elementary School to help others a world away.

Shana completed her Master's thesis on the role of parents in schools, so she knew better than most that kids do better academically and emotionally when parents take an active interest. "By being present at school, we tell our kids that school is important," she explains. Her research revealed that it's not just finances or competing obligations that keep parents from getting involved. In fact, often it's that they don't know where to start. Shana decided to ask the school if she could apply to create an O Ambassadors club. In order to join, kids had to answer one question: "Why do you want to become an O Ambassador and take action to make the world a better place for all children?" Applicants drew pictures and performed skits. Shana's son Evan, then in Grade 4, wrote a heartfelt poem called "I Can Make A Difference."

The dozens of kids who joined the club decided to raise $5,000 for a community in Ecuador. They sold reusable shopping bags and held a "$2-a-day" campaign — one third of the world's population lives on less — encouraging students and staff to contribute. To top off their efforts, the school principal volunteered to become a sundae if the students met their target. Sure enough, four months later, she showed up in her "sundae best" — whipped cream, chocolate sauce and cherries. The O enthusiasm was contagious. Shana cherishes a phone message from one girl who asked, "Is it too late to change the world? I want to sign up."

There's no telling what can happen when schools reach beyond the Three Rs to the Three Cs. We think of High Tech High International, a school in San Diego, California, where every student completes two hundred hours of volunteer service; international studies and overseas travel are integral to the curriculum. Then there's Easter Sun Academy, in Boulder, Colorado, where students study Mandarin Chinese, world music and dance. The O Ambassadors there raised $866 selling CDs featuring club members performing in Chinese. And there's Glebe Montessori School where kids built and supported a school by fundraising with pizza days and musical performances and sales of homemade greeting cards.

Service with a Smile

We ask a lot of our schools. Reading, writing and arithmetic, for starters. Increasingly, though, many want schools to teach values and ethics and citizenship — filling in where parents falter. Some want schools to stick to the basics. Others argue that teachers have a responsibility to turn young people into active and empathetic citizens. We agree it starts in the home but also know that schools can play an influential role. Classrooms that encourage service help students develop a strong sense of social responsibility and citizenship skills. Getting involved at a young age increases the chances kids will volunteer when they grow up. (Bonus marks: Students who "learn" to serve usually do well academically and socially.)

During the past decade, we've helped thousands of North American schools foster local and global links, setting up volunteer programs in schools and helping develop service-based curriculum. The two of us, along with our

Jack Nigro, Craig's Grade 9 teacher, with his daughter on a school trip

fellow teams of facilitators and speakers, have also met millions of students on our We Day speaking tours. Crucial to the success of any of these programs is the inspiration of teachers, administrators and parents.

Thanks to Mom and Dad, we've watched countless students step delicately into the world. We give the same thanks to teachers who dared to push beyond the Three Rs. Craig thinks fondly of Jack Nigro, his Grade 9 homeroom teacher. Marc, conversely, has never stopped tipping his hat to Lou Paonessa.

Lou was the director and producer of many musicals at Marc's high school. He helped students find their voice and embrace the spotlight. Under Lou's tutelage, the once shy Marc appeared in a couple of plays. The pair also worked on the school newspaper where few things were ever black or white. Marc served as editor and Lou as staff adviser. Lou will never forget taking a call at home about a letter to the editor. Marc wanted to know if he should print a note that urged the Catholic high school to install condom machines in the boys' washrooms. As a Catholic educator, Lou knew he should not condone birth control. And yet he felt it would be "negligent" to ignore the issue. He encouraged Marc to write a counterargument and print the pieces side by side. Marc published the stories on the front of the paper. If there was controversy, he figured they could snip out the offending articles and still distribute the paper. As if on cue, administrators seized the papers as soon as they hit the hallways. The vice principal eventually allowed them to circulate—minus the offending articles. Throughout the fallout, Lou stuck by his student. Marc will be forever thankful to his teacher for showing him that there are times when authority — even a respected authority — can and should be challenged.

Craig found his champion in Jack Nigro. Like all good teachers, Jack considered the world a classroom. By the time the two met, Craig was increasingly in conflict with educators who begrudged the time Free The Children stole from his academics. Jack first saw Craig on a TV news clip featuring a speech he made to the Ontario Federation of Labour that raised $150,000 for Free The Children. After the event, a journalist had asked Craig how he managed to combine school and activism. Craig struggled to answer.

At the time, Jack was teaching at Mary Ward Catholic Secondary School, a government-funded neighborhood school that allowed self-directed learning. Kids attended class once each week, working at their own pace during the remainder of the time. The school was a draw for athletes, actors and musicians. So why not activists? "Out of the blue, I called Craig," Jack recalls. "I wanted him to come take a look." At the time, Craig was contemplating a scholarship to a prestigious boys' school that thought

Craig's activism would make him a role model for other students. Like we mentioned earlier, the school had warned him that he could not miss classes for Free The Children work. After lengthy consideration, Craig decided to study at Mary Ward where Jack proved he was willing to advocate on his behalf at every opportunity. On one occasion, Craig missed an assignment because he was in San Francisco to attend Mikhail Gorbachev's State of the World Forum. Craig shared the stage there with Jane Goodall and others. "The teacher was not happy and I had to mediate," Jack remembers. "I had to say, 'Here is what he did with Bill Gates and Gorbachev and how we can help Craig take these experiences and make them fit into the curriculum.'" Craig will always be grateful for Jack's willingness to negotiate. "I think it's important sometimes to challenge how education should happen," Jack says. "I think those who embraced Craig's situation learned a lot about the value of experiences that take place outside the classroom."

Like Jack, we believe schools must embrace kids who are "different" — sports stars and would-be idols and, yes, social activists. "I'm waiting to pack up my kids and take them to Africa with me to build a school," he says of his young family. "I want them to be there when it opens, to see the look on their faces when it is finished."

Volunteer Now. But How?

In 1999, Ontario, a province in Canada, announced that high school students would have to complete forty hours of service before graduation. The legislation prompted

AFTER-SCHOOL SPECIAL

Playing volleyball? Volunteering? Rocking the tuba in the school band? Researchers surveyed 1,259 teens in the U.S. about their extracurricular activities. The good news is that kids involved in extra activities had higher grades than those who did not participate. But not all endeavors were created equal.

Jacquelynne Eccles and Bonnie Barber looked at participation in five types of activities. Two years later, they studied how this influenced such things as marks, absenteeism and college attendance. Teens who participated in pro-social activities such as church or volunteer work "reported less involvement in problem behaviors," showed "better academic performance and greater likelihood of being enrolled full-time in college at age twenty one" than those who weren't involved in extracurricular activities. These students also reported liking school more and had higher grades in Grade 12. Teens involved in other after-school activities responded similarly, except for those on sports teams.

Teens that played on school teams in Grade 10 also reported the same benefits, except by Grade 12, all tended to drink alcohol. It's theorized that school athletes identify with a "cool" group and, therefore, feel compelled to engage in other "cool" activities."[4]

many questions. Top of the list: How could "volunteerism" be "mandatory?" Where would kids find the time? What was the point? The government hoped students would catch the fever of civic participation and become life-long volunteers. Unfortunately, educators had no idea how to respond, and there weren't enough volunteer gigs to go around. Some sixty thousand students were combing Toronto for opportunities to chip in. By the end of that school year, students — many with top marks — faced not graduating because they had yet to acquire their volunteer hours.

Irate parents flooded call-in shows: Many placements required kids under eighteen to work with an adult; parents didn't have time. Some parents coaxed friends to vouch for service never completed. Others created bogus jobs — mowing a friend's lawn or walking a dog or painting a fence — that were light on altruism. What counted as volunteering? Parents couldn't fathom what kids were supposed to learn from licking stamps or delivering flyers. The Toronto District School Board, which is the fourth largest school board in North America, was stumped. It had tens of thousands of students with nowhere to volunteer. Eager to press forward, they invited us to help design a program to create volunteer opportunities while perhaps even generating enthusiasm for the government initiative.

In response, Volunteer Now was born. Our goal was to show teens how to identify and then meet the needs of their communities. Three times a year, we sent our facilitators — recent college grads who had been active volunteers — into high schools to meet with "Volunteer Ambassadors" — team captains and cheerleaders and flute players and other student leaders. We

created print resources for the Grade 10 students called *Take Action!* and *Take More Action!* We discussed social issues and coached kids to give speeches, combat apathy and launch action plans. In turn, these kids transferred their newly acquired skills to other students.

The program, which continues today, was more than a glorified pep rally. It encouraged kids to find or create placements where they could combine their gifts with their passions. Students set up their own volunteer tutoring programs, organized environmental cleanups, started after-school sports leagues, arranged social justice speaker series and designed websites about social issues. Some kids even devoted themselves to helping others meet their community-service requirements. They would load students and parents on buses en route to polluted parks or homeless shelters. The program has since spread to fourteen school boards and employs ten full-time facilitators who travel from school to school.

School-based community-service projects can have a long-lasting influence when students define and develop their plans. It makes a significant difference when kids understand the issues, develop relationships with the people they're helping and see the benefits of their work. When the project is done, the significance of their efforts is reinforced if they get to discuss their work and celebrate their accomplishments —a reminder of how much schools can do when they reach beyond the basics.

Roots and Wings

We are thrilled to be a small part of a huge movement that's working to foster service learning in schools. As we've traveled across North America, we have visited some amazing programs. One school, for example, requires students in Spanish class to work through their lessons with Spanish-speaking seniors. Other biology students have worked to clean up a stream so that salmon can spawn. When students return from the field, they're encouraged to talk and write about what they've learned. Allow us to tell you about a couple of other inspiring schools.

Ohlone Farm boasts one acre, many overflowing gardens, twelve chickens, two sheep, a pair of goats and an enthusiastic student body. A local paper once described the Palo Alto elementary school as a "place where there's no assigned homework, feelings are important and artichokes and goat cheese are a part of learning."[1] On a visit to Ohlone, you might find students tending tomatoes, or else feeding goats or chickens or sheep or maybe selling produce in the school's "Everything Shop" that earned $6,500 during a recent year. You might also see kids absorbed in daily sharing circles.

Working the farm is not an extracurricular activity at the public school. Instead, it is embedded deeply in the curriculum. Kids learn biology from real life. The life cycle of a pumpkin teaches lessons in science. Weighing pumpkins during harvest is a math lesson, as are the transactions that occur when they are sold. Once a week, each class goes to the farm that includes a native Ohlone Indian habitat with a pond surrounded by orange poppies, wild strawberries and coyote brush. Kids touch, smell and talk about the plants that grow there. Social studies lessons are held outdoors on land where the Ohlone Indians once lived. For a taste of the tribe's food, students use stones to mash sunflower seeds and squish berries into seed cakes.

The school is a draw for many wealthy families in the Silicon Valley — including the Hewletts and the Packards. Apple co-founder and CEO Steve Jobs sent his kids to Ohlone, as have our long-time supporters, Craig and Libby Heimark. Principal Susan Charles says the privileged choose her public school over private options because they "want their children to have a social conscience. They want their kids to give back." The school for the privileged also draws families from East Palo Alto, where parents are more likely to be blue-collar workers than tech tycoons. Susan ensures that students are responsible for themselves, for each other and for their communities. Grade 4 and 5 students let the animals out of their shelters each morning, get them fed and put them back at the end of the day. The older students show younger students how it's done. Tending crops and especially animals fosters responsibility and empathy. "If you don't take care of the plants and they die, it's not the end of the world. You just plant more lettuce and more tomatoes and who really cares. But you can't say 'who cares' about animals. You have to really take care of

WHERE SCHOOLS CAN BEGIN

When it comes to school fundraisers, we've discovered almost anything goes. Here is a place to start:

Vow of Silence

An opportunity to raise awareness on children's rights issues and stand in solidarity with youth who do not have a voice. The Vow of Silence campaign can be done individually or as a group. Being silent can mean speaking no words out loud. It can also mean no form of communication — no talking, e-mail, text messages, hand gestures, writing notes, miming, sign language, saying words without making the sound, etc. Each individual's level of comfort and commitment will determine how they choose to participate in the Vow of Silence campaign.

Brick by Brick

By raising money to build schools through Brick by Brick, students bring education to children who never had the chance to go to school before. This is an important first step in development for communities living in poverty. When you sign up for Brick by Brick, students choose the specific country they want to support. Free The Children sends a campaign kit, including a wall-sized poster to track the fundraising progress and a step-by-step guide to the campaign. Then during the year, build the school one brick at a time by throwing fundraisers and awareness campaigns about education issues.

One Night Out

With an estimated three million homeless people in the United States, the One Night Out campaign raises awareness about homelessness in our cities. On Feb. 25 of each year, we urge students to spend the night in the school gym to reflect on the challenges facing the homeless. Following the event, we challenge students to take meaningful action to raise awareness and help the homeless in their communities. This action could be, for example, a presentation to the student body on homelessness or a clothing drive for a local shelter.

Halloween for Hunger

An annual campaign to alleviate local hunger and raise awareness of global poverty. Started by Jonathan White and first adopted by Free The Children in October 2000, Halloween for Hunger challenges communities to think globally and act locally. Every year, youth from across North America collect non-perishable food items by going door-to-door.

them." Susan recalls the day an old sheep named Jasmine died. "The kids went crazy." They held elaborate memorials. "Children who grow up in urban areas don't know about the cycle of life. Most kids think food comes from a grocery store." Although many school boards do not introduce "service learning" until senior grades, Susan believes educators need to start young. By high school, she says, "kids already feel beaten up by academic requirements. Community service becomes one more requirement. If they approach it with that attitude, it won't stick. We want it to stick."

A Community of Caring Kids

Southridge School in British Columbia, Canada, is another place where service is a part of learning from the first day of school until the last. From kindergarten to Grade 12, all students are required to help out in their neighborhood. (Remember, you can get a head start with early childhood education.) Most studies feature an "action" component. Geography and biology classes, for example, go on field trips to learn about logging and mining. Every Friday, older students serve food at the mission, chatting with the lunch crowd as they work. They arrive with sandwiches made earlier in the day by younger students.

The school supports dozens of community initiatives. A service co-ordinator oversees projects and scouts opportunities to integrate service learning into the government curriculum. A Grade 1 class learning about homelessness organized a hot chocolate sale and blanket drive. A Grade 6 class decided to support a Haitian orphanage after learning about the extreme poverty in that country. (This was before the devastating earthquake.) With the help of a teacher, kids collected bed linens, toys, clothing and other supplies to ship to the orphanage. The students participated in the "Haiti Club" until graduation when they passed on stewardship to an incoming Grade 6 class.

When tragedy hit the school, it was almost expected that the community of children would respond with courage and compassion. Junior school principal, Laurel Middelaer, lost her daughter Alexa in a tragic accident. The toddler and her aunt were struck by a car while feeding horses at the side of a road. Julia Greer and her classmates wanted to show their support.[2] They decided that in Alexa's honor they would make and sell bracelets to raise money for the children's hospital where she spent her final days. The grieving principal was touched deeply. "This is born of their own initiative and compassion," she said. "This community has provided a layer of unexpected healing."[3] The simple gesture was born of the fabric of compassion built into the curriculum of this very special school.

"What we would hope for is that when these kids are in careers—whether it's business, a medical profession, law, or whatever they choose — that they don't judge their success on financial status, and instead understand the influence that they have beyond themselves," says Drew Stephens, head of the school. "We want them to know their choices can be powerful."

Educators like Drew Stephens and Susan Charles demonstrate that teachers have the power to transform children into active global citizens. Parents like Shana Stegner Bode remind us that schools should embrace passionate parents and use their enthusiasm to organize a charity run or to start a social issues club or to book an exciting, world-changing speaker.

Parents dispatch kids to school with a nutritious lunch, a kiss on the forehead and unspoken hopes for the future. We also dare to dream. We imagine what the world would be like — what their future could be — if courage, compassion and community were a part of every curriculum. We'd love every kid to study the Three Cs and to learn through service that Gift + Passion = Better World.

SMALL ACTIONS › EVERY DAY

1. GET INVOLVED:
Broadly show an interest in your child's education. Ask about their report card, go to a Parent Teacher Association meeting, show up for concerts and other events.

2. GET SPECIFIC:
Ask your children, their teachers and school administrators how they encourage community service. If they have days dedicated to helping out, offer to be one of the helpers.

3. VOLUNTEER:
Donate your time in the classroom or to organizing social justice events or even coaching a team or leading the choir.

4. PUT YOUR MONEY DOWN :
Donate your money to bring in inspiring speakers or support field trips.

5. DONATE RESOURCES:
Buy books about heroes or computers to link a classroom to the world.

6. SWEAT THE DETAILS:
Scrutinize the curriculum. If there isn't a service component, discuss its importance with teachers, school administrators and maybe even trustees. Get active in the school council and push for reforms.

7. DID YOU KNOW?
Looking for more about service learning? Here are two websites worth a peek: www.servicelearning.org www.communityservicelearning.ca.

A Very Patriotic Community

Robert Kennedy, Jr. is known as a staunch environmentalist and for his ceaseless groundwork fighting for communities. As an attorney specializing in environmental law, he has put clean water at the core of his mission. Here, he recalls a story he has shared with his own children from time to time. A story that illustrates what dedication and passion meant to him when he worked with the village of Crotonville, but more importantly, what it means for the next generation.

I'M A PROUD FATHER OF SIX. Since my kids were little, I've been sharing with them my passion for the environment and my fight to protect it, in the hopes that they will find their own passions in life — and that they'll understand that they too can help protect those passions, whatever they may be.

Over the years, we've enjoyed family vacations in national parks across North America, from Yosemite to Algonquin to the Everglades. We've hiked, skied, rafted, snowshoed and canoed our way across this great continent and back again. And I believe that these experiences are among the greatest gifts I can give my kids.

Let me digress and tell you a story. It's one that I've told my children now too many times to count.

When I started working for the protection of the Hudson River in 1983, the waters were in bad shape. It had been nearly 20 years since local riverkeepers had begun fighting back in the courtroom against corporate polluters who'd

turned the Hudson into a national joke.

One of the enclaves of the Hudson's commercial fisheries is a little village called Crotonville, New York, located 30 miles north of New York City. By the mid-'60s, the people of Crotonville had been fishing the river continuously since Dutch Colonial times. They used traditional fishing methods that had been passed from the Algonquin Indians to the original Dutch settlers of New Amsterdam and on through the generations.

These weren't powerful people or wealthy environmentalists; they were fisherman, factory workers, carpenters and laborers. Most of them had little hope that they'd ever bring their families to Yosemite or Algonquin or the Everglades. For them, their environment was their backyard. It was the bathing beaches and the swimming holes of the Hudson.

In 1966, Penn Central Railroad began vomiting oil from a four-and-a-half-foot pipe in the Crotonville rail yard. The oil went up the river and blackened the beaches. It made the local shad fish taste like diesel so they couldn't be sold at the fishing markets in New York City. Two million fish were dying each and every day.

For the people of Crotonville, the pollution was an assault not only on their livelihoods, but on their community, their values and, most importantly, their families.

One night in the summer of 1966, 300 men and women from Crotonville came together in the only public building in the town, bent on figuring out what to do — how to save their community, the river they'd built their history on and, in turn, their children's futures.

This was a very patriotic community. It had the highest mortality rate of any town in the United States during World War II. The entire male population joined the marines the day after Pearl Harbor. These were not radicals or militants; they were people whose patriotism was rooted in the bedrock of America. But they had been to the government agencies established to protect Americans from pollution — the Corps of Engineers, the U.S. Coast Guard, the conservation department — and they were given the bum's rush.

So that night their patriotism wavered.

Frustrated and helpless, they began to talk about violence against the corporate polluters. Someone suggested they put a match to the oil slick that was coming out of the Penn Central pipe and burn it down. Someone else said they should roll a mattress up, jam it up the pipe and flood the rail yard with its own waste. They talked about dynamite, about arson and about brute force.

But for each man and woman who was there that night, a family awaited them at home. And for each of those families, there were children who lived and breathed in their parents' image — who, like almost all children, accepted without question that mom and dad always know best.

That night, those men and women decided not to turn to violence. Instead, they discovered and started pushing for the enforcement of a long-forgotten law called the 1888 Rivers and Harbors Act, which, unbeknownst to anyone at the time, stated that it was illegal to pollute any United States waterway — punishable by a large cash penalty.

And one by one, the community started taking the polluters to court, and winning. For each case they won, they earned enough money to pay for the legal costs of the next. And slowly but surely, they began to turn the Hudson back into a vibrant and healthy body of water. The Hudson River is now the richest waterway in the North Atlantic. It produces more pounds of fish per acre and more biomass per gallon than any other waterway in the Atlantic Ocean north of the equator.

When I joined the fight in '83 as their attorney, the Crotonville riverkeepers had made incredible progress with little money and resources — fighting some of the wealthiest and most intimidating corporate entities in America. Since then, we've forced the polluters to pay more than $4.5 billion in remediation, and we've set up our advocacy organization, Waterkeeper Alliance, in locations around the world to protect natural waterways from pollution.

The reason I've shared this story with my kids time and again is to remind them that anyone can change the world, no matter the odds against them. And the reason I share it with you now is to remind you and I that, as adults, parents and mentors, showing the next generation that we're passionate about something and that we're willing to work peacefully to fight for it is one of the greatest gifts we can give our children.

For evidence of that, you need look no further than the children of those patriotic Crotonville citizens who took on the big business polluters back in '66. Today, those children are adults, leading the charge to protect our waterways in Crotonville and across the globe, and sharing their passions with children of their own.

"

Since my kids were little, I've been sharing with them my passion for the environment and my fight to protect it."

Robert Kennedy, Jr.

How to Live Faith Through Service

Through service, we make the world a better place. Even those who are not religious say that acts of kindness inspire faith in humanity.

ALL WAS QUIET WHEN we slipped through a screen door at the home of John and Liane Niles. We stepped over baby gates, around stuffed animals and on top of squeaky toys before we found John in his living room cradling a sleeping six-month-old baby boy. The infant woke when we entered and greeted us with a dimpled smile. It was as if he wanted us to scoop him up and take him home. It was tempting! John told us the baby had been taken at birth from his mother, a drug addict. John and Liane would care for him until a permanent home could be found. Stretched out on a nearby blanket was a new arrival in a bright red sleeper. The baby was wheezing from a chest infection. Abandoned by his mother, he'd been briefly in the care of his grandparents. When they couldn't cope, they turned to the Children's Aid Society, which placed the boy with the Niles Family.

John Niles is a minister with the United Church. For almost two decades, his house has served as a Children's Aid Society "emergency home." During that time, the Niles have sheltered the city's youngest and most vulnerable children — some one thousand babies and toddlers. We've come to think of the couple as the Guardian Saints of the Little Things.

The couple's stories are filled with heartbreak and hope. John told us of opening his door late one Friday to find two emaciated children. Tracy, five, and her two-year-old

brother, Jamie, had lice and scabies. Feces caked their scrawny bodies, as if "they had swum in a mud puddle and then sat in the sun to bake dry." Police had scooped up the children during a raid on a crack house, where the pair shared a torn mattress with addicts. Before tucking the children into a real bed, John and Liane gave them a bath. "An army of lice began to frantically crawl up my arm," he recalls. The next day, Tracy awoke to the smell of bacon and eggs and the sight of Liane doting on her brother. "Will you please be my mommy and daddy?" she cried. "Can we stay here forever?"

John's heart broke, as it had before and it would again. Although John and Liane rarely care for such children for long, they strive to make their home a place where love lives and a child belongs, if only for a couple of days.

Like few people we've met, John and Liane live their faith through service. Not content to study and preach the scriptures, John infuses his every action with a belief in, and service to, God. We were eager to talk to him because he's been a temporary guardian of one thousand children, of course, but also because he is a father of five ("three conceived, two received"),

John Niles opens his house as an "emergency home"

GOD IS IN THE DETAILS

In the world of John and Liane Niles, little things make all the difference. A few Niles' household statistics hint at the magnitude of 3,500 days and nights on call:

49,150 Extra meals and bottle feedings.

21,000 Additional loads of laundry.

6 Worn out washers and dryers.

54,000 Diaper changes.

19,350 Phone calls and meetings with social workers, placement workers, supervisors, physiotherapists, family court judges.

10,000 Amount of times they've asked, "How could someone have done this to a child?"

100,000 Number of smiles, giggles, hugs and "I love you's" they've received in return. [1]

all of whom serve their community in one way or another.

John didn't set out to be a minister, nor did he plan to open his house to so many wee ones. His father had been an orphan, "desperate for some place to belong," which may explain why John made it his mission to help the vulnerable. He went to college where he met Liane, who was also studying social work. (Great hearts think alike.) He landed a job, but God was calling. John went on to earn his doctorate in theology and became a minister. Service has consistently been the focus of his ministry and the center of his family life. "We have always known that because we have been blessed, we ought to be a blessing," John explains. "This is what we have modeled as a family. It is only natural our children would want to participate."

From the beginning, everyone in the home took responsibility for the children who passed through. The Niles kids took on feedings and diaper changes, just as they sang lullabies and comforted tears. They dragged themselves out of bed to greet late-night arrivals. "We let them so they know why we do the work we do," John says. He wanted his children to see "how important it is to be compassionate and caring."

When the Niles children realized these babies and toddlers had nothing, they created Kits for Kids. Now children who arrive at emergency homes receive a bag containing diapers, wipes, a toothbrush, teddy bear, toys and pajamas — items acquired thanks to the "power of positive begging." The Niles kids were known to use their own money to prepare bagged lunches for the homeless. They also volunteered at the food bank, a drop-in center for homeless teens and at an after-school program for at-risk children.

Through service, the Niles children came to appreciate why caring for others is the right way to live. "They internalized the lesson we tried to teach them," John says, "To 'love people and use things (not love things and use people).'" Every time they found a way to live this lesson, their social consciences blossomed.

It's probably no surprise the Niles children followed in their parents' footsteps. Alyssa became a neonatal nurse at the hospital where she once volunteered. Sarah decided to study social work, but first traveled to Senegal where she volunteered with homeless boys and former child slaves. She also spent time in Beijing where she worked in the first Christian orphanage to open in fifty years. After returning to Canada, she earned her degree and took a job working with aboriginal children. John is extremely grateful that his children have had opportunities to experience the many ways service deepens faith. "In life, it is not what we think or say that counts. It is what we do about what we think or say that counts. Our life is made manifest by every action we take."

Silver Linings and the Golden Rule

How does John stay hopeful in the face of so many wounded and discarded children? We have been asked the same question about our work in slums and war zones. How do we move forward despite human deprivation, the scourge of HIV/AIDS and the devastation of war? The short answer: Work renews our faith. In *Me to We*, we wrote of teachers who spent their own money to help at-risk students in urban centers of America. We shared stories of aid workers who toiled past the point of exhaustion to care for desperate people in refugee camps. Such stories of compassion and courage stir the soul. Inspired by faith, people meet the worst with their best. Through service, we make the world a better place. Even those who are not religious say that acts of kindness inspire faith in humanity.

One of Craig's favorite comic strips features two frogs on a lily pad.

"Why, when God is so powerful, does He not do something to help the less fortunate?" the younger frog asks.

"I don't know, my son," the older frog responds.

"Why haven't you asked Him this when you pray?" the young frog persists.

The older frog turns to his son and says, "I've never asked Him because I'm afraid He'll ask me the same question."

John reminded us that Jesus served in many ways. Most faiths are dedicated to service, in fact. Charity, or *zakat*, is a pillar of Islam: Muslims give a percentage of their belongings to the poor and make regular donations to those in need. The Mishna, which contains Jewish oral law, underlines the importance of helping. The Torah mandates responding to the needs of the poor and the sick, be they Jews, strangers or enemies. Everyone is obliged to do *tzedakah*, or righteous deeds, to help repair the world. This idea, reflected in all faiths, is summed up in the simple phrase we learned in our own church as young children, "Do unto others as you wish them to do unto you."

It's one thing to encourage service; it's another thing to actually serve. Churches promise young people that regular attendance will yield

We were born to make manifest the glory of God that is within us. It's not just in some of us; it's in everyone."

Marianne Williamson
Author

salvation and a closer relationship with their Lord. Kids rally in the name of God but rarely in the name of service. A recent study found that only about 30 percent of teens had been involved with their congregation on a mission team or with a service project.[2] It raises a troubling question: What good are scriptures and hymns if we neglect to live their messages?

When Craig was nine, he joined a group of friends and went to a local Bible camp where counselors advised their charges to stop watching *Star Trek* because it featured alien species that could never have been created by God. This was how he was told he could best live the messages in the Bible. Craig was bewildered. For starters, he loved *Star Trek*! Plus, he couldn't help but compare Bible camp to Boy Scout expeditions where kids learned how to protect the environment and give to the local community. Even at nine, Craig realized he felt closer to God when lending a hand.

There are compelling reasons for religious leaders to encourage youth to get out in their communities. A landmark study in 2007 found that the best way to deepen a teen's faith is by presenting them with opportunities to help people in need. Researchers from the School of Social Work at Baylor University surveyed 631 adolescents from thirty-five Protestant churches in six states.[3] Teens reported that service infused their lives with purpose and meaning, which in turn influenced their faith. Hands-on work was revealed to be far more influential than filling pews, reading scripture or participating in church retreats. The deepest connections are established when youth meet and work with the people they're helping. The degree of influence such experiences have on shaping

faith increases with involvement. Level 1 might be to pitch in with adult mentors on a fence-painting project. Level 2 could be to help at a shelter or soup kitchen. Level 3 would involve ongoing connections — Meals on Wheels, for example — in which the volunteer establishes a relationship with the person he or she is assisting.[4]

We can use this study as a blueprint to build faith through service. Of course, we can send our kids to Bible camp so they might grow closer to God. But we might also consider helping them help others closer to home so that they might deepen their faith. Our good friends, the Weiss family, have devoted endless hours to their synagogue. Julie Weiss and her children are long-serving volunteers with Out of the Cold, a program that counts on churches, synagogues, mosques and other houses of worship to feed the homeless. Julie started to help out when her daughter, Jordana — a youth member of the board of directors of Free The Children — was ten. Some helpers cook for the homeless, others set out mattresses. The Weiss family ensures visitors get set up with toiletries. The neat thing about Out of the Cold is that it rotates from synagogue to mosque to church — all faiths working together.

Keeping the Faith

In our house, lessons in faith were implicit rather than explicit. We discussed "right" and "wrong," but never "thou shall not." It wasn't until we were much older that we even learned how faith and service shaped the way our parents see the world. In subtle ways, they passed on their beliefs.

SMALL STEPS FOR LEADERS OF FAITH

A pastor leading a congregation in Haiti after the earthquake

1. Consider organizing a social justice fair. Kids can research local and global issues and then present their findings to other members of the church.

2. Set aside an evening to hear a guest speaker on a social justice issue.

3. Organize a movie night. Invite kids and their parents to share in a movie with a social justice theme. Sell popcorn and tickets with proceeds going to a charity chosen by the group.

4. Be as thoughtful and intentional and resource-generous in creating avenues to encourage social responsibility as you are with other components of the religious curriculum.

5. Consider approaching other faith organizations to share in a community project.

When we were well into our teens, Dad first told us that in his mid-twenties he'd headed to France in search of his hero, Jean Vanier. The Canadian hero founded L'Arche, a spiritual community for men and women with developmental difficulties. By day, Dad ran a workshop in which he helped men make lamps. At night, he slept on a couch in Vanier's office. Every morning, Vanier's mother would come in to greet Dad, kiss him on the cheek and say thank you. At one point, Dad figured he might make his mark by getting his charges to work faster. After all, the more lamps they had to sell, the more money the community would earn. "They didn't really listen to me," recalls Dad, who realized soon enough that the profits of production had little to do with money.

If Dad remained humble about his time with Vanier, Mom stayed mum on her early volunteer work. It was long after Marc was at university that we first learned she had left teaching for four years to work with Young Christian Workers. She'd operated a shelter for street kids. Later, she volunteered in Mexico and once represented Canadian women at an international conference in Lebanon. It wasn't until we were rifling through a box of photos and saw a picture of her on the steps of a derelict building with a bunch of long-haired young people in ripped jeans that we had a clue to her past. "Were those the homeless people?" we asked in wonder.

"It was the '60s," she replied. "Everyone dressed that way!"

When we were born, Mom and Dad decided religion would be a part of our lives, particularly if it led us to serve. So they were predictably supportive when Marc, at thirteen, asked to spend part of his summer helping people with leprosy and teenaged mothers in the slums around Kingston, Jamaica. Marc was considerably younger than other participants, so he set up a meeting to make his case to Fintan Kilbride, the priest-turned-teacher in charge of the program. He and Marc struck up a lasting friendship.

Fintan had devoted his life to helping the poor. He'd worked in Trinidad, Haiti, Nicaragua and Nigeria. He'd taught in six high schools. He'd built a hospital, three schools and founded a teacher training college. When the Biafran War began, he organized shipments of food and medicine. He took part in dangerous flights, and he once walked away from a devastating crash. In Canada, he taught high school and set up Students Crossing Borders, a program that enables young people to volunteer in less developed countries. On top of all this, he was a world champion racquetball player! When Fintan passed away in 2006, a colleague called him "an extraordinary example of a Christian disciple in the modern age. His life was always about peace — his life in the classroom and on the street."[5]

Later, at eighteen, Marc found himself in Klong Toey, the slaughterhouse neighborhood of Bangkok. He wanted to flee, but stayed, in large measure because of the influence of Father Joe Maier, a whiskey-drinking, cursing Catholic priest who helped children living amid poverty, drugs, gang violence and child sex abuse. For thirty years, Father Joe has slept in a shack in the slum. "That's where Jesus would be," he once explained. "You can't live uptown."[6] Father Joe has opened thirty-three preschools and also founded a center that provides housing for

homeless kids who've been rescued from abusive parents or orphaned by AIDS. He is a man of great character, compassion and tolerance. "I've only learned to be a Christian by learning from the Muslims and Buddhists: Tolerance and calmness and peace," he once said.[7] Seventy thousand children have graduated from Father Joe's preschools. "They know how to read and write. ... We've given them a gift they'll never, ever lose. ... What a glorious way to spend your life. ... This is what priests are supposed to do." Father Joe, like Fintan, led by example. By watching Father Joe in action, Marc could tell what he believed.

Gather the Children

When Craig was five, he began to walk to church with his friend. It was close to our house and had a wonderful young priest who did uncanny impressions of *The Simpsons*. Between sermons, he led kids in the congregation in regular games of hockey. Religion was the added bonus of Craig's twice-weekly outings. Rev. Phelan Scanlon would call forward the many children in his congregation and direct his sermons their way. Rather than drawing directly from the Bible, he'd sample from a current movie or TV show. Other times, he'd preach with a puck. He served as goalie and referee in the basement

GIFTS THAT GIVE BACK

Parents often ask us how we approach the holiday season. Our answer? "Very carefully." We all know that money can't buy happiness, yet we still hit the malls on the hunt to find something for someone who has everything. Here's a wish list of sorts featuring gifts that give back:

1. The gift of time: Let a loved one know your family will be volunteering at a local organization in their honor.

2. Holiday baking: If you are a baker, consider getting your kids to help you fill a platter to donate to a local mission.

3. Adopt a village: Donate to an overseas project on behalf of a loved one.

4. Comfort and joy: Turn a holiday open house into a party that collects donations or canned goods for a local charity.

5. Presents of presence: Instead of a gift exchange, consider pooling resources to buy gifts for a community hamper program.

floor hockey matches, making sure no one was ever picked last.

At the age of twelve, Craig was rather impressionable when he headed to Asia to investigate child labor. What he discovered there prompted questions that he wrestles with still. When Craig arrived in Dhaka, Bangladesh, he was drawn into a world where children were enslaved, chained to looms, beaten, whipped, starved and cast into the streets.

Eight-year-old Muniannal, for example, worked in an alley in Madras, separating used needles gathered from hospitals and the streets for their plastics. She worked barefoot, oblivious to the risks. When she pricked herself, she dipped her hand into a bucket of dirty water. It tore Craig apart. How could adults treat children this way? Why would God let this happen? Where was God? Craig asked similar questions during a tour of the red-light district in Bangkok with a human rights worker. What could he do in the face of so much evil? How could he help when there was such a profound disregard for the humanity of children?

One evening, as dusk fell on Calcutta, he saw an arrow pointing to the Mission of the Sisters of Charity. Threading through a labyrinth of dusty alleyways, he found the doorstep, slipped through a gate, crossed a bustling courtyard and climbed a staircase into a door that was slightly ajar. Stepping into a prayer room, he discovered several nuns in front of a simple altar. Craig asked if he might meet Mother Teresa but was told she was tired. When he was invited to return, he started to explain that it was his last day in the city. At that moment, Mother Teresa walked past. She reached out her calloused fingers to grab Craig's hands. "What brings you all the way

to Calcutta?" Calling on his courage, Craig explained. "We have come to meet working children. We have come to learn about their lives and how we might help them." He told her about all of the kids he'd met. "The poor will teach you many things," she replied.

Mother Teresa walked with Craig to a bench where she listened to his stories about the working children. Craig was excited but managed to speak slowly and clearly. When she looked into his eyes, Craig burst into tears. When she held his hands, he felt the embrace of a living saint. "I have a favor to ask," he said nervously. "Could you please include in your prayers the children who live on the streets and work every day?" Mother Teresa led Craig to a blackboard in the prayer room and pressed chalk into his hands. "PLEASE PRAY FOR CHILD LABORERS," he wrote.

We're convinced Mother Teresa took time with Craig because she recognized that youth are the only hope. "Even after I pass away, there will be young people committed to continuing the mission of helping the poorest of the poor," she said. As Craig walked away, he began to see the streets of Calcutta in a hopeful light. Mother Teresa's steady and unyielding compassion opened a pathway through the poverty and

sickness. She was proof that small, meaningful actions can change the world.

Many people hold up Mother Teresa as an extraordinary example of selflessness. In doing so, unfortunately, some decide they will never match her sacrifice, never enjoy a close relationship with God. So why bother, they ask. The amazing thing about Mother Teresa is that she was remarkably human. Some people have asked us if we still consider her a role model now that it's known she questioned God's existence. "Jesus has a very special love for you," she wrote to a confidant in 1979. "As for me, the silence and the emptiness is so great that I look and do not see, listen and do not hear."[8] Who among us has not questioned God's existence? Who among us does not live with doubts? No matter how alone and isolated Mother Teresa felt, her answer was the same: I must serve. Even when she felt abandoned by God, she continued her work. Her determination to serve is an inspiration to us in our work. When asked, we say we don't serve because we are faithful — we are faithful because we serve.

SMALL ACTIONS › EVERY DAY

1. PRACTICE WHAT YOU PREACH:
You can talk at your kids all you like. What they learn, though, is what you live.

2. SHOW YOUR FAITH:
Volunteer at your child's church, temple or mosque. If a youth group does not exist, create one. Help kids find a way to reach out as a team into the community.

3. BE INCLUSIVE:
Ask local faith leaders to include children in the service.

4. BUILD BRIDGES: Donate your money to bring in inspiring speakers or support field trips.

5. SERVE SIDE BY SIDE:
Join your kids in faith and service. In this way, they'll see it's important to you — just as it's important to the community.

6. TEACH THE GOLDEN RULE:
No matter what you believe, teach your children to do unto others as you wish them to do unto you.

7. LEARN ABOUT ANOTHER FAITH:
Read a book with your children about another faith that is practiced in your community but with which you are not very familiar. Teach them about different religious holidays and when they are celebrated.

Light a Candle to Dispel a Little Darkness

*The winner of the Nobel Peace Prize in 1984, **Archbishop Desmond Tutu** is a South African cleric and activist who rose to worldwide fame during the 1980s as an opponent of apartheid. He is also committed to stopping global AIDS and has served as the honorary chairman of the Global AIDS Alliance. Here he talks about a true hero, his mother.*

WHEN I WAS JUST A SMALL BOY, I was sitting in a South African ghetto township, maybe thinking I didn't count for too much. But I soon learned that each one of us is a glorious original and has the capacity to be God's special partner. At a tender age, I discovered it isn't doing spectacular things that makes you remarkable in the eyes of God, but instead, it is when you light just one candle to dispel a little bit of darkness that you are doing something tremendous. And if, as a global people, we put all the little bits of good together, we will overwhelm the world. In my young life, there were many key individuals and moments that embodied this spirit for me, but three standout in my mind, and I want to share them with you.

As a child I had tuberculosis and went to the hospital for nearly two years. During that time, about once a week, Trevor Huddleston, a priest

who became a renowned anti-apartheid activist, came to see me. He lived in Sophiatown, as a member of a religious community, and he shared the life of the poor and deprived people. I wasn't aware of it then, but his actions made a strong impression on me. In South Africa it was unusual to see a white person caring for a black township urchin like myself, and his example contributed to a lack of bitterness I felt against whites. Trevor touched my life and I'm so very grateful because he was a tremendous champion of goodness and the dispossessed. Through small examples of his humanity, he cared for others and for me; he was one of the first strong examples for me of someone working those little bits of goodness.

Now, the next experience was one I shared with many black South African kids. Because of the turbulence in my own country, I was very greatly influenced by the heroic struggles of African American sports people, Jackie Robinson especially. I think I was about nine when I picked up a tattered copy of *Ebony* magazine that happened to describe how Jackie broke into major league baseball to play with the Brooklyn Dodgers. I didn't know baseball from Ping Pong, but I could read, and here was the story of a man who had overcome enormous adversity and suffered tremendous abuse for simply following his dreams. His example, the way he had made it against all those odds, made me feel several inches taller. Jackie Robinson left the impression that we should do what we can, because in the end, by standing up to that bully, you win a little victory for righteousness and you give just one other person the example to stand up for truth.

My greatest mentor through everyday examples of goodness was my mother. And while I have said to many, many people that I resemble her physically (she, too, was stumpy and had a large nose, you see) it has been one of my missions in life also to resemble her in her spirit, in her generosity, and in her concern for others.

Our family was of modest means, but my mother was a wonderful cook and she never cooked just enough for our hungry family. She always imagined that there might be somebody who would come to our house and who would need to be fed. This was her way of showing her great heart and empathy for other human beings, through her wonderful cooking. And her generosity extended to far more than food. She almost instinctively had a way of comforting whoever was getting the worst side of an argument, and with good intention my wife aptly called her the Comforter of the Afflicted.

My mother was a quiet hero whose greatest achievements were never obvious to the outside world. Through each of my role models I have learned to trust in the love and the example of others and that we are made for interdependence. I have also learned that we are made different, capable of our own special miracles, not in order to be separated but to know of our need for each other. True happiness is not when you are there only for "number one," but when you are there for others. It is a very simple but powerful truth that leadership and greatness emerge when one is able to follow the Lord's words and to, figuratively perhaps, wash the feet of others.

❝

My mother was a quiet hero whose greatest
achievements were never obvious to the outside world."
Archbishop Desmond Tutu

THINKING OUTSIDE THE BOX

How to Make Connections in a Wired World

If parents and teachers are connected, they can help kids connect. Keep up on the latest technology, learn how to use it and get your kids to help. It will make a world of difference.

A WHILE BACK WE RECEIVED a pretty cool invitation. We were asked to meet the cast of *Degrassi: The Next Generation*, the wildly successful TV soap opera for teens that airs in 150 countries. It's a gritty show that deals with coming of age in a non-Hollywood kind of way. The people behind the show were looking for a charity to support and were eager to hear about our work. Excited and nervous, we imagined the possibilities — perhaps they might mention Free The Children on one of their episodes! We dismissed the notion, aware that plot twists about boyfriend stealing and unplanned pregnancies were much more likely to draw an audience than any storyline about raising money for less fortunate kids a world away.

The *Degrassi* kids had scripts to memorize and autographs to sign, but we'd convinced ourselves they'd welcome the chance to step up for our charity. Marc made his pitch and invited questions. Instead ... crickets; nothing but silence. Marc felt like a substitute teacher who had failed to make a good impression. Eventually, Jake Epstein — he plays Craig, the demon-wrestling beefcake on the show — put up his hand, as if he was in a *Degrassi* classroom:

"Could we build a school?" Marc wasn't entirely sure what he was asking. "The *Degrassi* cast?"

"Yeah," Jake said. "How would we do that?"

The cast of *Degrassi* building a school in Kenya

Marc thought he was asking how much money they'd have to raise.

"$8,500." Jake clarified his question: "Can we go to Kenya and build the school?" Marc practically cheered.

The teens started to brainstorm ways to raise money. One actor, a deejay by night, volunteered to host a fundraiser at a local club. Another offered to bake and sell cookies. It was like any meeting of students at any high school, the difference being that this one featured actors who play students at a fictional school. The kids were trying to find a way to pair their gifts with this newly discovered issue. (Though they'd yet to learn it, they were essentially working through Gift + Passion = Better World.) They joked about building a "*Degrassi*" in Kenya.

"The stars aligned," Ben Rotterman would tell us later. "We thought we would make a documentary of this trip." The executive producer of MTV Productions assumed correctly that the *Degrassi* kids would be embarking on an authentic dramatic journey. "We had a chance to marry celebrity with a life-changing experience." It would be ridiculously expensive to send a documentary crew to Kenya. It was a gamble, to be sure, but it was one Rotterman was eager to make.

To be honest, a lot of us at FTC had been pretty down on TV, or at least its influence on kids. Like most of you, we know the research: Junior couch potatoes have shorter attention spans and have been found to engage in less imaginative play. Television unplugs them from life at large. It takes them away from sports and reading. And, of course, if they're sitting on the sofa, they're less likely to get up to help. Watching television has also been shown to desensitize children, which makes them less likely to act in the face of injustice.[1]

The average kid will witness more than eight thousand murders on TV before he finishes grade school.[2] Books and careers have been devoted to the effects of violent and sexual content on these impressionable viewers. The evidence convinces us that violent programming — and threatening video games — increases violent behavior in children. Some producers insist they're simply reflecting reality, but it ain't so. Murder represents more than half of the crime shown on TV, yet it accounts for 0.2 percent of crimes reported by the FBI.[3] The American National Television Violence Study found that 40 percent of violence is perpetrated by "good characters," while more than half of the victims show little pain or suffering, further desensitizing children to its true effects.[4]

Unfortunately, the media also teach our children stereotypes — especially about people who are "different" — with perilous results for our world. Many kids are aware of racial differences by the time they are two. By age three, they may attach value judgments to these differences, perhaps thinking a man with another color of skin is scary or strange. Soon, children learn to stereotype based on gender or disability or color. The Media Awareness Network suggests that before long, kids will pick up stereotypes from books, television, movies, magazines, newspapers and the Internet. The media dictate what races are important or not, based on how they are portrayed or not. By age ten, students may hold stereotypes about people in other countries.[5] The media rarely give the developing world more than a passing mention unless there's a famine or an earthquake or some other unspeakable tragedy — depictions that increase the distance between "us" and "them."

And yet media bring the world into our living rooms, teaching us about war and peace, storms and calms, scientific discoveries and religious devotion. "Almost everything we know about people, places and events that we cannot visit first hand comes from the media," writes Kathleen Tyner and Donna Kolkin in *Media and You: An Elementary Literacy Curriculum.* "Television, film and now the Internet have become the storytellers of our generation: These stories tell us about who we are, what we believe and what we want to be."[6]

Get With the Program

When parents approach us for advice on the subject, we join them in bemoaning the *Gossip Girls* and the *Grand Theft Autos* and so much sexually over-the-top programming. Yet it's next to impossible to ignore TV and the Internet with Facebook and Twitter, so it would be irresponsible of us to advise parents to "Turn it all off." Instead, we urge you to get plugged in — stay up on the latest gizmos and gadgets. Make it your responsibility to raise media literate children. We're not talking about tutoring your kids in HTML or Flickr but instead coaching them to decipher all the angles at play.

Teach your kids to be critical of information. Show them that a news story is just one of many perspectives. In fact, encourage them to research both sides of a story. Guide them to alternative sources of information and entertainment. Help them to distinguish fact from fiction.

When it seems appropriate, have a conversation about bias. Talk about how the media champions some individuals and sidelines others. Just as you taught them to "bust" a television commercial, get them to consider the following when it comes to media:

1. Who wrote or produced the report? What kind of education or experience has this person had?
2. Who was the intended audience of the report?
3. What was its intent? Why was it written? What main point is the author trying to argue?

Explain that books and stories and websites are not always accurate; sometimes their statistics are outdated and incorrect. Encourage your kids to check out a variety of sources.

Media savvy kids can't help but be better citizens. We encourage parents and teachers to show children that it's possible to use the Internet to spread social justice messages. The Web puts local and global contacts at their fingertips, plus it presents limitless possibilities for enhancing outreach activities. Almost everyone can access the Web, whether at home, school, the library or an Internet café. If kids find a cause, they can use e-mail to create mailing lists, e-newsletters and online action alerts. Older kids might even want to set up a website to make their group and its issue known. MySpace, Facebook and Twitter are changing the way charities raise money and spread information about injustice. They can also get the word out in a hurry. Remember the Sea of Pink? Thanks to technology, it formed over night.

Advances are coming fast and furious — perhaps too fast for the slow adapters among us. If parents and teachers are connected, they can help kids connect. Keep up on the latest, learn how to use it and get your kids to help. You don't need to invade their MySpace or get in their Facebook, but you can talk to them about what they are doing online.

Lessons Learned the Hard Way

It turns out *Degrassi* did go to Kenya. A few months after our first meeting with the actors, an intrepid cast traveled to Kenya on what would be a transformative journey. Ray Ablack plays "Sav," a naïve but well-meaning transfer student from a rival school. In real life, Ray admits he was also a bit guileless. "I thought I would give people in Kenya all this help and they would be so grateful." During the last two weeks of August 2007, he arrived in Kenya with castmates and "classmates" Nina Dobrev (Mia), Marc Donato (Derek), Dalmar Abuzeid (Danny), Jamie Johnston (Peter), Jake Epstein (Craig) and Charlotte Arnold (Holly J).

None of them anticipated how hard it would be. After just a few days in Africa, Ray was vowing to change his ways. During a three-mile walk to collect dirty water, he came to appreciate the value of clean tap water. When he returned to "civilization," he was going to take five-minute showers — not twenty! Plus, he was going to stop complaining about the lack of clothing in his overcrowded closet — it seemed sort of ridiculous after meeting kids dressed in tatters. In one village, ragged children rushed out to greet their visitors. Ray snapped pictures with his digital camera and then shared the images with the swarming kids. "They didn't recognize themselves," he recalls. "These little kids had never seen what they looked like." He was humbled. "I didn't even realize they would give me so much more than I was hoping to give them. They opened my eyes to all of the things I take for granted."

Rotterman knew a "do-gooding documentary" was unlikely to grab an audience. The sad truth is that infomercials featuring emaciated Africans are more likely to make you switch the channel than to change the world. "Hollywood keeps telling us that audiences want violence and sex, but the single way to grab people and get them cheering is not sex or violence, it's empathy," Rotterman explained. "The stories they respond to are the ones that are about fitting in or choosing to get their own way." *MTV Presents: Degrassi in Kenya* was an instant hit. The thirty minute documentary played weekly for a year, and is now in demand around the world. It inspired a second documentary, *Degrassi in Ecuador*, and there are plans for more social justice programming.

Ray returned from Kenya "really bitter" about excess. He felt bad about the water in his drinking glass and the generous helpings set before him on the kitchen table. It irritated him that his younger siblings wouldn't finish the food on their plates. "I'd see how long I could go without eating, without drinking water." Ray's self-righteous starvation worried his parents and annoyed his friends. Eventually, though, he slipped back to pretrip habits of consumption and indifference. Furious with himself, he made a desperate call to Free The Children. "I thought if I stuffed envelopes or something it would keep me on the straight and narrow." Instead, we encouraged Ray to share his experiences. During the next five months, he visited students in Grades 4 to 8 to talk about his struggles to change his life.

The popularity of the Kenya documentary forced us all to stop and ask why programmers insist on bombarding kids with violence, sexual innuendo, an over emphasis on looks and the accumulation of stuff. The success of *Degrassi* proves young viewers are hungry to explore the pressing issues of our times. The experience prompted Ray to question future role choices. "Why don't we give kids something inspiring and positive?" he asked. "It's not like kids are going to complain and say, 'But we want to see some more killing.'"

So what can parents do? With so many channels and websites and technologies, it seems there's almost no point in complaining. Where would you begin? You could start by helping kids make sense of the noise. Equip them to find truth in the spin. Seek out, then guide them to the movies and the TV programming and the websites that will help them to discover the world and their place in it.

TUNE IN TO THE TAKEAWAY MESSAGES

U.S. President Barack Obama often reminds parents that the government can't turn off the television and make a child do her homework. Instead of zoning out in front of the flat screen, get engaged. A few things to think about:

1. Screen time: Decide on some household rules.

2. Press pause: Don't let the media spoon-feed your children. Stop programs to challenge points. Show your kids how to research. Explain that there's usually more than one side to the story.

3. Do it yourself: Let older kids try their hand at making a short video. By learning how it's done, they'll come to understand how stories are shaped and edited for consumption.

4. Be selective: Help your kids find programs with a social justice theme. Stick around with them to watch.

5. Turn it off: Consider instituting a screen-free day of the week — no TV, no computers, no video games.

DID YOU KNOW?

The average home in the U.S. is stocked with twenty-six different electronic devices — computers, televisions, DVD players and telephones, for starters.[9]

Online, Canadian students spend an average of fifty-four minutes a day instant messaging, fifty minutes downloading and listening to music, forty-four minutes playing online games and thirty minutes on schoolwork — often all at the same time![10]

TV or Not TV? That is the Question

We've met lots of parents who've banned TV and the Internet from their homes or have set tight controls. We were surprised to discover that MTV guru Ben Rotterman doesn't let his preteens, a boy and a girl, watch television (except for a few choice, pre-selected DVDs). The Rottermans have also kept the Internet out of their home. "Pop culture is still taking hold," he confesses. "Even if we restrict their exposure to content we find objectionable or worrisome, they will still get it somewhere else." But at least there are rules and concerns, he says. "They can keep that in the back of their mind as they go out into the world."

It would be next to impossible to raise Luddites and TV-phobes. Despite all efforts, the outside world creeps in. We think that the best parents can do is set guidelines and help kids develop the critical thinking required to watch TV or use the Internet with a strong dose of caution and cynicism. This means raising a kid who can turn a critical and informed eye to all that they read and watch. Start a dialogue with your kid about what is appropriate or inappropriate. If you don't pay attention, you'll lose the battle without even putting up a fight.

Let your children watch the news with you and then discuss it. Kids are often confused by what they see on TV. If you don't want your children to read or watch something, explain why. If they like watching cartoons, start a conversation about the violence. Help kids question commercials and advertising. Stick around, so you can help them figure it out. Don't be afraid to say "No." As U.S. President Barack Obama has said repeatedly, it's up to us to make kids turn off the TV and put away their video games. "These are things that only a parent can do," he's said. "These are things that parents must do."

Stay in the loop on what teenagers are watching and surfing. Figure out what is holding their attention. Discuss the sites they visit. Try to get them talking about what they find cool, confusing or complex. When it comes to technology, they are probably your best teachers. Bring them on side — you'll need them there if your terms and limits are going to stand a chance. Of course, you'll also have to play by your own rules. You can't tell kids you don't want them to watch TV violence, then watch back-to-back *Law & Order* episodes. Explaining your concerns is just as important as controlling access to the mouse or the remote.

We know all of this makes us sound a tad curmudgeonly. We admit we're cautious, but we are equally excited by technology's ability to make connections. We cheer such projects as Regent Park TV, a network that hit the online airwaves in 2006 to give kids a chance to tell their own stories. RPTV is the creation of the Regent Park Focus Youth Media Arts Centre, a community center that produces newspapers and video segments on issues important to the neighborhood. Kids write, shoot and edit their own short videos and post them online using the hugely popular video sharing site YouTube. Their videos have covered a diverse array of subjects including crime, bullying, police relations, cultural conflicts and teen homelessness. "It's the kids who are defining what they want to do," says the program's co-ordinator. "They're really excited about producing."[7]

Vote With Your Remote

About twenty years ago, people made fun of Tipper Gore when she launched a campaign to get music companies to voluntarily label albums and cassette tapes (yes, tapes) containing explicit language. Frank Zappa called her a "cultural terrorist," and she was accused of being a puritan and a censor. In the face of critics, she persuaded her husband, Al Gore, to hold Senate hearings on the subject. "We should be deeply concerned about the obvious cumulative effect of this cult of violence that has captured the public's imagination and pervaded our society," she wrote in her book titled *Raising PG Kids in an X-rated Society*.[8] Almost two decades on, she remains an awesome example of how parents can take on industry.

Our experience with *Degrassi* and MTV taught us that TV producers respond to their audiences. After the success of the Kenya expedition, MTV agreed to make more documentaries. Why? Well, for lots of reasons but especially because the ratings were good and the feedback effusive. When you see something you like on TV or the Web, tell somebody in a position of influence. People rarely speak out in favor of the good stuff, so it will make your feedback all the more valuable. Voice your concerns when you don't like something, too. Vote with your remote. With so many channels competing for attention, you always have options. If *Gossip Girl* doesn't get the ratings, producers will eventually figure out that the lying, cheating, over-sexed heroines are missing their mark with teens.

We've been working hard to get our message out on TV and the Web. But some

opportunities just fall in our lap. Craig got tapped for a cameo on *Degrassi*. Just as we'd dared to hope, the make-believe high school created a Free The Children chapter. Playing himself, Craig delivered an impassioned speech about helping impoverished children in Africa. As the storyline went, two girls were inspired to organize a daylong fast to raise money. It all unraveled — we told you it was a soap opera — when one girl tried to sabotage the fundraiser by giving out pizza to the hungry fasters. In the nick of time, Craig appeared. "What are you doing?" he demanded. "There are four hours left in the fast!" It was a fun experience and great opportunity, though Craig is still waiting to hear from Steven Spielberg about his next gig. Still, the episode proved popular. The show worked not just because it was about issues, but because it told real stories about kids trying to do good even when life gets in the way.

Degrassi **cast members Raymond and Dalmar building a school in Kenya**

SMALL ACTIONS › EVERY DAY

1. GET CONNECTED:
Log onto: www.freethechildren.com or www.metowe.com, two sites where you can get the scoop on international development, stay on top of global issues, share your actions with other youth activists and have your say.

2. SCREEN YOUR SCREENS:
Don't let your kids settle in front of a TV or computer unless you know what they are watching or surfing.

3. MEDIA SAVVY SUBVERSION:
Teach kids all the angles. Who is behind the media, what they're selling and why. Kids who are wise to what is going on are less likely to be duped.

4. SEND A MESSAGE:
Praise producers when you like something; complain when you don't.

5. STAY CURRENT:
Do your best to keep up with the latest technology and social networking tools. It's hard to guide your kids when you don't know what they're talking about.

6. VOTE WITH YOUR REMOTE ... AND YOUR MOUSE:
If you don't like what you're seeing, turn it off. Model this behavior and your kids may learn to do the same.

Follow Your Passion

*Philanthropist **Jeff Skoll** was the first president of the Internet auction firm eBay. He has used his wealth to advance social justice throughout the world by creating the Skoll Foundation, the Skoll Centre for Social Entrepreneurship at Said Business School at Oxford University and the Skoll World Forum. In 2004, he founded Participant Media, a global media company that inspires and compels social change. Its first four films —* Syriana, Good Night and Good Luck, North Country *and the documentary* Murderball *— received 11 Oscar nominations in 2006. Participant's projects continue to be acclaimed, challenge and change the world.*

LOOKING BACK, I recall three childhood events that set me on my life's path.

I learned to read in kindergarten with the help of my mom, a teacher. By the time I was thirteen or fourteen, I was reading books usually read by adults. I especially loved epic historical novels by authors such as James Michener, Leon Uris, Edward Rutherford, Aldous Huxley and Ayn Rand. They gave me a real sense of the sweep of time, where the world was going, and the challenges we might face, including pollution, over population, militarization and famine.

I was fifteen when my father was diagnosed with kidney cancer. As he was taking stock of his life, he told me he didn't regret that he might die, but he did regret he hadn't done what he had wanted to do in his life. My dad spent so much of his life working, lots of hours building his business. But there was more he'd wanted to do: travel, live on a boat, see the world. Thankfully, my dad survived

and went on to pursue some of his other dreams. But his regrets, and his belief that we should try to live our dreams, had a huge impact on me.

In high school, I had a teacher who asked us to consider what we wanted written on our gravestone. It was a powerful assignment and I gave it a lot of thought: "To make a difference in the big issues of the world and have a good family life." Once I knew the answer, I figured I could work backward and find a way to make it happen.

My goal was to become a writer. I hoped to write books that would get people interested in world issues that affected us all. But I didn't think it would be a great way to make money. I didn't want it to be my profession but rather my passion. Somehow I needed to bridge the financial gap. My family didn't have much money. I

needed to be entrepreneurial. When I was in high school, I pumped gas to pay my way through the University of Toronto, where I studied electrical engineering. After graduating in 1987, I started my own businesses but I realized I would need more business knowledge to achieve financial independence. So I headed to Stanford University in California. After graduating with an MBA, a friend named Pierre Omidyar asked me to help with a new business that involved trading and selling items on the Internet. At first I said no. It seemed like a bad idea. But the job I had taken in the newspaper industry convinced me there just might be some potential. So, Pierre and I left our full-time jobs and I joined eBay as the company's first president.

Five years later, I left the company a billionaire

and began to revisit the idea of writing stories that would inspire people to get involved. The more I thought about it, I realized I didn't have to do the writing myself. Instead, I'd hire writers and filmmakers to spread the message about the problems facing our world. I decided to start a media company for the good of society. When I came to Los Angeles in 2003 to pursue this idea, I expected a lot more skepticism. But everyone — writers, producers, actors and directors — were interested in making films and documentaries about the issues they cared about. What they needed was somebody outside Hollywood who was willing to take a financial risk.

We've had many successes but I'm most proud of the documentary, *An Inconvenient Truth*. I knew that climate change was one of the biggest issues in the world and one of the most urgent. As it happened, we were fortunate to convince former vice president Al Gore to get involved. The documentary won two Oscars in 2007 and is now part of school curriculum the world over. The film has made such a difference in the issue and making people aware of the perils of climate change.

I'm amazed sometimes when I think of how that documentary has dramatically extended the discussion on climate change. I'm also very pleased to see how films like *North Country* have advanced women's rights and films like *Charlie Wilson's War* and *The Kite Runner* have helped us better understand the current situation in Afghanistan.

I think back to those words I envisioned as a high school student on my gravestone. We can each be so powerful if we put our minds to work and follow our passions.

"

We can each be so powerful if we put our minds to work and follow our passions."

Jeff Skoll

THANKS A MILLION

WHEN WE BEGAN THIS BOOK, we sat down at the kitchen table with Mom and Dad and a tape recorder. We pressed "Record," then asked them many questions about how we were raised. The tape reveals long minutes of dead silence. Mom could not begin to imagine recording her thoughts on parenting. But when she clicked off the recorder, the stories started to flow. She told us about her mother, Mimi, who at ninety-six is a beacon of benevolence. She shared stories of her grandparents. Dad told us about his father, a man who worked every day in a convenience store so he could send his son to university to get a better chance at life.

Eager to find out more about our childhood, we explored our family tree. At its roots, we found compassion, courage and community, all of which support our efforts today. Mom and Dad taught us that we are grounded in something much larger. One day — soon, but not too soon! — we will have children of our own. We hope that when they find their roots, they too will find a way to grow and flourish in a better future.

No family is perfect, least of all ours. We had our moments, like every family. Mom and Dad were conventional parents in almost every way but one. They sent us forth with the belief that we could do anything, not just for ourselves but also for others. Mom and Dad gave us the tools to explore, question and try to change the world. For that, we say "Thank you." To Grandma and Grandpa, "Thank you." To Mimi ... and, well, you get the idea.

Your kid needs you in the very same way. Teach your children about courage, compassion and community. They are your legacy and our best hope for the future.

The world needs your kid.

EPILOGUE

His Holiness the Dalai Lama addressing students at We Day

MORE THAN A DECADE AGO a conversation with the world's most famous monk rocked the foundations of our world. Not so long ago, we rocked him right back. At least 32,000 of our closest friends did. But more about that later.

First, the long ago discussion with His Holiness the Dalai Lama. As we mentioned earlier in this book, we had only recently started Free The Children when we were invited to meet him in Stockholm along with philosophers, historians, teachers and religious leaders. We were there to consider a single but profound question: "What is the greatest challenge facing our time?" Poverty. War. The disparity between rich and poor. There were many answers offered that week. We suggested it could be the failure to educate millions of the world's children.

The Dalai Lama suggested that the greatest challenge facing our time was not weapons of mass destruction or terrorism or ethnic cleansing. "It is that we are raising a generation of passive bystanders," he said. He argued that children are afraid to stand up for what they believe in. Instead of raising their voices against injustice, they remain silent. This did not bode well for our future.

Over the past decade, his words lingered in our hearts and his warning stuck with us as we built Free The Children. How could we do our part to raise, not bystanders, but active participants? While our work has been inspired and shaped by the values and lessons of our parents, teachers, mentors and friends, it was the concerns of the world's most famous monk that have often driven us forward.

We owe much to this man who has given so much to the world. But how do you thank the monk who renounces all worldly possessions? This is where the rock concert for social change comes in. But it was much more than that.

In fall 2009, more than 32,000 middle and high school leaders gathered in two stadiums, with millions more watching a televised broadcast and webcast. These all-day "We Days" featured keynote speakers including three Nobel Peace laureates, world leaders, humanitarians and amazing musical acts. Even the Jonas Brothers performed. More than 2,200 schools sent student delegations. It was a free event, but as an entry fee the school made a commitment to a year-long series of social justice actions focused on local and global causes. As this book goes to print the student leaders were well on their way to exceeding the goal of achieving more than one million hours of service, and raising funds to adopt ten villages overseas touching the lives of 100,000 people.

For us, the most exciting and poignant moment of We Day was welcoming our most honored guest speaker: His Holiness the Dalai Lama. It seemed impossible but it was true. All these years after meeting him in Stockholm, he agreed to join us in North America to address the thousands of gathered young people. He'd heard about our annual gathering of student leaders — then in its third year— and graciously offered to share his words on compassion and service. It was, quite honestly, a dream come true.

Our team had choreographed the entire day of events — musical performers and inspirational speakers — down to the minute. We anticipated the Dalai Lama would rush in, and then rush out. Then on the day we got word that our special guest was going to be early. Not a little early. But thirty minutes early. We learned that he had decided to take leave of the group of adults he was meeting with to come early to our event. He was excited to address all of the young people.

With little warning, a motorcade of police vehicles came screeching to a halt outside the arena, and an advance team of security and bomb sniffing dogs spread out around us. After the security team surrounded the stage, the Dalai Lama exited the car, walking slowly in his crimson and golden robes. He was obviously tired, and older than we remember him. As he approached, he looked up and smiled in recognition. He took our hands, we each bowed slightly, and then he embraced us. Within moments we realized that he wasn't as tired as we assumed, as his advance team had suggested. Instead, he was bursting with energy to address the students. He kept asking, as he waited backstage, "Can I go on? Soon? Wow. There are so many young people. Can I go on now?"

When the cheering students saw him they leapt to their feet. In a trickle that led to a tidal wave, one-by-one they bowed their heads. Within moments 32,000 young people were standing in respectful silence, reverence and awe. In words that echoed throughout the stadium, he greeted the gathering with the traditional Tibetan greeting, *Tah-shi de-leh*.

The stage was designed so a large group of children could sit around his feet. As requested, we'd provided a chair so he could sit to conserve his energy. But after returning the bow to the appreciative audience, His Holiness walked past the empty chair, up to the very edge of the stage. He came so close to the edge that his security team worried he was going to trip over wires and teeter onto the audience.

In words filled with a mix of laughter, sober reflection, and gratitude of spirit, he told the young crowd about making the 21st century one of peace. That is what young people must do. Strive for greater peace and deep compassion. And in a very poignant moment, he also told the students that he recognized his own mortality.

"My life was not an easy one. At age 16, I lost freedom. At age 24, I lost my country. I remain as a refugee," he said. "Inside I felt fear and distrust. But during these periods, my source of strength is compassion and respect for others' rights." He also said that his generation had failed to find peace. The generation of bystanders he long ago worried about now have the world's future in their hands. He hoped they could do better. When the spiritual leader was finished speaking, the youngsters erupted in appreciative applause. The Dalai Lama bowed to them.

That moment was our humble gift to the Dalai Lama. On that day, he witnessed the energy and hope of thousands of students who will continue his teachings of compassion and justice. In that moment, he did not seem so tired. He stepped off the stage with his arms outstretched and with a giant smile. He looked hopeful and happy.

It is in appreciation of the Dalai Lama's words and his life's work, that we echo his message in this book. Young people must become active citizens today. Not tomorrow, or when they turn eighteen-years-old or some day after. We can't wait. The world can't wait. We have important work to do now.

SMALL ACTIONS EVERY DAY

100 Tips to Raise Global Citizens

Before you head off on your journey, we offer you the 100 greatest hits from the lessons in this book. We hope they will inspire you and your family to nurture compassion, courage and community.

1. EARLY TO RISE:
Set the alarm twenty minutes early to avoid the morning rush. With luck, you'll spend less time hustling your kids out the door and more time checking in with them about the day ahead. Connecting leads to caring.

2. EVERY CONTRIBUTION COUNTS:
Enlist your children to aid with chores. Young kids especially love to "help." Let them know their efforts are important to the running of your household. Helpers around the home are helpers around the neighborhood.

3. DINNER-TIME CONVERSATION:
Encourage kids to discuss highlights and low points in the day. Get them talking about small injustices they've witnessed, then help them figure out how to react — and act.

4. DINNER AND A MOVIE:
Set aside a family night to play games or watch a movie or to make a meal together. Go international! Cook a meal from a world away. Watch a movie about a different culture.

5. TURN COMMUTES INTO COMMUNICATION:
Make the backseat of the car a no iPod, gadget-free zone. Encourage your kids to talk. If they won't, take the lead and share stories from your day.

6. NOT-SO-RANDOM ACTS OF KINDNESS:
Show your kids the beginning steps of living *me* to *we*. Open a door for someone. Help someone who is short of change. Buy lunch for a stranger.

7. IF THEY'RE HAPPY AND THEY KNOW IT:

Help your children name what they are feeling. Once they can articulate their own emotions, encourage them to think about the feelings of others. When they care for others they will want to help them.

8. HOW WOULD YOU FEEL IF ...?

It's a question that's perfect for every occasion. Ask kids to put themselves in someone else's shoes — happy or sad.

9. CHAMPION A PET PROJECT:

Caring for an animal — large or small — is a natural way to nurture compassion in a child. In the same way, older children can be asked to tend to younger siblings.

10. MAKE THANKS A HABIT:

Invite every person around the dinner table to express gratitude for something that happened during the day.

11. SHARE QUIET ACTS OF EMPATHY:

Morally courageous people don't often make front-page news. Don't let that stop you from highlighting acts and decisions that are worth celebrating.

12. STEP BACK SO THAT A KID CAN STEP UP:

If you are forever tying his shoes, he might never try on his own. If you always intervene in playmate squabbles, she may never attempt to work things out on her own.

13. HAVE PATIENCE FOR TRIAL AND ERROR:

Spilt milk is truly no cause for tears, especially if it's the result of an ambitious preschooler learning to self-serve. Help your child deal with the consequences. "Here's a cloth to mop up ..."

14. PRESENT OPTIONS:

Let your child choose — when safe and possible — and stand by his choices. Doing so demonstrates your faith in his abilities.

15. BOTTOM FEEDERS:

Move the plates to a low shelf so the kids can set the table. No matter what the task, enlisting kids to do chores teaches them to contribute.

16. WILL WORK FOR COIN:

If you give your kids allowance, make sure they divide it into three: Save some. Spend some. Share some.

17. OF COURSE YOUR CHILD IS GIFTED:

Every kid is. Your challenge and joy is to help them discover their talents.

18. DON'T RUSH:

Let your child discover her own abilities at her own speed.

19. MAKE ROOM TO EXPLORE:

Your talents are your talents. Give your kids the freedom to find their own way to shine.

20. TAKE AN INTEREST IN THEIR INTERESTS:

If your child is fascinated with dinosaurs, take them to the library or the natural history museum. No matter the flavor of the month, help her explore.

21. NO PAIN, NO PAIN:

Pushing and pulling a kid to practice only works for so long. Help him find his groove.

22. ENCOURAGE EFFORTS, NOT RESULTS:

Marks and scores are only important to a point. At the end of the day, the real goal is for the child to feel a sense of accomplishment.

23. MODEL OPTIMISM:

Tell your children you have faith in them and believe they can succeed.

24. SHOW AND SHARE:

Encourage kids to show off their talents to friends, family and community.

25. TALK ABOUT THE HEADLINES:

When you are reading the morning paper, point out stories of interest to your children. Discuss the influence of individuals you read about — and the difference they are making in the world.

26. SHAKING UP THE NEIGHBORS:

Point out growing concerns in your community. Clip out articles that relate to these concerns. Find websites that explain.

27. DON'T PREACH:

There's a fine line. If your kids stop listening, you'll know you've crossed it.

28. TALK THE TALK:

Identify local injustices and discuss how your family might respond. Consider what the community could be doing.

29. WALK THE WALK:

Take steps as a family to contribute to a solution. Budding environmentalists might decide to change energy-sucking light bulbs around the house.

30. GO GLOBAL:

Help kids understand they are part of the world at large. Reach out to immigrants and refugees by inviting them to coffee or dinner. Get a pen pal in a developing country.

31. LEAD, THEN GET OUT OF THE WAY:

There are many ways to support children as they take their first steps to pursuing their passions for helping. Children learn by example, of course. But they are also usually open to guidance that helps them on their way.

32. CHARITY BEGINS AT HOME:

Give them a corner of the basement to work on their project. Show your support by stocking the "office" with supplies.

33. BE A CHEERLEADER:

Be sensitive to the fact kids may feel overwhelmed at times, especially if they run into opposition. In such moments, remind would-be activists why they got involved in the first place.

34. BUY THE PIZZA:

Never underestimate its importance to eager volunteers, hungry for change.

35. IDENTIFY TARGETS:

Help your young activists establish achievable goals. Break large projects into smaller pieces. Make sure the action is both fun — though not superficial — and do-able.

36. LET THINGS GO WRONG:

Allow them to make mistakes. Don't always clean up their messes.

37. FREQUENTLY ASKED QUESTIONS:

Aspire to be your child's go-to person for answers. Be honest when you don't know the answers — find them together.

38. START SMALL:

Model small actions for your children. Smile at the people you pass on the street. Strike up a conversation with a stranger. Do a favor for a friend.

39. A PLACE TO START:

Help your child identify an issue about which they care deeply. Help them brainstorm ways they may make a difference. Help them to answer the following questions: Who will help? Friends? Parents? What tasks will require the help of others?

40. WHERE IN THE WORLD?

Hang a map of the world on a wall in your kitchen, family room or your child's bedroom. When you discuss issues with your kids, help them locate the country you are discussing.

41. TO WHOM IT MAY CONCERN:

Help your child write a letter to tell others what they think about an issue. It could be a note to request information, a thank-you card or a letter to a politician or a newspaper editor.

42. BE A FRIEND:

Suggest that your child offer to show a new student around — introducing them to friends and teachers.

43. DEFEND A FRIEND OR A STRANGER:

Teach your kids to stand up to bullies, or to protect those who are being bullied.

44. WHERE DO YOU SEE YOURSELF IN FIVE YEARS?

Take the proverbial question and apply it to your family.

45. POLL THE FAMILY:

Ask your kids how they define success. Their answers may surprise you.

46. TALK AMONGST YOURSELVES:

When you see an example of someone who has achieved success on their own terms, point it out to your kids. Discuss how the individual's actions differed from the more traditional.

47. HAPPILY EVER AFTER:

Find movies — both fictional and not — that highlight a similar message.

48. WATCH YOUR BALANCE:

Help kids see that there's more to life than marks. In the same way, show them that it takes more than money to make the world go around.

49. BUY NOTHING:

Get your kids to commit to going an entire week without buying anything that you don't absolutely need.

50. CLEAN HOUSE FOR A CAUSE:

Go through your home and collect things your family no longer uses. Ask the kids to find clothes and toys that they've outgrown. Donate them to a local woman's shelter or service organization.

51. PUT THE FUN IN FUNDRAISING:

Hold a garage sale and donate profits to charity. Ask family members, including relatives, for donations. Think about having other events at your garage sale such as face painting or a lemonade stand.

52. GIVE A GIFT THAT KEEPS ON GIVING:

Next time you're trying to find that special something for someone who has everything, consider making a donation to an international charity in his or her name.

53. BUST AN AD:

Talk to your kids about advertising. Discuss what an ad is trying to sell. In no time, your kids will be deconstructing messages and talking about products in a different way.

54. GO BEHIND THE SEAMS:

Learn about the people who make the products you purchase and where they come from. Let your conscience guide your purchases and shop fair trade.

55. PRACTICE GRATITUDE:

Help your child start a gratitude journal. Every day, get them to write down three things that make them happy.

56. SAY THANKS:

Make a list of people whom you are grateful to for being in the lives of your child. Can't think of any? Ask yourself: Who supports them? Who mentors them? Who's always there to help them reach their goals?

57. BE A MORAL COMPASS:

Teach children the principles of good decision making, as well as the differences between right and wrong. Such discussions are vital in providing children with a sense of ethics and morality.

58. SCHEDULE MEANING FIRST:

Schedule blocks of time for your family to volunteer together. Do not sacrifice this time.

59. PENCIL IN A PASSION:

Make sure your children's days aren't only filled with sports and languages and music. Set time for commitment to community.

60. TOP OF THE LIST:

Create a new family tradition: As you raise your own family, carry on old traditions and create new ones that make a difference.

61. ENCOURAGE YOUR KIDS TO RECRUIT:

It's easy to ask others to help out for a worthy cause.

62. BEGIN CLOSE TO HOME:

Show your child how to enlist a sibling to a cause.

63. NO PLACE LIKE HOME:

Make it easy and tempting for your teen to entertain at home.

64. SUPERVISE BUT DON'T INTERFERE:

Help them get to where they need to be.

65. STAY IN THE LOOP:

Find out what your kids are doing and why. Encourage other parents to get involved.

66. SHARE THE JOY AND THE JOBS:

Help your child ensure every pal they enlist to a cause has a job to do.

67. LEND A HAND:

Help someone who may be dealing with hardship in life. Encourage your child to write a letter to an elderly relative.

68. ... OR AN EAR:

Arrange for you and your child to visit a nursing home and spend time with someone who has no family nearby. Listen closely — storytelling is therapy for the loneliest soul.

69. FILL A POCKET WITH LOVE:

If you are a poet, a teller of jokes, or simply a kindhearted soul, sneak a note into the pocket of a loved one who hasn't been feeling well lately. It is guaranteed to bring a smile to his or her face.

70. DO A GOOD DEED:

With your child, help elderly neighbors with chores. Make sure to reflect how you feel at the end of the task. More than likely, you will all be inspired.

71. CELEBRATE TRANSITIONS:

Honor your child as he ages by marking milestones and passages in a symbolic way.

72. FIND THE RIGHT RITES:

Help your teens do what is hard and confront what they fear.

73. REWARD WITH RESPONSIBILITY:

Make adolescence about doing, not being done for. Prepare kids for adulthood by making them take charge.

74. AROUND THE BEND:

Encourage your teens to step into the great unknown so they can test themselves and expand their horizons.

75. ... AND BACK AGAIN:

Be open and attentive to what they have learned about the world. Help them share their experiences and newfound wisdom with others.

76. HIT THE ROAD:

Go on a volunteer vacation to Kenya or China or Ecuador and build a school or a well. Encourage a gap year to volunteer.

77. JUST LIKE YOU:

Think of the mentors in your life. Ask yourself why they played a significant role in your development. Consider how you might model their actions in your own relationships with young people.

78. A WORD OF THANKS:

Show your kids how to write a note of appreciation.

79. SEEK SUPPORT:

If your child doesn't have any mentors, find some. Look to valued coaches, community leaders, trusted teachers or faith leaders.

80. IF IT TAKES A VILLAGE ... CREATE ONE:

From time to time, find a reason to gather the people who are important in the life of your child. Throw a party on their tenth birthday, for example. Let everyone celebrate your child, not just school chums.

81. GET INVOLVED IN SCHOOL:

Broadly show an interest in your children's education. Ask about their report cards. Go to a Parent Teacher Association meeting. Show up for concerts and other events.

82. GET SPECIFIC:

Ask your children, their teachers and school administrators if they encourage community service, if they have days dedicated to help out. If so, offer to be one of the helpers.

83. SIGN UP:

Donate your time in the classroom or to organizing school justice events or even coaching a team or leading the choir.

84. PUT YOUR MONEY DOWN:
Donate your money to bring in inspiring speakers.

85. DONATE RESOURCES:
Buy the school books about heroes, or donate a computer that will help link a classroom to the world.

86. SWEAT THE DETAILS:
Scrutinize the curriculum. If there isn't a service component, discuss its importance with teachers, school administrators and maybe even trustees. Get active in the school council and push for reforms.

87. PRACTICE WHAT YOU PREACH:
You can talk at your kids all you like. What they learn, though, is what you live.

88. SHOW YOUR FAITH:
Volunteer at your child's church, temple or mosque. If a youth group does not exist, create one. Help kids find a way to reach out as a team into the community.

89. BE INCLUSIVE:
Ask local faith leaders to include children in service.

90. BUILD BRIDGES:
Once you have that youth group, look for — or create — opportunities where they can meet and socialize with groups from other faiths.

91. SERVE SIDE BY SIDE:
Join your kids in faith and service. In this way, they'll see it's important to you — just as it's important to the community.

92. TEACH AND LEARN THE GOLDEN RULE:
No matter your faith: Do unto others as you wish them to do unto you.

93. LEARN ABOUT ANOTHER RELIGION:
Read a book with your children about another faith in your community.

94. GET CONNECTED:
Log onto www.freethechildren.com, a site where you can get the scoop on international development, stay on top of global issues, share your actions with other youth activists and have your say.

95. SHOW THEM ALL THE ANGLES:
Teach kids to ask tough questions. Kids who are wise to what is going on are less likely to be duped.

96. SEND A MESSAGE:
Praise producers when you see programs that encourage social change.

97. STAY CURRENT:
Do your best to keep up with the latest technology and social networking tools. It's hard to guide your kids when you don't know what they're talking about.

98. VOTE WITH YOUR REMOTE ...
and your mouse: If you don't like what you're seeing, turn it off. Model this behavior and your kids may learn to do the same.

99. A JOURNEY OF A THOUSAND MILES BEGINS WITH A SINGLE STEP ... BE THE CHANGE!

100. JOIN THE MOVEMENT

ME TO WE PARENTS

Join the parenting movement at metowe.com.
Stay up-to-date with parenting tips for the whole
family. Find blogs, recipes and articles on the
Three Cs. Log on to post your own stories to
share with other parents.

Visit metowe.com/movement/parents

Follow Craig on His Adventures*

Stay up-to-date with Free The Children:

 twitter.com/craigkielburger

 facebook.com/craigkielburger

 youtube.com/freethechildrenintl

*Craig is still nudging his older brother to join Facebook and Twitter.

ACKNOWLEDGEMENTS

In true Me to We spirit, this book represents the collective efforts of an extraordinary team of individuals whom we are honored to call friends. As the three co-authors of the book, we were supported by many dedicated people who helped make this project a reality.

We are especially grateful for the leadership and vision of the extraordinary Sue Allan, who served as the editor as well as a writer and researcher on this mammoth project. Without Sue, this book would not have come to fruition. Sue's considerable writing, researching, interviewing and editing skills ensured that every page speaks to the mission of this book. Her sense of humor and compassion are evident throughout, as is her keen eye for detail and a good story. We are deeply moved by her dedication and the countless hours she devoted to this project. As mom to James and Will, Sue shows us every day what it means to raise kids who care and contribute.

Special thanks to Barb Williams for her creative cover design capturing the whimsical dream of childhood and to Marisa Antonello and TurnStyle Imaging for their creative energy; Dr. Dorothea Gaither for her attention to detail while copyediting the manuscript; Eva Haller for serving as an invaluable mentor, resource and connector to persons and ideas; and to Scott Feschuk for being a great support and injecting humor where needed.

Me to We Books is grateful to the dedicated team at Douglas & McIntyre and Greystone Books. A special thank you to Scott McIntyre, Rob Sanders, Richard Nadeau, Susan Rana, Carra Simpson and the whole team.

Thanks to the Me to We Books team of Russ McLeod, David Johnson, Marc Henry, Don Lane, Olga Kidisevic, Stacey Sleightholm, Matthew Ng, Andrew Garcia and Dan Yu. This revised North American edition would not have been possible without the passion, dedication and meticulous supervision of Ryan Bolton. His countless hours are deeply appreciated. The layout and design is the result of the great vision of Carl Neustaedter and the creative and design expertise of Frances Data. Me to We Books would not be possible without our friends and supporters at Participant Media, especially Jeff Skoll, Jim Berk, Bob Murphy, Jeffrey Ivers, Karen Frankel and Ricky Strauss.

This book was several years in the making. We would like to thank the following individuals for their help during our research: Katharine Spears, Susan Mohammad and Liisa Tuominen. We are also grateful for the design expertise of Paula McLaughlin. Thanks to those who offered suggestions on the manuscript, including Julie Weiss, Kim Plewes, Anne McIlroy and Andrew Duffy. We would also like to thank the almost two hundred people who shared their insights and expertise. Included in this group are many esteemed academics, thinkers and teachers. All our thanks to Tim Kasser, Mary Gordon, Dan Kindlon, Samuel Oliner, Jonathan White, Thomas Armstrong, Dr. Alvin Rosenfeld, Wendy Ellis, Rev. John Niles, Bret Stephenson, Lou Paonessa and Jack Nigro. We would also like to acknowledge the writings of professors Charles A. Smith, Nancy Eisenberg, Dan Dolderman and Mary Pipher. Thanks to Katherine Cheng, formerly of Do Something and the Brick Awards, for connecting us to so many young world changers. We'd like to extend our appreciation to the many inspiring families we interviewed. Thanks to the dozens of FTC staffers who answered our questions during the early stages of our research. Although not everyone we interviewed will find their names in these pages, their insights contributed to the finished project.

Thanks to the activists and philanthropists who contributed personal stories: Jane Goodall, Archbishop Desmond Tutu, Mia Farrow, Elie Wiesel, Jane Fonda, Jason Mraz, Monica Yunus, Betty Williams, Sol Guy, Ethan Zohn, Eva Haller, Jerry White, Steve Nash, Robert Kennedy Jr., Jeff Skoll and Robin Wiszowaty.

This book represents the experiences of Free The Children's more than fifteen years of work in the field of human rights and youth empowerment. We are especially grateful for the support of our board of directors, including our chairs, Michelle Douglas and Eva Haller. Thank you to Chris Besse, Mary Eileen Donovan, Charlotte Empey, John Gaither, Ed Gillis, Gregory Harmandayan, Adrian Horwood, Stephanie Kay, Kathy Sarafian, David Sersta, Lara Steinhouse, Jordana Weiss, Andrew Black and the Virgin Unite team, Juliet Bryan-Brown, David Cohen, Josh Cohen, Amy Eldon Turteltaub, Craig Heimark, Libby Heimark, Mary Lewis, Jessica Mayberry, Beverly Cooper Neufeld, Richard Prins, Ernan Roman, Hal Schwartz, Megan Sidhu, Dick Simon, Neil Taylor, Prof. Jonathan White, Monica Yunus, Heidi Hopper and Jim Baller.

The work of Free The Children and Me to We would not be possible without the dedication of many team members who work tirelessly on its mission. Free The Children is blessed to have the tremendous vision and leadership of Dalal Al-Waheidi, who has become family. Me to We's activities have been built by the unwavering dedication and hard work of Renee Hodginkson. Thank you to the leadership team of Victor Li, Janice Sousa, Erin Blanding, Lloyd Hanoman, Shobha Sharma, Peter Ruhiu, Michelle Hambly, William Qi, Erin Barton-Chéry, Dan Kuzmicki, Lindsey Coulter, Sapna Goel, Allison Sandmeyer, Ashley Hilkewich, Scott Baker, Robin Wiszowaty, Marianne Woods, Kate Likely, Rann Sharma, Alex Apostol and Louise Kent.

Our gratitude goes out to all the organizations and individuals who believe in Free The Children's mission.

We are thankful for the encouragement and support of Leonard Kurz and the Kurz Family Foundation; David Aisenstat and the Keg Spirit Foundation; Julie Toskan-Casale and the Toskan Casale Foundation; David Stillman and the Howie Stillman Young Leadership Fund; ONE X ONE; the Solo Family Foundation; the Boyd Foundation; the Sanam Vaziri Quraishi Foundation; Kerry Shapansky and the team from Pareto; Sharon Geraghty, Michael Akkawi and Jackie Taitz from Torys LLP; Micheline Villeneuve and Suzana Bulhoes and the team at Air Canada Kids' Horizons; Linda Schuyler and the team at Epitome Pictures; Darcy Rezac and the Vancouver Board of Trade; Dave Krysko, Pascale Audette, Nicole Rustad and team at Club Penguin and the New Horizon Foundation; The Caldwell Family and Caldwell Investment Management; Theresa Beenken; Jennifer Clarkson and the The National Speakers Bureau; Jeff Church, Mike Stone and the Nika Water team, Thomas Lundgren and The One, Chris Besse and the team at Nelson Education; Lorne Silver and the team at the *Toronto Star*; Marianne Taggio and the team at Educators Financial Group; Gerry Connelly, Chris Spence, Jeff Hainbuch, Allan Hux, Mark Lowry and the Toronto District School Board students, principals and teachers.

We also remain thankful for the support of Greg Rogers, Mike Consul and the Toronto Catholic District School Board family, Farah Perelmuter and the Speakers Spotlight team, and Bob Lato and the team at Adventure Learning. We are privileged to count as friends Odette and Cristelle Basmaji and the Jacob team; David Krieger and the Nuclear Age Peace Foundation; Sally Osberg, Lance Henderson, Richard Fahey, Laura Vais, Kimberly Tripp, Bridget McNamer, Kelly Creeden and the rest of the team at the Skoll Foundation; Lorraine Frost and Dennis Mock and the educators at Nipissing University; Veronica Atkins, Abby Bloch, Jacqueline Eberstein and the Robert C. and Veronica Atkins Foundation.

We would like to extend special thanks to Oprah Winfrey, Katy Davis, Letty Tranchum,

Tim Bennett, Annie Streer and Christina Timmins from Harpo. Thank you as well to the team at CTVglobemedia especially Susanne Boyce, Mark McInnis, Jessi Cruickshank, Ben Mulroney, Tanya Kim, Karen Barzilay, Michelle Crespi, Jon Taylor, Morely Nirenberg, Seamus O'Regan, Marie Bourbonnais, Faith Feingold, Jordan Schwartz, Matthew Garrow, Nanci MacLean, Pat DiVittorio and our friends at *Canadian Living*, including Susan Antonacci, Miriam Osborne, Kathryn Dorrell and Lynn Chambers.

Much appreciation to our corporate and organizational partners, especially the team at National Bank Financial Group, Investors Group, Telus, the Baby Girl Project, Filmplan International II; Freelife International Friends of Iqbal; Gibson Foundation; Crofton House School; Sullivan Entertainment; DDB/Rapp Collins; Love Quotes; Lloyd A. Fry Foundation; Sudbury Minga for Maasai; Universal McCann; World Medical Relief; Nokia and Royal St. George College.

We thank the following individuals for their support, guidance and friendship: David Baum, Chris and Tania Carnegie, Oliver Madison, Shelley Lewis Hood, Tre Armstrong, Mia Farrow, Brett Wilson, Victor Chan, Jennifer Tory, John Fraser, Sarah Raiss, Joseph Koch, Karen Radford, Tammy Mock, Tim Broadhead, David Bray, David Kilgour, David Walsh, Ellen MacAdam, Evan Soloman, Farley Flex, The Rt. Hon. John Turner, Patrick Johnston, Donna Cansfield, Premier Dalton McGuinty, Rebecca Amyotte, Steve Miller, Janelle McFarlane, Jeffrey Latimer, Reed Cowan, Richard Irish, Walter Green, Kim Samuel-Johnson, Terry Reeves, Elaine Silver, Marion Stewart, Linda Rosier, Giovanna Chianello, Clive Metz; Mike (Pinball) Clemmons, the Joyal family the Kurylowicz family, the Rothney Family, the Evans-Toyne family, the Van Dusen Kelley family, the Narayen Family, the Young Family, the Jorgenson family, and the Weiss family. And a tribute to Virginia Benderly and Joe Opatowski, our friends whom we all miss dearly.

Very special thanks to the Segal Family, the Hopper-Dean Family, the Malo Family, the Heimark Family and the Tory Family for their tremendous friendship.

Thank you to dozens of remarkable educators including Rick Centritto, Kristen Evans, Doris Ciaravella, Diana Sutej, Lori Adams, Tania Carducci, Bruce Downey, Paul Sullivan, Geoff Grant, Lori DiMarco, Marg Weigel, Beth Carey, Philip Marinelli, Vanessa Taylor, Chris Sleeth, Rosemary Tough, Brenda Stromberg, Alex Shum, Sally Petrovic, Eva Muresan, Martin Herbst, Rob MacKinnon, Anita Watkins, David Thwaits, Rebecca Patkau, Marlene Morrow, Amy Reesor, Doug McLaren, Jodi Kuran, Lynn Larkin, Lucy Rinaldi, Katy Whitfield, Charis Kelso, Lisa Perrotta-Huhse, Alison Harrington McCabe, Katie Hamilton, Kate Somers, Darryl Hobbs, Rebecca Fleisig, Aly Hirji, Lesley Gage,

Azniv Marie Harmadayan, Kimberly D'Souza, Kailey Laurenson, Daniel Oster, Shawna Howsen, Megan Oxley, Deborah Walker, Theresa Cosentino, Patsy Young, Cathy Chant, Alison Conroy, Rita Digiocchino, Laura Roth, Alexandria Dorsaneo, Melinda Orris, Irene Maier, Heather Allison, Alice Leafblad, Allison Burke, Dennis Devorick, Heather Kirk, Linda Michalski, Laurie Beggs, Michelle McMillan, Jenn Brown, Shana Bode, Patty Wyman, Katrina Fugate, Betsy Yager, Eileen Day, Ed Mahoney, Mary Jo Houck, Darci Keyser, Kristy Waldman, Taylor Hoffman, Renee Laporte, Lynn Rudolph, Luanne Ruonavar, Josephine Hudson, Michael Totten, Enzina Karas, Nancy DiGregorio and Chris Spence.

Shelley would like to thank her husband, Glen McGregor, and daughters, Cleo and Scarlet, for serving as a testing ground for many of the ideas in this book. She is grateful for their support during the long writing process. Much love to Orv and Liz Page and to Julie Mason and Don McGregor for showing us how to raise kids — and grandkids — who care and contribute. And deep gratitude to her brother Glenn for his optimism and caring heart.

Finally, Shelley thanks Craig and Marc, and their parents, Fred and Theresa, for sharing their inspiring and unique stories with so many in the hopes that it will make a difference in the world.

Craig and Marc would like especially to thank Shelley Page for her incredible hard work, determination, love and patience, which made this book possible. Since our paths crossed nearly a decade ago, she has joined us in far-flung destinations while juggling the joys of parenting with writing. With grace and a smile, she has embraced our working style of idealistic passion.

Thanks to Roxanne Joyal for her years of partnership and support.

Love to our Mimi, who remains our biggest fan.

We would not be where we are today without the love and support of our parents, Fred and Theresa. Thanks for *everything*, Mom and Dad!

ENDNOTES

LESSON 1

1. Niles, John. *The Art of Sacred Parenting*. White Knight Books, 2006.
2. Kelly, D.C. "Parents' Influence On Youths' Civic Behaviours: The Civic Context of the Caregiving Environment." *Families in Society 87*, no. 3 (2006): 447-455.
3. Bekkers, René. "Giving and Volunteering in the Netherlands: Sociological and Psychological Perspectives." Proefschrift Universiteit Utrecht, 2004.
4. An excellent summary of this research on parental role models appears in: Eisenberg, Nancy. *The Caring Child*. Harvard University Press, 1992.
5. Smith, Charles. "First Steps to Mighty Hearts: The Origins of Courage," Journal of the National Association for the Education of Young Children. (January 2005).
6. Zann-Waxler, C., Radke-Yarrow, M. and Chapman, M. "Development of Concern for Others." *Developmental Psychology* 28. (1992): 126-36.
7. Gibran, Kahlil. *The Prophet*, Alfred A. Knopf: New York, 1973.
8. Duncan, Greg J., Hill, Martha and Young, Jean W. "Fathers' Activities and Children's Attainments." Paper presented at the Conference on Father Involvement, October 10-11, 1996, Washington, D.C.
9. Kindlon, Dan and Thompson, Michael. *Raising Cain: Protecting the Emotional Life of Boys*. Ballantine Books, 1999.
10. Severn Suzuki speaking at UN Earth Summit 1992." www.youtube.com.

LESSON 2

1. National Institute of Child Health and Human Development Survey. *Journal of the American Medical Association*. April 25, 2001.
2. Lynn Hawkins, D., Pepler, Debra J. and Craig, Wendy. "Naturalistic Observations of Peer Interventions in Bullying." *Social Development* 10, no. 4 (2001): 512-527 (16).
3. Kindlon, Dan and Thompson, Michael. *Raising Cain: Protecting the Emotional Life of Boys*. Ballantine Books, 1999.
4. Oliner, Samuel and Oliner, Pearl. *Towards a Caring Society: Ideas into Action*. Greenwood Press, 1995. This book contains an overview of important research on parenting and empathy.

5. Gordon, M.C. "The Role of Parenting Styles in Developing Social Responsibility." *Dissertation Abstracts International* 65 3-B (2004): 157.

6. Kestenbaum, R.; Farber, E. and Stroufe, L. "Empathy and Related Emotional Responses." *New Directions for Child Development* 44 (1989): 51-64.

7. Hinchey, F. S., and Gavelek, J. R. Empathic Responding in Children of Battered Women. *Child Abuse and Neglect* 6 (1982): 395-401.

LESSON 4

1. Pipher, Mary. *Seeking Peace: Chronicles of the Worst Buddhist in the World.* Riverhead, 2009.

2. Damon, William. *Greater Expectations: Overcoming the Culture of Indulgence in Our Homes and Schools.* Free Press, 1995.

3. Zeidner, M. and Schleyer, E.J. "The Big-Fish-Little-Pond Effect for Academic Self-concept, Test Anxiety and School Grades in Gifted Children." *Contemporary Educational Psychology*, 24 no. 4 (1998): 305-329.

4. Fern, T.L. "Identifying the Gifted Child Humorist." *Roeper Review*, 14 no. 1, (1991): 30-34.

LESSON 5

1. Rader, Dotson. "Leonardo DiCaprio, Hollywood Outsider." *The Sunday Times*, January 11, 2009.

2. Lynch, Lorrie. "Leonardo DiCaprio talks to USA Weekend." *USA Today*, September 17, 2007.

LESSON 6

1. Caprara, G.V., Barbaranelli, C., Pastorelli, C., Bandura, A. and Zimbardo, P.G. "Prosocial Foundations of Children's Academic Achievement. *Psychological Science*, 11, no. 4, (2000): 302-306.

LESSON 7

1. Smith, Charles. "First Steps To Mighty Hearts: The Origins of Courage." *Young Children* vol. 60, (2005): 80-87.

2. Ibid.

3. Ibid.

4. "The Man in the Red Bandana: Family, Survivors Bonded by Man's Heroism." CNN.com.

5. "America is 'Grateful' to Flight 93 heroes: A 'Wave of Courage' During Doomed Assault on Hijackers." CNN.com.

6. Smith, Charles. "First Steps to Mighty Hearts," 80-88.

7. Ibid.

8. Gansberg, Martin. "Thirty-Eight Who Saw Murder Didn't Call the Police." *The New York Times*, March 27, 1964.

9. "Remembering Kitty Genovese." *Weekend Edition*, National Public Radio, March 13, 2004.

10. Keltner, D. and Marsh, J., "We Are All Bystanders." *Greater Good Magazine*. Fall/Winter 2006- 07.

11. Darley, J.M. and Latané, B. "Bystander Intervention in Emergencies: Diffusion of Responsibility." *Journal of Personality and Social Psychology*, 8 vol. 4. (1968): 377-83.

12. Oliner, Samuel. "Can Love Save The World?" *Yes Magazine*, 2002.

13. Oliner, Samuel. *Do Unto Others: Extraordinary Acts of Ordinary People*, Westview Press, 2003.

14. Fried, SuEllen and Fried, Paula. *Bullies, Targets and Witnesses: Helping Children Break the Pain Chain*. M. Evans and Co., 2003.

15. Nelson Mandela Announces AIDS Project With Princess Diana Fund. *The Body: The Complete HIV/ AIDS Resource*. www.thebody.com, Nov. 4, 2002.

LESSON 8

1. Schwartz, Barry. "Buyer Beware: Are We Training Our Kids To Be Consumers Rather Than Citizens?" *The Washington Post*. April 8, 2007; Clark, Eric. *The Real Toy Story: Inside the Ruthless Battle for America's Youngest Consumers*. Free Press, 2007.

2. Kindlon, Dan. *Too Much of a Good Thing: Raising Children of Character in a Permissive Culture*. Miramax, 2003.

3. Kasser, T., Cohn S., Kanner A.D. and Ryan, R.M. "Some Costs of American Corporate Capitalism: A Psychological Exploration of Value and Goal Conflicts." *Psychological Inquiry* 1 vol. 18. (2007): 1-22.

4. Chaplin, L.N., John, D.R. "Growing Up in a Material World: Age Differences in Materialism in Children and Adolescents." *Journal of Consumer Research* 34. December 2007.

5. Dunn, Elizabeth W. and Aknin, Lara B. and Norton, Michael I. "Spending Money on Others Promotes Happiness." *Science* 21 vol. 319 5870 (2008): 1,687 – 1,688.

6. Ibid.

7. Pan, Philip. "Worked Till They Drop; Few Protections for China's New Laborers." *The Washington Post*. May 13, 2002.

LESSON 9

1. Hofferth, S. and Sandberg., J. "How American Children Spend Their Time." *Journal of Marriage and the Family* 63 (2001): 295-308.

2. Rosenfeld, Alvin and Wise, Nicole. *Hyperparenting: Are You Hurting Your Child By Trying Too Hard?* St. Martin's Press, 2000.
3. Rosenfeld, Alvin. "The Over-Scheduled Family." Address to St. Luke's School, Nov. 15, 2006
4. Popenoe, David. "We Are What We See: The Family Conditions For Modeling Values for Children." *The Parenthood Library* (1998).
   http://parenthood.library.wisc.edu/Popenoe/Popenoe-Modeling.html

LESSON 10

1. Kang, Esther. "Girl Power." *Chicago Magazine,* January 2008.
2. Lichter, Daniel T., Shanahan, Michael J. and Gadner, Erica L. "Helping Others: The Effects of Childhood Poverty and Family Instability on Prosocial Behaviour." *Youth Society* 34. 2002: 89.
3. Luks A. and Payne, P. *The Healing Power of Doing Good.* Fawcett Columbine, 1991.
4. Schwartz C. and Sender R. "Helping Others Helps Oneself: Response Shift Effects to Peer Support." *Social Science and Medicine.* 48 (1991): 1,563-1,575.
5. Corporation for National and Community Service, Office of Research and Policy Development. "The Health Benefits of Volunteering: A Review of Recent Research." Washington, D.C., 2007.
6. White, Jerry. *I Will Not Be Broken: Five Steps to Ovecoming A Life Crisis.* St. Martin's Press, 2008.
7. Tam, Jackie. "Cody Enriches Many Lives With His Giving." *The Ottawa Citizen.* August 14, 2007.
8. Brooks, Robert and Goldstein, Sam. R*aising Resilient Children: Fostering Strength, Hope and Optimism in Your Child.* McGraw-Hill, 2001.
9. Lichter, Daniel T., Shanahan, Michael J. and Gardner, Erica L. "Helping Others: The Effects of Childhood Poverty and Family Instability on Pro-social Behavior." *Youth Society* 34, (2002): 89.
10. McClelland, D., McClelland, D.C. and Kirchnit, C. "The Effect of Motivational Arousal Through Films on salivary immunoglobulin A." *Psychology and Health* 2 (1988): 31-52.

LESSON 11

1. Pipher, Mary. *Reviving Ophelia: Saving the Selves of Adolescent Girls.* Ballantine, 1995.
2. Stephenson, Bret. *From Boys To Men: Spiritual Rites of Passage in an Indulgent Age.* Inner Traditions International, Ltd., 2006.

LESSON 12

1. Neufeld, Gordon and Mate, Gabor. *Hold On to Your Kids: Why Parents Need to Matter More Than Peers.* Vintage Canada, 2005.

2. Rosenberg, Steven, McKeon, Loren and Dinero, Thomas. "Positive Peer Solutions: One Answer for the Rejected Student." *Phi Delta Kappan* 81, no. 2 (1999): 114-18.

LESSON 13

1. The following citations provide an excellent review of research on the impact of mentoring on young people:

    LoSciuto, L., Rajala, A. K., Townsend, T. N. and Taylor, A. S. "An Outcome Evaluation of Across Ages: An Intergenerational Mentoring Approach to Drug Prevention." *Journal of Adolescent Research* 11 (1996): 116-129.

    Davidson, W. S., and Redner, R. "The Prevention of Juvenile Delinquency: Diversion from the Juvenile Justice System" in Price, R.

    H., Cowen, E. L., Lorion, R. P., and Ramos-McKay, J. (eds.), F*ourteen Ounces of Prevention: Theory, Research and Prevention.* Pergamon, 1998.

    McPartland, J. M., and Nettles, S. M. "Using Community Adults as Advocates or Mentors for At-risk Middle School Students: A Two-Year Evaluation of Project RAISE." *American Journal of Education* 99, (1991): 568-586.

    Reisner, E., Petry, C. A. and Armitage, M. *A Review of Programs Involving College Students as Tutors or Mentors in Grades K-12.* Policy Studies Associates, Inc., 1998.

2. Tierney, J. P., Grossman, J. B., and Resch, N. L. Making a difference: An impact study of Big Brothers Big Sisters. Philadelphia: Public/Private Ventures. (1995)

3. Canadian Centre for Teaching Peace, www.peace.ca

4. Landers-Potts, Melissa and Grant, Linda. "Competitive Climates, Athletic Skill and Children's Status in After-School Recreational Sports Programs." *Social Psychology of Education* 2, no. 3-4, 1997.

LESSON 14

1. Hong, Susan. "The Ohlone Way." Paolo Alto Weekly. May 8, 2007.

2. Holmes, Tracy. *Surrey North Delta Leader.* September 25, 2008.

3. Ibid.

4. Eccles, Jacquelynne S. and Barber, Bonnie L. "Student Council, Volunteering, Basketball, or Marching Band: What Kind of Extracurricular Involvement Matters?" *Journal of Adolescent Research* 14 no. 1 (1999): 10-43.

5. Scales, P.C., Blyth, D.A., Berkas, T.H. and Kielsmeier, J.C. "The Effects of Service-Learning on Middle School Students' Social Responsibility and Academic Success." *The Journal of Early Adolescence* 20, no. 3 (2000): 332-358.

LESSON 15

1. Niles, John. *How I Became Father to 1000 Children*. White Knight Books, 2005.
2. Smith, C., with Denton, M. L. *Soul searching: The religious and spiritual lives of American teenagers.* Oxford University Press. 2005
3. "News Community Ministry Powerful Factor in Maturing Teens' Faith." Baylor University. January 22, 2007.
4. Camp, Ken. "Study says Teen Faith Shaped More by Hands-on Ministry than Worship." *American Baptist Press*. February 8, 2007.
5. The quote is from Ted Schmidt, a fellow teacher.
6. *Religious and Ethics News Weekly*, www.pbs.org, June 4, 2004.
7. Ibid.
8. Van Biema, David. "Mother Teresa's Crisis of Faith." *Time*. August 23, 2007.

LESSON 16

1. Drabman, R.S., and Thomas, M.H. "Does Media Violence Increase Children's Toleration of Real-Life Aggression?" *Developmental Psychology* 10 (1974): 418-421.
2. Huston, A. C., Donnerstein, E., Fairchild, H., Feshbach, N. D., Katz, P. A., Murray, J.P., Rubinstein, E. A., Wilcox, B. L., and Zuckernan, D. *Big World, Small Screen: The Role of Television in American Society*. University of Nebraska Press, 1992.
3. Bushman, B. J., and Huesmann, L. R. "Effects of Televised Violence on Aggression" in D. G. Singer and J. L. Singer (Eds.), *Handbook of Children and the Media*. Sage Publications, 2001.
4. *National Television Violence Study*. University of California, Center for Communication and Social Policy. Sage Publications, 1998.
5. "Why Teach About Media Literacy?" Handout from Media Awareness Network, media-awareness.ca.
6. Tyner, Kathleen R. and Kolkin, Donna Lloyd. *Media and You: An Elementary Literacy Curriculum*. Educational Technology Publications, 1991.
7. Kielburger, Craig, Kielburger, Marc and Shankaran, Deepa. *Take More Action: How to Change The World*. Me to We Books, 2008.

8. Gore, Tipper. *Raising PG Kids in an X-rated Society*. Abingdon Press, 1987.
9. Consumers Electronics Association of America. As quoted in Pew Internet and American Life Project Presentation: How the Internet is Changing Consumer Behavior and Expectations, www.pewinternet.org/PPF/r/64/presentation_display.asp
10. Moscovitch, Arlene. *Good Servant, Bad Master: Electronic Media and the Family*. Vanier Institute of the Family. 2007

PHOTO CREDITS

Vito Amati, Stan Behal, Marc Bryan-Brown Photography, Michael Collopy, Chris Dowsett, Andrew Eccles/JBG Photo, Christina Gapic, V. Tony Hauser, Goh Iromoto, Jeff Jewiss, Richard Lam, Wayne Mah, Dave Meisner, the Steve Nash Foundation, Phil Ogynist, Shelley Page, Greg Paupst, Kim Plewes, Travis Price, Scott Ramsey, Manuela Stefan, Pat Young, and Free The Children staff.

INDEX

ABOUT FREE THE CHILDREN

FREE THE CHILDREN
children helping children through education

Free The Children is the world's largest network of children helping children through education, with more than one million youth involved in its innovative education and development programs in 45 countries. Founded in 1995 by international child rights activist Craig Kielburger, Free The Children has a remarkable record of achievement, initiating community-based development projects around the world and inspiring young people to develop as socially conscious global citizens. Today, through the voices and actions of youth, Free The Children has built more than 500 sustainable schools in developing countries around the world. Under the Adopt a Village model, Free The Children supports the communities by providing primary education, health care, alternative income projects and clean water to create sustainable communities.

Visit www.freethechildren.com to learn more.

ABOUT ME TO WE

 me to we

Me to We is a new kind of social enterprise for people who want to help change the world with their daily choices. Through our media, products and leadership experiences, we support Free The Children's work with youth creating global change. Every trip, organic and free-trade T-shirt, song, book, speech, thought, smile and choice adds up to a lifestyle that's part of the worldwide movement of *we*.

Me to We offers choices that allow people to create ripples of positive change. What's more, Me to We is designed to help bring Free The Children's already low administrative costs to zero. Half of its annual profits are given to Free The Children with the other half reinvested to sustain the growth of the enterprise.

Visit www.metowe.com to find out more.

ᨸᨺ me to we
SPEAKERS

Bring a speaker to your child's school, your parent and educator association or your workplace conferences—and take away all you need to "be the change."

The team at Me to We Speakers has traveled the world to discover the most inspirational people with remarkable stories and life experiences.

From community activists to former child soldiers to social entrepreneurs, our roster of energetic, experienced speakers are leading the *me* to *we* movement: living and working in developing communities, helping businesses achieve social responsibility and inspiring auditoriums of youth and educators to action. Their stories and powerful messages inspire, motivate and educate.

They leave audiences with a desire to take action and make a difference. They'll make you laugh, cry and gain new perspective on what really matters. Be warned: their passion is contagious!

Visit www.metowe.com/speakers to learn more.

ᕊᕊ me to we
TRIPS

If you want to really experience another culture and truly see the world, take a Me to We Trip. Seek out a volunteer travel experience as a family, faith group or corporate getaway that radically changes your perspective, while positively transforming the lives of others.

Our staff live and work in the communities you'll visit, coordinating schoolbuilding and supporting development in participation with local communities. On a Me to We Trip, you'll learn leadership skills, experience new cultures and forge truly meaningful connections.

Over 3,000 adventurous people of all ages have chosen to volunteer abroad with us. You'll do incredible things, like building schools and assisting on clean water projects. You'll meet exuberant children excited at new possibilities for learning, and be immersed in local communities in ways never otherwise possible.

And best of all, you'll have memories that last a lifetime.

Visit www.metowe.com/trips to learn more.

Free the Children
Craig Kielburger

This is the story that launched a movement. *Free the Children* recounts twelve-year-old Craig Kielburger's remarkable odyssey across South Asia, meeting some of the world's most disadvantaged children, exploring slums and sweatshops, fighting to rescue children from the chains of inhumane conditions. Winner of the prestigious Christopher Award, *Free the Children* has been translated into eight languages and inspired young people around the world.

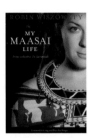

My Maasai Life
Robin Wiszowaty

In her early 20s, Robin Wiszowaty left the ordinary world behind to join a traditional Maasai family. In the sweeping vistas and dusty footpaths of rural Kenya, she embraced a way of life unlike she'd ever known. With full-color photographs from her adventures, Robin's heart-wrenching story will inspire you to question your own definitions of home, happiness and family.

Take Action! A Guide to Active Citizenship
Craig and Marc Kielburger

Want to begin changing the world? *Take Action!* is a vivid, hands-on guide to active citizenship packed with the tools young people need to make a difference. Accomplished human rights activists Marc and Craig Kielburger share valuable tips and advice from their experiences as founders of Free The Children and Me to We. Ideal for Grades 8–10, *Take Action!* shows that young people don't need to wait to be the leaders of tomorrow—this journey begins *now*.

Take More Action: How to Change the World
Craig and Marc Kielburger with Deepa Shankaran

Ready to take the next step? *Take More Action* is our advanced guide to global citizenship, empowering young people to be world-changers—around the world or in their own backyard. Brilliantly illustrated and packed with powerful quotes, stories and resources, *Take More Action* includes invaluable material on character education, ethical leadership, effective activism and global citizenship. Ideal for Grades 10 and up, *Take More Action* paves the way for a lifetime of social action.

The Making of an Activist
Craig and Marc Kielburger with Lekha Singh

Warning: this book will change you. Full of vivid images and inspiring words, travelogues, poems and sparkling artwork, *The Making of an Activist* is more than just a scrapbook of Free The Children's remarkable evolution. It's a testament to living an engaged, active and compassionate life, painting an intimate portrait of powerful young activists. Explore the book. Catch the spark.

It Takes a Child
Craig Kielburger and Marisa Antonello; Illustrated by Turnstyle Imaging

It was an ordinary morning like any other. Twelve-year-old Craig Kielburger woke to his alarm clock and hurried downstairs to wolf down a bowl of cereal over the newspaper's comics before school. But what he discovered on the paper's front page would change his life—and eventually affect over a million young people worldwide. *It Takes a Child* is a fun, vibrant look back at Craig's adventures throughout South Asia, learning about global poverty and child labour. This incredible story truly demonstrates you're never too young to change the world.

Visit www.metowe.com/books to learn more.

metowe.com/books

The Buy a Book, Give a Book promise ensures that for
every Me to We book purchased, a notebook will be given
to a child in a developing country.